BEGINS WITH THE OBOE

A History of the
Toronto Symphony Orchestra

BEGINS WITH THE OBOE

A History of the

Toronto Symphony Orchestra

RICHARD S. WARREN

UNIVERSITY OF TORONTO PRESS
Toronto Buffalo London

ISBN 0-8020-3588-4

Printed on acid-free paper

National Library of Canada Cataloguing in Publication Data

Warren, Richard S.
 Begins with the oboe : a history of the Toronto Symphony
 Orchestra / Richard S. Warren.

 Included bibliographical references and index.
 ISBN 0-8020-3588-4

 1. Toronto Symphony Orchestra.   I. Title.

 ML205.8.T72T73 2002   785′.06′2713541   C2002-901111-6

Photographs are from the Toronto Symphony Orchestra archives, or are used with kind
permission of Dr Fred Fallis, Frank Harmantas, and Brian Pickell.

University of Toronto Press acknowledges the financial assistance to its publishing program
of the Canada Council for the Arts and the Ontario Arts Council.

University of Toronto Press acknowledges the financial support for its publishing activities
of the Government of Canada through the Book Publishing Industry Development
Program (BPIDP).

To Marian

Contents

Foreword

In 1976 the administration of the Toronto Symphony Orchestra wisely decided that an archives section should be installed for the retention of important documents to maintain the history of the orchestra. Richard Warren volunteered to be the archivist. In 1995 Richard decided that it was time for a book giving a more in-depth account of the Orchestra's colourful history. After seven years of intense research and writing that chronicle has arrived.

I knew Richard personally from his first year with the orchestra; his enthusiasm and dedication have been an inspiration to musicians, administration staff, directors, and myself alike. He and I often discussed the works of English composers, especially Elgar, for whom we had a kindred fascination. Richard was also greatly interested in the historical fortunes of other orchestras, particularly the BBC Symphony Orchestra and the City of Birmingham Symphony Orchestra, both of which were founded in his lifetime.

What many of us would not give to have witnessed first-hand the work of the great conductors of the past. For me in particular, the chapters on Luigi von Kunits, Ernest MacMillan, and Walter Susskind provide a fascinating glimpse into the minds and musical souls of men who guided the orchestra through such important times.

Richard's invaluable, dedicated service to the Toronto Symphony Orchestra is revealed through the pages of this illuminating volume, which faithfully narrates the complex course of the orchestra's history, relishing the good times while not white-washing the not-so-good. Everyone who cherishes the Toronto Symphony Orchestra will also cherish this book. Happy reading!

Sir Andrew Davis
Music Director, Lyric Opera, Chicago
Conductor Laureate, Toronto Symphony Orchestra

Preface

The title of this book – *Begins with the Oboe* – could be a crossword clue, but within the world of symphony orchestras this phrase is a fact of life. Once the orchestra has assembled on stage, the concertmaster will arise and look toward the principal oboe to indicate that he requires the 'A' to be played. At this signal, the principal oboist plays the 'A 440' and the members of the orchestra tune their instruments. Then the rehearsal or concert is ready to proceed.

I have often given thought to writing a book on the history of the Toronto Symphony Orchestra, but I always came up with the excuse that an archivist is too close to the scene to give a fair record of events. However, since a close friend who is also the archivist of a major orchestra in England successfully completed a volume for his orchestra, I adjusted my thinking, and decided to make a similar attempt.

This book is intended as a history of the Toronto Symphony Orchestra: a chronicle of achievements, challenges, and outstanding events during the past eighty years. My aim, in writing this history, was to give the reader an enlightening and accessible insight into the Orchestra.

On a few occasions I deviate from the main theme of the book in order to describe a certain personality, such as a conductor or a guest artist. I have done so because I feel that this additional information adds colour and provides another level of interest to the association of performance between orchestra and artist.

Acknowledgments

I am deeply indebted to the many friends and associates who have been so very helpful in my endeavour to write this book. My thanks go especially to Joanne Harada, who over the past three years patiently put words and letters in the correct order; Pat Wardrop, who straightened out the historical content; Beresford King-Smith, whose inspiration prompted me to take the plunge in writing this book; Dr Tim Maloney, Music Division of the National Library of Canada, for assistance with the Sir Ernest MacMillan Archives; Neil Cory, Senior Music Producer, CBC Radio Music Department; Gail Donald, Co-ordinator, English Radio Network Archives; William Littler, music critic, *Toronto Star*, for the very informative interview he gave me on his many years of reviews with the TSO; to Bill Harnum, Suzanne Rancourt, Ruth Pincoe, and all their colleagues at University of Toronto Press, for all the hard work they have put into the production of this book; to Walter Homburger, who for many years has kept informed about the history of the orchestra; and finally to Loie Fallis, Roberta Smith, and all members past and present of the TSO music department, for their undying support in making this project possible, and to all members, past and present, of the orchestra, who, through conversations and recorded interviews, have enriched my knowledge of the TSO.

BEGINS WITH THE OBOE

A History of the
Toronto Symphony Orchestra

CHAPTER ONE

Prelude

Toronto
Symphony Orchestra
FRANK S. WELSMAN, Conductor.

Mme. JOHANNA GADSKI
Soprano Soloist

First Concert

Season 1908-9

Tuesday Evening, December 8th, 1908

MASSEY MUSIC HALL.

Music is in the air – you simply take as much as you require!

EDWARD ELGAR

In 1920 Edward Johnson (1878–1959), the eminent Canadian tenor and Metropolitan Opera star, said, 'I want to see Toronto produce and maintain a full time professional symphony orchestra. This city is a very important metropolis of North America and it therefore needs and must have one.' Undoubtedly, Johnson was well aware of the unsuccessful attempts made over the past sixty years.

The musical situation in Toronto before the advent of the present Toronto Symphony Orchestra is important because it encompasses the many elements that led to the orchestra's eventual formation. During the latter half of the nineteenth century the musical life of Toronto was dominated by choral music, owing in large part to the rich tradition of choral singing that had been brought by many British immigrants from their homeland. The Toronto Philharmonic Society was not a single organization, but rather a series of successive societies. The first was organized in 1845 by John McCaul (1807–86) and was for a time the centre of musical life in the city. Over the next ten years, performances of oratorios along with some instrumental selections were organized and conducted by various musicians including James P. Clarke, James D. Humphreys, Henry Schallehn, and George W. Strathy at a number of locations in the city, including St Lawrence Hall, the Royal Lyceum Theatre, and City Hall. However, the organization folded in 1855 because of financial problems. After many attempts, the Philharmonic Society was revived in 1872, with McCaul as president and James P. Clarke (1807–77) as conductor, for a performance of Handel's *Messiah* given at Shaftesbury Hall in February 1873. That year Frederick Torrington (1837–1917) took over as conductor and in following years the Society presented Canadian premieres of Mendelssohn's oratorios *Elijah* (1874) and *St Paul* (1876), and Charles Gounod's *La rédemption* (1882, the year of its composition).

At this time concert orchestras were assembled for each performance from a core of regimental, theatre, and band musicians, augmented by amateur and professional musicians borrowed from neighbouring communities. Even then, specific instruments were sometimes missing and consequently the balance was often unsatisfac-

Frank Welsman (1873–1952)

tory. Regular rehearsal was almost impossible; programs were restricted to works ten to twenty minutes in length, and symphonies were represented by single movements. By the turn of the twentieth century, visits by American and European orchestras formed the real basis of the musical season for Toronto. A number of American orchestras, including the Boston Symphony, the Theodore Thomas Orchestra, and the New York Philharmonic, made regular visits to Toronto, on many occasions joining forces with local groups such as the Toronto Mendelssohn Choir. Without a doubt, these visits stimulated a desire by local musicians for a well-established symphony orchestra of their own.

During this time several attempts were made to create a permanent orchestra. The first group to call itself the Toronto Symphony Orchestra appeared in 1890–1, under the baton of Francesco D'Auria (1841–after 1913), an Italian conductor who also taught voice at the Toronto Conservatory of Music. Then, in 1900, organizers announced the formation of an orchestra under the leadership of Frederick Torrington. This orchestra was to present regular concerts and to tour within Canada and abroad. Unfortunately, the first concert of the Toronto Permanent Orchestra, given after extensive rehearsals, also proved to be its last. The following year, another Toronto Symphony Orchestra, conducted by James Dickinson, gave a single concert before it too folded for lack of financial support.

In 1906 the situation began to look a little brighter. That year Dr Edward Fisher (1848–1913), the director of the Toronto Conservatory of Music, called a meeting to discuss the possibility of forming an orchestra. The outcome was a decision to organize financing and invite a prominent musician – Frank Welsman (1873–1952), a former student of the Conservatory – to join the teaching staff. Welsman accepted the offer and, in an agreement with Dr Fisher, formed an orchestra under the auspices of the Conservatory. The musicians of the Toronto Conservatory Symphony Orchestra were drawn from faculty members, students, and talented amateurs. After two successful

MUSICAL FESTIVAL OF THE EMPIRE

PRESIDENT
HIS EXCELLENCY EARL GREY, P.C., G.C.M.G.

———

THE ARENA, MONTREAL
MONDAY, TUESDAY & WEDNESDAY EVENINGS,
MARCH 27, 28, 29, 1911, AT 8.15.

———

THREE GRAND FESTIVAL CONCERTS
UNDER THE DIRECTION OF DR. CHARLES HARRISS

———

THE SHEFFIELD CHOIR OF ENGLAND
TWO HUNDRED VOICES

———

"THE DREAM OF GERONTIUS"
CONDUCTED BY THE COMPOSER
SIR EDWARD ELGAR

GRAND MISCELLANEOUS FESTIVAL CONCERT
CONDUCTED BY
DR. HENRY COWARD

CORONATION EMPIRE CONCERT
CONDUCTED BY
DR. CHARLES HARRISS

—

ARTISTS
MISS JENNIE TAGGART	MISS MAUD WILLBY

LADY NORAH NOEL

MISS GERTRUDE LONSDALE	MISS ALICE HEELEY
MR. HENRY TURNPENNEY	MR. WILFRID VIRGO
MR. ROBERT CHARLESWORTH	MR. ROBERT CHIGNELL

———

SOLO ORGANIST AND CHORUS ACCOMPANIST
MR. J. EDWARD HODGSON, Mus. Bac., F.R.C.O.

———

THE TORONTO SYMPHONY ORCHESTRA
SEVENTY PERFORMERS

CONDUCTOR
MR. FRANK WELSMAN

———

CONDUCTORS
SIR EDWARD ELGAR, DR. HENRY COWARD and DR. CHARLES HARRISS
Heintzman Piano used exclusively by the Sheffield Choir on their Canadian Tour

3

Playbill from Montreal performance of *The Dream of Gerontius* conducted by Edward Elgar; the concert was repeated in Toronto on 4, 5, and 6 April 1911.

seasons, the connection with the Conservatory was dropped, and on 8 December 1908, the new Toronto Symphony Orchestra presented its first official subscription concert. The following morning, Toronto newspapers were full of praise not only for soloist Johanna Gadski, the Wagnerian soprano from the Metropolitan Opera, but also for the outstanding performance by the orchestra. At this time an Executive Committee was formed under the chairmanship of Herbert C. Cox (the president of Canada Life Assurance), giving the orchestra a firm financial foundation. The orchestra's success continued through eight seasons, and featured well-known guest artists including Fritz Kreisler, Mischa Elman, Eugene Ysaÿe, Jan Kubelík, and Serge Rachmaninoff. Apparently Rachmaninoff came totally unprepared for a Canadian winter and, convinced by Welsman that a fur coat was required, was taken to Holt Renfrew to purchase a suitable garment. They had nothing to fit his tall stature so he settled for the best possible fit – the sleeves ended midway between his elbow and wrist, and the coat reached just below his knees.

On 4 April 1911 the orchestra took part in a performance of Sir Edward Elgar's *The Dream of Gerontius* conducted by the composer. This concert was part of a three-day Musical Festival of the Empire, and was one of six performances of this program to be presented in Montreal and Toronto. After the concert, Elgar, who was at the end of an intensive North American tour and was not enjoying the best of health, travelled directly to New York to embark for England. Shortly after his return he was present at the Queen's Hall in London for the premiere of his Symphony No. 2 in E flat major.

With the outbreak of the First World War in 1914 the activities of the orchestra were curtailed. The Executive Committee was of the opinion that monies needed for the support of the orchestra should instead be directed toward the war effort, and suspended future plans for the orchestra. Frank Welsman, however, felt that the orchestra should continue to function as well as possible under wartime conditions and took on the duties of both administrator and music director-conductor. During the first three years of the war the conditions became increasingly difficult and audience support fell off. In the summer of 1918, Welsman finally gave up what seemed to be an endless struggle, and Toronto's first permanent symphony orchestra came to an end. A few years would pass before the musicians of a Toronto orchestra would again be able to tune to the A played by the principal oboist.

The success of this first Toronto Symphony Orchestra left a deep impression on the musicians. The opportunity to perform together and to build a first-class orchestra was imbedded in their memories. Within a few years, some of them would decide to attempt to form yet another permanent symphony orchestra.

THE ORCHESTRA

1st VIOLINS	CELLOS	BASSES	BASS CLARINET
M. Garten	J. Sterin	C. Rose	Dr. J. Pilcher
B. Clarke	S. Mondzak	D. Schmidt	
Ph. Rosenfield	O. Roberts	J. J. Woods	**BASSOONS**
G. Milligan	G. Bruce	L. F. Addison	Dr. G. R. MacRitch·
M. Roth	H. Jenning	A. E. Ranson	F. E. Dennis
L. Gesensway	H. S. Saunders	F. E. Knaggs	
E. Johnson	C. H. Curtis	F. H. Carver	
A. Gesensway	H. F. Palmer		**TRUMPETS**
C. P. Causton			E. Boucher
H. J. Taylor			E Smeall
J. van Vugt			W. Tong
E. S. Knaggs			
A. Koldofsky			
M. Fogie			**HORNS**

THE NEW SYMPHONY ORCHESTRA

The New Symphony Orchestra is the result of a voluntary effort on the part of Toronto musicians who decided that a Symphony Orchestra could be established if the musicians united in the spirit of co-operation, and if the citizens were sincere in their oft repeated regrets that no such organization existed in Toronto. This splendid movement on the part of the musicians who decided to demonstrate the possibilities of the scheme, so far as they were concerned, became a reality through the great desire of men to study and present the glories of symphonic music. When they decided to organize they lost no time in approaching Mr. Luigi von Kunits, and in soliciting him to be their conductor, which position Mr. von Kunits most graciously accepted. The conductor and the musicians of the New Symphony Orchestra began their work and have continued it to date without consideration of financial return. Their one aim has been to prove that the musicians are ready and that an orchestra can be organized by Toronto musicians.

The need of an orchestra is constantly admitted by all who have any interest in the development of music, not only in our city, but in Canada.

2nd VIOLINS		HORNS
B. Stansfield		R. L. Jose
K. Sturm		W. Voisey
J. Dubinsky		W. Morris
M. Solway		D. Karp
H. L. Vansickle		J. C. Crown
H. S. Tweedie		
V. F. Pellettiere		**TROMBONES**
E. W. Shrubsole		G. T. Blackwell
H. Beard		R. J. Dixon
M. Griss		J. Peel
G. Berul		
H. Aaron		**TUBA**
		T. B. Jones

VIOLAS	FLUTES	OBOES	TYMPANI and PERCUSSION
M. Blackstone			C. E. Culley
F. C. Smith			T. Burry
L. Richer			E. C. Whitney
S. Hoffman		R. H. Lodge	
M. A. Glionna	A. Fenboque	O. E. Woods	
L. Waizman	E. T. Smith		
H. G. Parkinson	N. Fontana	**CLARINETS**	**LIBRARIA**
B. Barshtz	H. J. Elton	W. Dudley	L. Waizman
H. Vearncombe		R. O. Causton	

Members of the orchestra for the 1923–4 season, from the program for the first Twilight Concert, 25 September 1923 at 5:00 p.m. in Massey Hall.

Luigi von Kunits

Mozart – the admiration of my youth, the desperation of my mature years, the consolation of my old age.

GIOACHINO ROSSINI

During the 1920s most of the professional musicians in Toronto were employed in the numerous theatres throughout the city. Many of these musicians were anxious to play classical repertoire, and a number of them had performed in the Welsman orchestra. In the early spring of 1922, these musicians met to discuss the possibilities of once again building a symphony orchestra. They delegated violinist Louis Gesensway and flutist Abe Fenbogue to approach Luigi von Kunits to see whether he would be willing to rehearse and conduct an orchestra.

Luigi von Kunits (1870–1931) was born and raised in the musically rich city of Vienna. He studied violin with Jakob Grün and Otakar Ševčik, composition with Anton Bruckner, and music history with Eduard Hanslick. At age eleven he had been asked by Brahms, who knew his father, to play second violin in one of the composer's string quartets. He was also acquainted with Karl Goldmark and Johann Strauss II. At age twenty-one he had the opportunity to perform his own violin concerto with the Vienna Philharmonic Orchestra. In 1893 he travelled to the United States to perform with an Austrian orchestra at the Chicago World's Fair, where he also won the best solo violinist trophy in open competition. Von Kunits decided to stay in the United States, where he taught violin first in Chicago (1893–6) and later at the Pittsburgh Conservatory (1896–1910). He was also concertmaster of the Pittsburgh Symphony Orchestra from 1897 to 1910. He spent the following two years touring in Europe as a violin soloist. During this time, he was offered the conductorship of the Philadelphia Orchestra, and he also received an invitation to teach at the Canadian Academy of Music in Toronto. He chose the less stressful position in Toronto for health reasons, and the Philadelphia position was given to Leopold Stokowski. Von Kunits remembered Toronto from performances the Pittsburgh Symphony Orchestra gave with the Toronto Mendelssohn Choir, and he felt that there was a great future for music in Toronto.

When von Kunits came to the Canadian Academy of Music as head violin teacher in 1912, he was well known for his superb playing and was equally renowned for his conducting abilities.

Von Kunits considered the request from the Toronto musicians and, sensing their determination and staunch enthusiasm, decided almost immediately to undertake the task. He knew most of the musicians and had personally taught many of the violinists. All the musicians in the new orchestra were professionals except for two: R.L. Jose, who played French horn, and Dr J. Pilcher, a bass clarinettist who was on the faculty of Wycliffe College. Rehearsals commenced in the fall of 1922, initially in the von Kunits home and later in the basement of Massey Hall. Because most of the musicians were employed full-time in the theatres, rehearsals were held in the morning. By the early spring of 1923, the orchestra was ready for its first concert. It was decided that the concert would begin at 5:00 p.m. and would last approximately an hour with no intermission; this would allow sufficient time for the musicians to return to their places of regular employment and, as publicity for the concert pointed out, time for the audience to reach home before evening dinner.

The musicians gave their first concert on 23 April 1923 in Massey Hall under the name New Symphony Orchestra. It is easy to imagine the anticipation, excitement, and apprehension on stage for this first concert, but von Kunits knew that the orchestra was ready to perform for the public. The principal oboe played an A and the orchestra tuned. Then Dr von Kunits stepped onto the podium, raised his baton, gave the downbeat, and they were away into the Overture to *Der Freischutz* by Carl Maria von Weber. The remainder of the program consisted of a *Slavonic Dance* by Antonín Dvořák, two *Hungarian Dances* by Johannes Brahms, and the Symphony No. 5 in E minor by Pyotr Il'yich Tchaikovsky.

1922–1923

Next morning the Toronto press was full of praise for both orchestra and conductor, confident that Toronto once again was on the threshold of having its own permanent symphony orchestra. Each musician received $3.95 for the concert and four rehearsals, but these musicians were performing for the sheer joy of being able to make music as part of a symphony orchestra. Two more concerts were planned and presented in May. Tickets were priced at seventy-five, fifty, and twenty-five cents, with no seats reserved within each section. All the music presented in this inaugural season was orchestral. There were no soloists, but the three programs included compositions by a number of major composers and covered a wide spectrum of international orchestral repertoire. All the works performed involve approximately the same instrumentation. The following announcement appeared in the first program.

> The New Symphony Orchestra is the result of a voluntary effort on the part of
> Toronto musicians who decided that a real Symphony Orchestra could be established

on a musical conception alone. That is, players who wished an opportunity to express themselves through playing symphonic music without considering the immediate financial returns, found themselves in a sufficient numbers to establish themselves as a Symphony Orchestra, and it is believed that there are in Toronto a sufficient number of people who understand and appreciate a Symphony Orchestra, to make a fair audience whenever it is announced that the Orchestra has a program sufficiently rehearsed.

The response to the initial concerts by the public was so good that in the summer of 1923 subscriber applications appeared for the 1923–4 season. H.C. Wotherspoon, who had been orchestra manager for the first season, was replaced by H.J. Elton, who left the flute section to assume this position.

1923–1924

The 1923–4 season witnessed several changes. The size of the orchestra increased from sixty-five to seventy-five musicians, and soloists were invited to perform with the orchestra. Concerts were scheduled to take place every other Tuesday throughout the season. Another innovation in this second season was a series of pre-concert talks, presented on Monday evenings prior to the Tuesday concerts in the Women's Art Association Gallery by Lois Wilson. Each lecture interpreted and explained the music being performed at the upcoming concert.

The first concert of the second season opened with the Overture to Wagner's *Die Meistersinger von Nürnberg* – undoubtedly Dr von Kunits was anxious to make good use of the enlarged orchestra. J. Campbell McInnes sang an aria from Handel's opera *Berenice* and the concert ended with Beethoven's Symphony No. 3 in E flat major ('Eroica'). A note in the program explained that there could be no encores, owing to the limited time allotted for these concerts. Other major works presented during the 1923–4 season included the Piano Concerto No. 5 in E flat major ('Emperor') by Ludwig van Beethoven, the Symphony No. 9 in E minor ('From the New World') by Antonín Dvořák, the Piano Concerto in A minor by Edvard Grieg, and two Tchaikovsky compositions – *Variations on a Rococo Theme* and the Symphony No. 6 in B minor ('Pathétique').

On 30 November, in response to widespread demand, the orchestra gave its first Pops Concert. This new venture was a good indication of the rapidly developing interest of the audience in the orchestra, and its resulting financial stability. The first financial statement issued by secretary-treasurer A.E. Gesensway, covering the period from 24 April 1923 to 6 December 1923, showed a balance of cash in hand of $259.19.

Toronto Symphony Orchestra with conductor Luigi von Kunits at the Arcadian Court in the Robert Simpson department store, circa 1929

Yet another undertaking of the orchestra's first full season was the formation of the Toronto Symphony Orchestra Women's Committee (now the TS Volunteer Committee). This strong, dynamic group, a continuing source of substantial financial support for the orchestra, was initiated in 1923 by Mrs Luigi von Kunits, who enlisted a group of women to form the Women's Orchestral Association of Toronto to secure interest in and finances for the New Symphony Orchestra. In 1924 this group joined with the Executive Committee of the orchestra to create the New Symphony Orchestra Association, the aim being to establish an efficient and capable organization that could sustain the orchestra. A.E. Gooderham was elected president of the new association and Mrs W.A. (Mary) Austin, who had been president of the Women's Orchestral Association, was chosen as one of the two vice-presidents. The Association agreed that the musicians should be paid at least $12.00 per concert, a substantial increase from the $3.95 they had been receiving.

For the next eighteen months there was no separate women's volunteer group, but it soon became obvious that one was needed. On 11 May 1926, a group of women who were members of the New Symphony Orchestra Association agreed to form a Women's Committee. The first president of the Women's Committee was Mrs J.F. Ross. The Women's Committee took over most of the responsibility for the ticket sales and introduced a plan for season tickets to be sold in book form at $10.00 for ten concerts. The innovation proved to be a great success.

In the second half of the 1923–4 season (January to May) twelve concerts were given. One interesting program involved two conductors, Ernest MacMillan and Frank Welsman, along with Luigi von Kunits as soloist, and included two Canadian works.

Overture	Ernest MacMillan
(conducted by Ernest MacMillan)	
Violin Concerto in E minor	Luigi von Kunits
(Luigi von Kunits, violin, conducted by	
Frank Welsman)	
Prelude and Love Death from *Tristan und Isolde*	Richard Wagner
(conducted by Ernest MacMillan)	

1924–1925   The 1924–5 season included the first orchestra concert for children, sponsored jointly by the Toronto Board of Education and the Toronto Catholic School Board. The concert took place on a Saturday morning at 10 a.m. in Massey Hall. The one-hour program included excerpts from compositions by Haydn, Edward German, Edward

Elgar, and Handel. Duncan McKenzie, the supervisor of music for the Toronto Board of Education, gave a short introduction to each piece. It could be said that this concert was the beginning of the TSO Education Programs, the development of which will be a continuing theme in later chapters. At the end of this third season a deficit of $2,200 was erased by a generous anonymous donor.

The first concert of the 1925–6 season opened with the concert overture *In the South* by Edward Elgar and also included the Piano Concerto No. 1 in B flat minor by Tchaikovsky, played by the well-known Canadian pianist Ernest Seitz. On 19 October 1925, a sincere and impassioned plea for maintaining the orchestra on a permanent basis appeared as an editorial in *The Globe*. The editorial was reprinted in the program for the second concert of the season.

1925–1926

> Once more our symphony orchestra has begun its modest season of twilight concerts with no positive assurance that the series planned can be carried out. This annual effort is a venture of faith only, faith in the community's civic pride and good taste, for no endowment fund or private guarantee exists to make certain the continuance of these artistic opportunities ... The New Symphony is a genuinely community affair, of the people, for the people, by the people, and its perpetuation depends entirely upon popular support ... 'Music is what awakes in us when we are reminded by the instruments.' We all need as much of this awakening to higher things as our daily grind makes possible, and there is no tranquilizing of the spirit or recreating joy in beauty comparable to that bestowed by this twilight hour dedicated to the supreme form of this supreme art.

On 10 November Frank Welsman returned to conduct a performance of the Double Concerto in A minor for Violin and Cello, op. 102, by Brahms with soloists Luigi von Kunits and Leo Smith. Halfway through this season there was a deficit of $2,073, but through a concentrated effort in ticket sales, along with more innovative programming, it was reduced to $641 by the end of the season.

November 1925 also saw the first attempt to broadcast a portion of one of the concerts. CKVL, a local radio station, began negotiations with the musicians of the orchestra and the musicians' union for permission to broadcast. Unfortunately, a final decision, which depended on a unanimous vote of the musicians, was not forthcoming, so the technicians removed their equipment and the broadcast fell through.

1926–1927

Frank Welsman returned as guest conductor in 1925

The 1926–7 season opened with a new concertmaster: Grant Milligan took over from Moses Garten, who had left the orchestra. Publicity was intensified and, with the inspiration of Association Committee Chairman A.E. Gooderham, corporate sponsorship was introduced. Leading soloists who appeared with the orchestra this season included British pianist Katherine Bacon, who performed the Piano Concerto No. 2 in G minor by Saint-Saëns, and Kathleen Parlow, the internationally acclaimed Canadian violinist, who played the Paganini Violin Concerto No. 4 in D major.

1927–1928

The beginning of the 1927–8 season saw a significant change: the New Symphony Orchestra officially became the Toronto Symphony Orchestra. The charter bearing the name 'Toronto Symphony Orchestra' was presented to the orchestra by Herbert Cox, who had been chairman of the TSO under Welsman. Cox also owned the library of the orchestra and had obligingly loaned scores and parts to the new TSO, which had not yet built up its own library. A number of problems that had developed as the orchestra grew in prominence were resolved through lengthy discussions between the orchestra management and the musicians' union. This meant that the orchestral musicians now received a more reasonable financial return for their efforts.

The 1927–8 season brought yet another change of concertmaster, when Donald Heins joined the orchestra. Donald Heins (1878–1949) was born in England, but on the advice of Pablo de Sarasate had gone to the Leipzig Conservatory to study with Hans Sitt. In Leipzig he also studied harmony with Gustav Schreck and orchestration with Richard Hoffman, and later in England he continued his violin studies with August Wilhemj. Heins came to Canada in 1902 and settled in Ottawa, where he taught at the Canadian Conservatory of Music and also directed the Conservatory orchestra. During his years with that orchestra, he conducted Ottawa premieres of a number of works from the standard orchestral repertoire. Donald Heins was also a composer, and on 31 January 1928 the TSO program included a performance of his

Concertino in D minor for violin and orchestra, with Heins as the soloist. Heins remained concertmaster until Ernest MacMillan became conductor in 1931, when he became both the principal violist and the TSO's first assistant conductor. This season also included a performance by lyric soprano Lady Eaton, singing an aria from the opera *Mignon* by Ambroise Thomas.

The 1928–9 season bought the orchestra's first evening performance: a non-subscription joint concert with the Schubert Choir of Brantford. The program consisted of short pieces for choir and orchestra. There had been many requests from concert-goers regarding the possibility of 8 p.m. performances, and perhaps this joint concert was a test of public reaction. On 29 January Ernest MacMillan was the guest conductor for a performance of Hubert Parry's *The Pied Piper of Hamelin*, and the Toronto Conservatory Choir joined the orchestra for this fine setting of Browning's poem. As with the preceding seasons, the orchestra ran a deficit of $3,000 to $4,000. An urgent appeal for 1,000 members to join the orchestra Association at a fee of $10 each underlined the need for additional funding.

1928–1929

In the fall of 1929 the TSO embarked upon a new venture in music making with a much larger audience than could be accommodated in Massey Hall. Sunday, 20 October marked the Toronto Symphony Orchestra's first radio broadcast across Canada on the CNR Radio Network. This initial effort was a success, with congratulatory telegrams and letters arriving from across the country. The following telegram was sent to Dr von Kunits by E.A. Weir, the director of CNR Radio.

1929–1930

> Dr von Kunits:
> Your performance magnificent. A wonderful representation on the air, for Canada.
> Entire programme outstanding success. Congratulations.
> E.A. Weir, Director of Radio.

Such success did not come easily. Special equipment had to be obtained from New York, and since Massey Hall was not completely soundproof, a broadcasting venue had to be found. The Arcadian Court, an expansive dining area on the eighth floor of the Simpson's department store, turned out to be highly suitable for broadcasting purposes, and C.L. Burton, president of Simpson's, generously made this space available to the orchestra. This first broadcast was not only a momentous occasion for the orchestra but also an important step for Canadian radio, and it marked the beginning of the TSO's long association with this media. Broadcast concerts took place on Sundays, which was most convenient for the musicians as there were no Sunday theatre performances. Much of the information about the program content for these broadcasts has since been lost; most likely the orchestra repeated music from that week's Massey Hall concert.

This season also included some outstanding concerts on stage. One was a performance of Edward Elgar's *Sea Pictures*, sung by the renowned English contralto Muriel Brunskill. Another was the North American premiere of Constant Lambert's *The Rio Grande*, with pianist Ernest Seitz and the Toronto Conservatory Choir, conducted by Ernest MacMillan. In addition, the children's concerts were resumed after a break of three years – an unfortunate disruption caused by the resignation of Duncan McKenzie as supervisor of music for the Toronto Board of Education. His position was filled by Emily Tedd, who had been his assistant.

1930–1931

During the 1930–1 season the venue for the CNR broadcasts changed from the Arcadian Court to the studios of CFRB Radio. The reason for the move remains a mystery, as no official documentation has survived. On 7 April 1931 a special full-length evening concert was given for the purpose of reducing the orchestra's deficit of $6,000. Both conductor and musicians donated their services, as did the Toronto Conservatory Choir, for this most ambitious program.

Overture	Ernest MacMillan
Symphony in D minor	César Franck
Violin Concerto in E minor	Felix Mendelssohn
(Léon Zighéra, violin)	
Prelude and Fugue in G minor	J.S. Bach, arr. Ernest MacMillan
St Patrick's Breastplate	Arnold Bax

This concert was significant for two reasons. One was that this would be the last time Luigi von Kunits conducted the orchestra, for he died six months later on 8 October 1931. The Franck symphony and the Mendelssohn concerto were two of his personal favourites. The other point of significance is that the program included two works by Ernest MacMillan, who was to be the next conductor of the TSO. In addition, the performance of *St Patrick's Breastplate* was a North American premiere. All in all, it was a prestigious event for the end of a season, and the end of an era.

Luigi von Kunits gave his life to music and devoted many hours of work to establishing a solid foundation for the orchestra. His dedication made it possible for the TSO to move on to a new stage of development under the leadership of Ernest MacMillan.

Sir Ernest MacMillan, Part 1

I am convinced that there are universal currents of Divine Thought vibrating the ether everywhere and that any who can feel these vibrations is inspired ...

RICHARD WAGNER

Ernest MacMillan (1893–1973), one of the most prominent figures of his time in Canadian music history, was born in Mimico, Ontario. He began organ studies at the age of eight and soon was performing in public. During a family sojourn in Edinburgh (1905–8) he continued his organ studies with Alfred Hollins, and also attended music classes at the University of Edinburgh. Back at home, he served as organist of Knox Presbyterian Church in Toronto for two years and then spent an additional year studying music in Britain. On his return to Toronto, he studied modern history at the University of Toronto and simultaneously served as organist and choirmaster at St Paul's Presbyterian Church in Hamilton. In 1914, he journeyed to Paris to study piano with Thérèse Chaigneau. The outbreak of the First World War in 1914 found him in Germany with the intention of attending the Wagner Festival at Bayreuth. He was consequently detained as an enemy alien, and spent most of the war in a prisoner-of-war camp at Ruhleben, near Berlin. However, he did not allow this confining situation to interrupt his music studies. During the first months of the war, while he was detained in Nuremberg, he wrote the first version of his String Quartet in C minor. Later, through the Prisoners-of-War Education Committee, he submitted a setting of Swinburne's ode *England* as part of the requirements for a doctorate of music from Oxford University. On returning home, MacMillan embarked upon an intense music career not only in Toronto and Ontario but also across Canada. Around this time MacMillan was becoming interested in conducting. In 1924 Luigi von Kunits invited him to conduct the TSO in a performance of his *Overture*. Von Kunits approved of MacMillan's conducting and in 1931, during his last illness, suggested that MacMillan should be his successor. MacMillan had already been booked to conduct the first two concerts of the 1931–2 season, owing to the serious condition of von Kunits's health, and on 23 October 1931 he was appointed conductor of the orchestra.

1931–1932   The appointment of Ernest MacMillan to the position of conductor only four days before the first concert of the new season did not result in a smooth transition. There had been a number of applicants for the position, and while the local press was of the opinion that MacMillan was the right choice, many people favoured Reginald Stewart, another serious contender. Like MacMillan, Stewart was of Scottish descent, and he had strong support. His conducting technique and interpretation were considered to be more mature. However, the orchestra committee's decision prevailed and MacMillan accepted without hesitation. The next day, he made his plans for the future of the orchestra known to the players – including some major changes in personnel. The musicians' immediate reaction was negative and they made it known that they did not appreciate MacMillan's high-handed attitude. Within the next day or two MacMillan realized the error of his ways, and on 24 October 1931 wrote 'Statement re Orchestra Situation,' which opens as follows:

> When last evening I announced my acceptance of the position as conductor of The Toronto Symphony Orchestra, I thought I was doing so with the unanimous support of the members of the orchestra. Had this not been so, I should certainly have refused or at least delayed my acceptance until we should have had time to come to a complete understanding on all points at issue. Having announced my acceptance, I was surprised to learn by chance today that some dissension had since arisen with regard to the reorganization which I outlined to the orchestra yesterday.[1]

MacMillan went on to suggest that the musicians had misunderstood his plans and that he had no intention of introducing measures that could be interpreted as destroying the pioneering work done by Luigi von Kunits.

MacMillan had little knowledge of professional orchestras or the temperament of musicians. He was, however, taking over an orchestra that had been well prepared and developed by a master. He soon realized that there was a lot to learn. He handled future situations with more diplomacy, but there were occasional incidents when MacMillan acted in haste and showed some insensitivity.

The first concert of the 1931–2 season, presented on 27 October, opened with the second movement from the Symphony No. 3 in E flat major ('Eroica') by Beethoven, played as a memorial to the late Dr Luigi von Kunits. The program included the Piano Concerto No. 1 in E minor by Chopin with soloist Ernest Seitz and Beethoven's Symphony No. 8 in F major.

Throughout his career Ernest MacMillan was an enthusiastic proponent of music education for young people. He wrote numerous articles on the subject and gave many speeches on music education throughout Canada. In an article for the Ontario Educational Association in 1944 he commented that the greatest function of school music was that of building future audiences: 'Music is not primarily something you do – it is something you live.'

Emily Tedd had been involved with Toronto school concerts since 1926, when she was appointed successor to Duncan McKenzie as supervisor of music for the Toronto Board of Education. It was in 1931 that the school concerts began to really flourish. Emily Tedd and MacMillan shared a strong desire to present music to schoolchildren with the emphasis and quality it deserved. The first concert on which they collaborated took place on 3 November 1931; details of that concert have been lost, but the second concert, presented on 1 December 1931, gives an indication of how varied and interesting the programs were.

Prelude to *Lohengrin*, Act III	Richard Wagner
'Berceuse' from *Jocelyn*	Benjamin Godard
Overture to *The Magic Flute*	Wolfgang Amadeus Mozart
Kol Nidrei	Max Bruch
Dances from *Henry VIII*	Edward German
Selections from the *William Tell* Overture	Gioachino Rossini

The programs began at 4:15 p.m. because the Toronto Board of Education would not relinquish school time for children to attend the concerts.

The 1931–2 season saw the first indications that the one-hour Twilight Concerts were coming to an end. Three or four concerts were given in the evening, commencing at 8:30 p.m. and lasting for two hours. There were also some changes in personnel. Donald Heins, who had been concertmaster under von Kunits, was appointed assistant conductor as well as principal viola. The new concertmaster, Elie Spivak (1902–60), had studied at the Paris Conservatoire and the Royal College of Music in Manchester. He spent a year in New York before moving in 1926 to Toronto, where he taught at the Conservatory and, from 1929 to 1942, played first violin in the Conservatory String Quartet. For the subscription concert on 10 November, Spivak gave an outstanding performance of the *Symphonie espagnole* by Édouard Lalo.

The second half of the 1931–2 season opened on 12 January with a concert featuring the well-known Chilean pianist Alberto Guerrero, who was the soloist for the colourful and exhilarating *Nights in the Gardens of Spain* by Manuel de Falla. On 20 January Reginald Stewart played the Piano Concerto No. 2 in C minor by Serge Rachmaninoff in a concert that was upgraded from a twilight to an evening event. The program also included the suite from Tchaikovsky's ballet *The Nutcracker* and Brahms's

Toronto Symphony Orchestra with conductor Sir Ernest MacMillan on stage at Massey Hall

Symphony No. 2 in D major. The concert for 23 February included a performance of the Symphony No. 2 in D major by Jean Sibelius. The program for this concert included a notice requesting the audience to kindly refrain from applauding between the movements of the symphony. Perhaps MacMillan was a little annoyed with the disturbance. An all-British program on 8 March included the Toronto premiere of *Benedicite*, a cantata by Ralph Vaughan Williams. Soprano Agnes Smith Kelsey and the Toronto Conservatory Choir joined the orchestra for this work. The final concert of the season was devoted to works of Wagner, including the overtures to *The Flying Dutchman* and *Tannhäuser*, and two other favourites, the *Siegfried Idyll* and the 'Ride of the Valkyries' from *Die Walküre*. This ambitious season could be counted a success – especially in the midst of the Depression.

1932–1933

Since A.E. Gooderham had decided to step down, the Board of Directors had to choose a new president. Vincent Massey, who was elected to take his place, immediately proposed that Col Gooderham, the man whose guidance and drive had done much to maintain the momentum during the first crucial years of the orchestra, be named Honorary President.

At a Board meeting in the late summer of 1932, MacMillan put forward a plan for the upcoming season and suggested that concerts should start at 8.30 p.m. and should be two hours long. He was also anxious to bring the size of the orchestra to ninety musicians. His plan had great merit. Movie theatre orchestras were rapidly becoming redundant with the advent of 'talkies' and subsequently musicians were available for evening concerts. A new and better salary scale was agreed upon for rehearsals and concerts, and these increased costs resulted in higher ticket prices: the new tickets ranged from 50¢ to $2.50 (a substantial increase from the previous 25¢ to 75¢). The Board accepted MacMillan's plan – a significant decision considering that Canada was still in the grip of the Depression. The program for the first concert showed both virtuosity and intensity – a clear indication that MacMillan's knowledge of repertoire was developing.

Overture to *Ruslan and Lyudmila*	Mikhail Glinka
Suite from *Water Music*	George Frideric Handel,
	arr. Hamilton Harty
Piano Concerto No. 4 in G major	Ludwig van Beethoven
(Viggo Kihl, piano)	
Symphony No. 1 in C minor	Johannes Brahms

Robertson Davies, who was a student at Upper Canada College when MacMillan took over the TSO in 1931, wrote, 'With MacMillan came rather a lot of Wagner and I recall feeling crushed under the intensity of the Liebestod.'[2] MacMillan was indeed a Wagner enthusiast and during his tenure he was to conduct many concerts devoted to the composer. A Wagner program on 6 December presented the Prelude to Act I, the Good Friday music, and the final scene from *Parsifal* followed by the final scene of *Die Meistersinger von Nürnberg*. The Toronto Conservatory Choir joined the orchestra for the two final scenes. MacMillan's great interest in Wagner later led him to publish an article entitled 'Hitler and Wagnerism,' in which he suggests that it is necessary to understand 'Wagnerism' in order to understand the perversions of Hitler. However, he argues for the continued acceptance of the superb music of a great composer, divorced from that composer's dubious and unoriginal philosophical ideas, and for music to be kept in the concert hall and out of politics.[3]

The season also included Brahms's Violin Concerto in D major, with Géza de Kresz as soloist, and Sibelius's Symphony No. 2. Canadian pianist, composer, and conductor Rex Battle had presented the TSO with the score and parts for Ernest Chausson's Symphony in B flat major, and the symphony was performed on 7 February. At the following concert on 21 February Rex Battle was piano soloist with the string section for the *Concerto Grosso* No. 1 by Ernest Bloch. In March, when spring is on the minds of most people, Elie Spivak and the orchestra appropriately gave a performance of Vaughan Williams's *The Lark Ascending*. The last subscription concert of the season was devoted to two Beethoven symphonies: No. 1 in C major and No. 9 in D minor with soprano Jeanne Pengelly, contralto Mabel Beddoe, tenor Julian Oliver, baritone George Lambert, and the Toronto Conservatory Choir. An additional concert added to the season on 4 April included the North American premiere of George Dyson's *The Canterbury Pilgrims*.

1933–1934

The opening concert of the TSO's twelfth season began almost where the previous season had left off, with a large portion of Wagner. The second half of the concert was devoted to a performance of Tchaikovsky's Symphony No. 5 in E minor. Wagner was well represented this season. Lord Bessborough, the Governor-General of Canada, and his wife were interested in Wagner's music, and asked to hear the all-Wagner program on 9 January 1934. At the end of the season an extra concert was added to commemorate the centennial of the city of Toronto. Half the program was devoted to Wagner and the other half to Beethoven's Symphony No. 9 with soprano Jeanne Pengelly, contralto Eileen Marshall, tenor Leslie Mardall, baritone George Lambert, and the Toronto Conservatory Choir.

The 1933–4 season also saw an increase in the engagement of international artists: Jeanne Dusseau sang *Three French Canadian Sea Songs* arranged by Ernest MacMillan and 'Abscheulicher' from *Fidelio* by Beethoven. The following concert on 5 December brought Ruggiero Ricci, a twelve-year-old violin prodigy. His performance of the *Symphonie espagnole* by Édouard Lalo received rave reviews and a standing ovation in Massey Hall. Harriet Cohen, the renowned English pianist, was the soloist for the Canadian premiere of Arnold Bax's *Symphonic Variations*. On 6 February Gregor Piatigorsky, the world-acclaimed Russian cellist, played the Cello Concerto No. 1 in A minor by Camille Saint-Saëns. In February or March the TSO, under the direction of MacMillan, performed at the Toronto Skating Club in a program entitled 'Carnival – Follies of 1934.' Guest skaters Sonja Henie and Karl Schaffer appeared in what was the first interpretation on ice of Maurice Ravel's *Bolero*. On 6 March the Toronto Conservatory Choir, the Madrigal Singers of Peterborough, and a schoolchildren's choir led by Emily Tedd joined forces with the orchestra for a performance of Gabriel Pierné's *The Children's Crusade*. For the last concert of the regular season Ernest Seitz, Viggo Kihl, and Alberto Guerrero were soloists for Mozart's Concerto in F major for three pianos, K 242. The orchestra had planned a short spring tour of western Ontario, including concerts in Kitchener-Waterloo and London. However, because of a disagreement between the Toronto and London musicians' unions over percentage pay from box office receipts, the tour was cancelled.

For many years TSO musicians had experienced difficulty in finding employment from April to September, when there were no regular concerts. This situation changed in the summer of 1934 when Reginald Stewart, in association with the Toronto Musicians Protective Association, founded a summer series of weekly Promenade Symphony Concerts given in Varsity Arena, on the University of Toronto campus. The orchestra of seventy-five to ninety musicians (mainly TSO members) was first known as the Promenade Symphony Orchestra. The Promenade Concerts continued until 1956, although the orchestra changed its name to the Toronto Philharmonic Orchestra in 1941.

1934–1935   MacMillan's devotion to Wagner was once again represented with two concerts of his compositions. The concert on 11 December presented the Prelude and 'Liebestod' from *Tristan und Isolde* and the aria 'Dich, theure Halle' (Dear Hall of Song) from *Tannhäuser* with Lotte Lehmann as soloist. The last concert of the regular season was a Wagner evening of opera in concert, consisting of the Prelude and Act I of *Lohengrin* in the first half, and excerpts from Act III of *Die Meistersinger* in the second half. Although the main season had come to a close, the month of April was a busy one. On 12 April the annual benefit concert was given to raise money for the orchestra's Sustaining Fund. This was followed on 23–4 April by two concerts with the Toronto Mendelssohn Choir for the Choir's Spring Festival at Maple Leaf Gardens. On the first night the choir sang selections from the *Liebeslieder Waltzes*, op. 52, by Johannes Brahms and the 'Sanctus' from Bach's Mass in B minor, and the orchestra played the Symphony No. 4 in F minor by Tchaikovsky. The program for the second night consisted of a selection of English folk songs and part songs and other choral works. On 27 April the TSO participated in a concert at Massey Hall that was part of the trans-Canada jubilee tour of the original Hambourg Trio: pianist Mark Hambourg, violinist Jan Hambourg, and cellist Boris Hambourg. The interesting program took full advantage of all three soloists.

Coriolan Overture	Ludwig van Beethoven
Two Romances for Violin	Ludwig van Beethoven

Violinist Albert Pratz became concertmaster of the orchestra in 1971

accommodated as the broadcast portion of the concert ran precisely from 9:30 to 10:30 p.m.

The season was one of highs and lows. On the plus side there were several interesting guest artists, including Jan Peerce, the celebrated tenor, on 8 November. On 15 November 1939 Albert Pratz, a gifted young violinist who was a member of the TSO and would later become concertmaster of the orchestra, played the Glazunov Violin Concerto in A minor. On 29 November, Heinz Unger was invited back to conduct the orchestra for a second time. Unger's conducting skills and interpretation had been well received the previous season, and at this concert, he again gave an outstanding performance, which included Brahms's Symphony No. 4 in E minor and the *Romeo and Juliet* fantasy overture by Tchaikovsky. Hans Kindler, the founder and conductor of the National Symphony Orchestra in Washington, made his conducting debut with the orchestra on 24 January 1939. On 7 February, George Enescu conducted the first half of the concert, and was the soloist for the Beethoven Violin Concerto in D major after the intermission. Two weeks later, Henry Swoboda, the Czech conductor, led the orchestra in works by Antonín Dvořák and Bedřich Smetana while MacMillan conducted the remainder of the program.

The Opera Guild of Toronto joined forces with the Toronto Symphony Orchestra in a complete concert performance of Wagner's *Lohengrin*. The opera was performed on 28 February and 2 March, with Sir Ernest conducting the first night and Ettore Mazzoleni on the podium for the second. The final subscription concert of the season was a request program with the nine-year-old pianist Valdine Conde as guest artist for a performance of the Liszt Piano Concerto No. 1 in E flat major.

The season ended with a deficit of almost $40,000, and the future of the orchestra was unclear. MacMillan was unhappy with the circumstances and began questioning his conducting ability in comparison with that of conductors such as Heinz Unger, Eugene Ormandy, or Leopold Stokowski. He gave thought to stepping down, and actually forwarded two letters of resignation (on 28 March and 11 April) citing the nervous strain caused by the difficult conditions, especially in view of the possibility of war. MacMillan had also written of his intentions to Arthur Judson of Columbia Concerts in New York in September 1938, but Judson advised him to be patient and to build on the foundation of his good work in Toronto, which would pay dividends in the long run. MacMillan, however, did make enquiries in London and New York about possible appointments. One of his justified complaints was the number of concerts in the season – there were only nineteen. He had asked the TSO Board to review the musicians' salaries with a view to raising the scale to allow for more concerts and additional personnel. During the summer of 1939 his strategy was to encourage the Board to adopt his scheme. However, with war imminent, he was apprehensive that symphony orchestras, like other arts organizations, might be seen as a low priority, and thus he distanced himself from confrontation as he prepared for the new season. Board member J.E. Hahn wanted to place the orchestra on a 'share' plan, similar to an arrangement made with von Kunits in the early days of the orchestra. MacMillan had the foresight to know that this would not be beneficial for the continuance of the orchestra. 'People need music,' he wrote, 'and need it badly in wartime.'[4] He was not prepared to see his orchestra suffer the same fate as the first TSO under Frank Welsman in 1918. Hahn retracted his position and MacMillan won the day. W.G. Watson, who had been elected President of the Board (a position he was to hold until 1953), agreed with MacMillan that for the next season the orchestra should be maintained at all costs.

During the First World War works by German composers had been almost forbidden, but the first concert of this season opened with two works by Beethoven: the *Coriolan* Overture and the Symphony No. 3 in E flat major ('Eroica'). It seems that music appreciation and understanding had risen to a more sophisticated level and compositions were accepted for what they were rather than rejected because of the country from which they originated. The concert of 5 December further demonstrated this musical acceptance, with performances of *These Things Shall Be* by John Ireland and the Symphony No. 9 in D minor by Beethoven. The first concert in the new year was to include works by George Butterworth, Mozart, and Brahms, but this was changed to a program of music by the Finnish composer Jean Sibelius. The concert represented an expression of support for the Finnish people in their strong and determined resistance to the invasion of Finland by Russian forces that began on 1 December 1939. The request program that brought the season to a close on 26 March included Tchaikovsky's Symphony No. 6 in B minor and his fantasy overture *Romeo and Juliet*. The programming for this first wartime season was not audacious. The Board, wanting to maintain good audience attendance, had approved a season that contained well known and accepted repertoire, and the season saw a slight but encouraging increase in ticket sales.

The children's concert on 1 November included a work that was, and still is, a favourite for young people's concerts – *The Carnival of the Animals* by Camille Saint-Saëns. Sir Ernest conducted, and had the audience join in singing 'There'll Always Be an Eng-

1939–1940

1940–1941

land.' For the opening concert of the subscription series on 29 October, William Primrose, the internationally acclaimed violist, returned to give an outstanding performance of *Harold in Italy* by Hector Berlioz, and also played the *Ballade for Viola and String Orchestra* by Canadian composer Godfrey Ridout. On 26 November, Sir Thomas Beecham made his debut with the TSO in a program of Beecham favourites, including *The Faithful Shepherd* (a suite of music by Handel, arranged by Sir Thomas), Frederick Delius's *On Hearing the First Cuckoo in Spring*, and two Mozart works – the Symphony No. 31 in D major, K. 297, and the Overture to *The Marriage of Figaro*. The evening ended with Brahms's Symphony No. 2 in D major. The concert was well received and there was much speculation about possible return visits, since Beecham was now resident in the United States and his visits would have benefited both MacMillan and the orchestra. The first concert of 1941 included the world premiere of *Symphonic Suite* by the Canadian composer and arranger Robert Farnon. The concert for 21 January had a British theme. The program included Ralph Vaughan Williams's cantata *Dona Nobis Pacem*. Walt Whitman's text for this choral work expresses the desire of all people for peace. The evening also featured a performance of Sir Ernest MacMillan's *England*. MacMillan wrote this work while in a prisoner-of-war camp during the First World War; it was first performed in 1921 by the Sheffield Musical Union with Henry Coward conducting. The Toronto Mendelssohn Choir gave the Canadian premiere in 1921 with the Philadelphia Orchestra at Massey Hall. On 4 February Kathleen Parlow, the internationally renowned violinist who was born in Calgary, played the Sibelius Violin Concerto.

A number of high school students had approached Emily Tedd to ask about the possibility of longer concerts with more adult content because school concerts no longer met their needs. Emily Tedd discussed this suggestion with MacMillan and they decided to arrange a full evening concert to see what response was generated. This first Secondary Schools concert took place on 11 February 1941. The program was a good mix of works including Edvard Grieg's Piano Concerto in A minor and the first movement of Vaughan Williams's *A London Symphony*. The admission price was forty cents and tickets could only be obtained at the high schools. The concert proved a success and a second was planned for 1 April.

At the beginning of the 1940–1 season Zara Nelsova, who had studied with Pablo Casals and Gregor Piatigorsky, became the principal cellist. Her brilliant playing had already made her a household name in Canada. On 18 March her dazzling musicianship was fully demonstrated in her performance of Schumann's Cello Concerto in A minor. The season had been a success and had strengthened the argument for continuing

Arthur Rubinstein made his debut with the TSO in 1941

orchestra performances during wartime. The total income for the season was $47,596 (including $10,000 from broadcasting fees) and the excess of revenue over expenses was $246, making an overall balance in hand of $2,507. Furthermore, two outstanding Canadian musicians – Kathleen Parlow and Zara Nelsova – had made their debuts with the orchestra.

1941–1942

The previous season had been reassuring, but the 1941–2 season was to be one of the most exciting to date. With the United States now fully involved in the war, many artists were limited to touring in North America and this situation was reflected in the season's programs. In November Kathleen Parlow returned to perform the Tchaikovsky Violin Concerto in D major. On 3 February Arthur Rubinstein made his debut with the TSO in a performance of Brahms's Piano Concerto No. 2 in B flat major. Joseph Szigeti came a month later to play the Brahms Violin Concerto in D major.

Because of the success of the two Secondary Schools concerts in the previous season, MacMillan and the Board decided to increase the number of student concerts to five, keeping the admission price of forty cents. In addition, a Student Council was formed, made up of two representatives from each high school in the city. At the first meeting, held at Jarvis Collegiate, Victor Feldbrill (who later became a well-known Canadian conductor) was elected president. The council also included another celebrated name in the musical world – Harry Somers.

Back in 1940 the orchestra management had begun negotiations with RCA Victor on the production of recordings. RCA was interested and it was hoped that a contract would be signed so that recording could commence in 1941. Much discussion took place between RCA and MacMillan regarding the selection of music to be recorded. MacMillan wanted to include the *Enigma Variations* by Edward Elgar, but RCA felt that four movements from *The Planets* by Gustav Holst along with Elgar's *Pomp and Circum-*

stance *Marches* would be more profitable. After many months of negotiation, the RCA choice of music was agreed upon and the recording sessions were finally undertaken on 27 March 1942. These recordings were made in Massey Hall late in the evening so as to avoid as much extraneous street noise as possible. Other changes that took place during the 1941–2 season included an alteration in the CBC broadcasting schedule. The CBC requested that the one-hour broadcast portion of the concerts begin at 9:30 p.m. Consequently, the symphony changed the concert time to 8:30 p.m.

This season also included a number of special events. A special Dominion Day concert celebrating the seventy-fifth anniversary of Confederation was picked up by the BBC in England for re-broadcast in the British Isles. Undoubtedly this was done so that the many thousands of Canadian Forces stationed there would have the opportunity to hear the concert. In August 1942, the orchestra was engaged by the IBM company for a concert at the Canadian National Exhibition, and in October 1942 they were back in Maple Leaf Gardens for two concerts with the Coliseum Chorus.

1942–1943

The season opened with a change of assistant conductor. Donald Heins resigned from the position, but remained a member of the viola section of the orchestra. Ettore Mazzoleni (1905–68) was invited by MacMillan to join the orchestra as Associate Conductor. Mazzoleni was born in Switzerland but moved to England as a child. While a student at the Royal College of Music, he had come into contact with Sir Adrian Boult and Ralph Vaughan Williams. Mazzoleni came to Canada in 1929 as music master of Upper Canada College, and in 1934 succeeded Donald Heins as conductor of the Toronto Conservatory of Music Symphony Orchestra. He had also been program annotator for the TSO, and was a brother-in-law of Sir Ernest.

In February 1942, when Herbert Austin Fricker resigned his position as music director of the Toronto Mendelssohn Choir because of poor health, MacMillan was invited to take over. The most significant change he made was to absorb the Toronto Conservatory Choir into the Mendelssohn Choir. This gave him the opportunity to perform large choral works with the TSO. The first concert of the reorganized choir with the orchestra was a performance of Handel's *Messiah* in December 1942. The concert on 19 January 1943 included two major choral works: *Blest Pair of Sirens* by Hubert Parry and Verdi's *Messa da Requiem*, composed in honour of Alessandro Manzoni. The *Requiem* was repeated on 25 April for a special Easter Sunday broadcast concert over the CBC national network in Canada and the Columbia Broadcasting System in the United States. Two more choral works were given in a special concert on 6 April: *For the Fallen* by Edward Elgar and Beethoven's Symphony No. 9 in D minor.

Sir Ernest MacMillan, Part 2

The trouble with music appreciation in general is that people are taught to have too much respect for music; they should be taught to love it instead.

IGOR STRAVINSKY

1945–1946

After six years of war, with all its uncertainty, anguish, and tension, it was time for regrouping and rebuilding. Musicians who had been away on active service with the Canadian Forces returned. Unlike the situation at the end of the First World War, the orchestra was still fully intact. President of the Board W.G. Watson and MacMillan had stressed the importance of music as a significant element in morale building during the war, and with determination and dedication had maintained regular concerts. The size of the postwar orchestra increased from eighty-one to eighty-four musicians.

This first postwar season totalled fifty-seven concerts (compared to thirty-nine in the previous season), including twenty-four Pops Concerts that were sponsored by the Robert Simpson Co. and broadcast by the CBC across Canada. The CBC paid $65,000 for broadcast of these concerts. The Toronto Board of Education also proposed the broadcast of five sets of Secondary Schools concerts at $500 per concert. This expansion in concert activity meant that the musicians' salaries were increased by almost 35 per cent and the administrative expenses by almost 50 per cent. For example, the rent for Massey Hall was almost double due to the extended use of the facility. The Board also approved an initial transfer of $3,000 from the Toronto Symphony Association general funds to establish the Toronto Symphony Orchestra Retirement Fund.

The opening concert of the season, as might be expected, was a 'Victory Programme,' but much of the 'international' music was somewhat unconventional. China was represented with *New China March* by Morton Gould, and England by the 'Gavotte and Cachuca' from *The Gondoliers* by Arthur Sullivan. Canada was represented by a waltz from the *Symphonic Suite* by Robert Farnon. The United States seemed to be the only country properly represented – with the *Liberty Bell* march by John Philip Sousa. The work chosen to end the concert, Beethoven's Symphony No. 5 in C minor, was also appropriate, as the opening three measures of the first movement had become a victory theme for the Allied Forces.

Engagements of guest artists were also substantially increased. To open the season resignation was both diplomatic and compassionate, but Elie Spivak was naturally hurt and distraught. After a few days, with extreme sadness, he submitted a letter of resignation. In his hand-written reply accepting Spivak's resignation MacMillan wrote, 'It will be a genuine pleasure to have you as guest artist in the coming season.'

The season offered a number of exciting concerts. On 18 November the Toronto Mendelssohn Choir joined the orchestra for a performance of Mendelssohn's *Elijah* with soprano Helen Simmie, contralto Eileen Law, tenor Albert Marson, bass John Brownlee, and boy soprano Barry Knibbs. In December the TSO and the Mendelssohn Choir again combined for two performances of Handel's *Messiah*, an event that has continued as a seasonal tradition for more than fifty years.

Eileen Farrell, the American soprano, made her TSO debut on 30 January in a Pops Concert conducted by Arthur Fiedler. Dame Myra Hess also made her TSO debut on 6–7 January playing the Piano Concerto No. 3 in C minor by Beethoven. On 13–14 April William Kapell performed the Rachmaninoff Piano Concerto No. 3 in D minor. Another important TSO debut in this season was by Isaac Stern, who performed the Prokofiev Violin Concerto No. 1. America's foremost (and reputedly Toscanini's favourite) tenor Jan Peerce joined the orchestra in a concert conducted by Ettore Mazzoleni. He sang the arias 'Il mio tesoro' from *Don Giovanni* by Mozart, 'Sound an Alarm' from *Judas Maccabeus* by Handel, and 'O Paradiso' from *L'africaine* by Giacomo Meyerbeer.

In 1947 MacMillan, who was a strong advocate of Canadian music, was appointed Honorary President of the Composers, Authors and Publishers Association of Canada (CAPAC). With CAPAC funds he proposed and conducted a special concert of Canadian music with the TSO, consisting of Healey Willan's Symphony No. 1 in D minor along with shorter works by Godfrey Ridout, Leo Smith, Claude Champagne, Jean Vallerand, John Weinzweig, and Maurice Dela. MacMillan made a strong appeal for patrons to come and hear music composed by Canadians, but unfortunately the attendance was disappointing. Financially the concert showed a deficit of almost $3,000, which was sustained by CAPAC. However, the doubling of the subscription concerts had proved a success and the financial situation at the end of the season was extremely healthy.

The season opened with a new concertmaster, Hyman Goodman, who had joined the orchestra in 1931. During the summer months, Massey Hall had undergone extensive restoration, mainly to comply with Toronto fire regulations, which required specific

1948–1949

Dame Myra Hess gave a special recital for the TSO musicians' Sustaining Fund in 1949

alterations beneath the stage. One requirement involved poured concrete, which in turn caused acoustical problems and deterioration. The staff said the hall would be ready for the TSO's opening concert on 22 October, but not without some inconvenience, because there were no new seats in the balcony.

The 1948–9 season had a number of important guest artists. On 1–2 February Clifford Curzon, the brilliant English pianist, played Mozart's Piano Concerto No. 24 in C minor, K 491, and the *Hungarian Fantasy* by Liszt. The previous month, Witold Malcuzynski, a world-acclaimed pianist from Poland, performed the Piano Concerto No. 3 in D minor by Rachmaninoff. Metropolitan opera stars also were featured. Eileen Farrell joined the orchestra for a Wagner night, and according to reviews the following day, her performance of the *Wesendonck Lieder* and three extracts from *Gotterdämmerung* was outstanding. Other members of the Metropolitan 'contingent' who made Toronto Symphony Orchestra debuts were Robert Merrill, Richard Tucker, and Nan Merriman. William Primrose, the eminent violist, gave fine performances of Arthur Benjamin's *Concerto on Themes by Cimarosa* and *Harold in Italy* by Berlioz. On 9 February, Myra Hess returned to Toronto to give a special recital for the TSO musicians' Sustaining Fund. On previous visits to Toronto Dame Myra had become quite friendly with MacMillan and Pearl Whitehead, a member of the Board, and discussion arose among them regarding the orchestra's Sustaining Fund. The resulting highly successful recital added almost $6,000 to the fund.

On 22 February the TSO and the Mendelssohn Choir joined forces for a significant historical performance of J.S. Bach's Mass in B minor, conducted by Sir Ernest MacMillan. The soloists included sopranos Lois Marshall and Mary Morrison, contralto Margaret Stillwell, tenor Pierre Boutet, baritone Donald Brown, bass Eric Tredwell, and Greta Kraus playing the harpsichord. On 8 March MacMillan conducted the orchestra and choir for a Secondary Schools concert in a predominately British program which included William Walton's *Belshazzar's Feast* and *Songs of the Sea*, op. 91, by Charles Villiers Stanford.

A sold-out Friday night Pops Concert in Massey Hall, 1949

The financial situation at the end of the season illustrates how corporations and the Toronto Symphony Women's Committee came forward to eliminate a deficit of $49,000. The Women's Committee donated $14,000 and corporations contributed the balance into the operating fund, enabling the TSO Association to show a surplus of $2,500.

1949–1950

Originality in programming for 1949–50 seemed to be non-existent in comparison to the previous season. Perhaps MacMillan had lost interest in contemporary works and especially in Canadian music. In past seasons he had introduced plenty of new music, much of which was British. Indications were that the standard of playing was becoming static, and that there would be little change in the foreseeable future. MacMillan and the Board were well aware of the type of music most patrons desired and were not about to embark on new policies that might cause a reduction in seat sales.

On 13–14 December, however, the orchestra did venture into a new field when the CBC Opera Company produced a concert version of George Bizet's *Carmen*. The conductor for this production was Nicholas Goldschmidt, with Herman Geiger-Torel as artistic adviser. The CBC Opera Company had been broadcasting operas from the Toronto CBC studios since 1948 but this presentation in Massey Hall was their first public peformance.

Pianist Benno Moiseiwitsch performed at two TSO concerts. On 6–7 December he played the Tchaikovsky Piano Concerto No. 2 in G major. The following 14–15 February he returned, rather unexpectedly, to play Beethoven's Piano Concerto No. 3 in C minor. Dame Myra Hess, the soloist for this February concert, had to cancel owing to a sudden illness and Moiseiwisch, who was on a North American tour, was fortunately available to fulfil the engagement. On 17–18 January Yehudi Menuhin played the Elgar Violin Concerto in B minor. Menuhin had recorded this concerto in 1932 with Elgar conducting.

1950–1951

Once again the programming was predictable, with the usual large helpings of Wagner, Tchaikovsky, and Mozart. However several exciting events enlivened the season. On 3 April, Walter Homburger's International Artists booked the TSO for a concert in Massey Hall under the baton of one of the world's great conductors of the time, Victor de Sabata, co-director with Toscanini of La Scala in Milan. Sabata's program was an interesting and innovative mix. The first half opened with Rossini's Overture to *La gazza ladra*, followed by an electrifying and inspiring interpretation of Brahms's Symphony No. 1 in C minor. After the intermission came the *Mother Goose Suite* by Maurice Ravel and Richard Strauss's *Till Eulenspiegels lustige Streiche*. The concert was an enormous success, and audience and critics alike were enthralled. The musicians were full of praise for Sabata and undoubtedly stimulated by the opportunity to work with a world-renowned maestro. Homburger commented that a number of audience members found it difficult to believe that this was the same TSO they were accustomed to hearing from week to week.

On 15 November the TSO was engaged for a performance of Verdi's *Requiem* by the Toronto Mendelssohn Choir with soprano Lois Marshall, mezzo-soprano Louise Roy, tenor Pierre Boutet, and bass Désiré Ligeti. The choir and orchestra joined forces again on 21 February for an all-British program consisting of Walton's *Belshazzar's Feast* and the Canadian premiere of Benjamin Britten's *Spring Symphony*. On 13 December the CBC called on the services of the TSO for a CBC Opera Company concert version of Verdi's *Rigoletto*, with Nicholas Goldschmidt conducting and Herman Geiger-Torel as artistic director. The TSO season, it appears, was saved from insignificance by the efforts of organizations that undertook to employ the orchestra.

This season opened with an important change. The Pops Concerts that had been sponsored by the Robert Simpson Co. for the past six seasons were now sponsored by Canada Packers Ltd. An announcement printed in the first program of the season stated that the concerts would continue in the same style and that twenty-six of the concerts would be broadcast.

1951–1952

The TSO was invited to participate in the 'Major Symphony Series' at the Masonic Auditorium on 27 November in Detroit. Other orchestras appearing in the series were the Boston Symphony Orchestra, the Chicago Symphony Orchestra, the Cleveland Orchestra, and the Philadelphia Orchestra. This would be the orchestra's first appearance in the United States, and was an indication that the TSO was regarded as one of the top orchestras in North America. In accordance with U.S. immigration regulations, the TSO submitted the names of all musicians and administrative staff who would be entering the United States. When the lists were returned, approval had been given to all but seven musicians. The Board and MacMillan agreed that the seven who were refused entry visas would be replaced for the concert. One musician was later cleared and so what eventually happened became known as the saga of the 'Symphony Six.' The concert in Detroit was a success and reviews in both the American and Canadian press were full of praise for the high quality of the symphony's musicianship. However, this was not the end of the affair.

Toward the end of the season when it came time to renew the musicians' contracts the Board and MacMillan decided that the six individuals who had been unable to go to Detroit due to the intervention of the United States government would not have their contracts renewed. The rationale for this decision was that the musicians had not fulfilled their contractual agreements, and that their status with U.S. immigration would cause further problems when the orchestra was invited to return to Detroit in the following season. The Board's announcement had repercussions not only in Toronto but nationwide, and the news media made banner headlines of the situation. There was a split within the Board in which two members resigned, and a number of subscribers cancelled their subscriptions. To make matters worse, MacMillan did not attend two of the Board meetings at which the whole matter was discussed, although it has been indicated that he briefed orchestra manager Jack Elton on what to report.

The whole situation became very muddied but the important issue was whether or not the six musicians should be kept on and replaced with substitutes as necessary for future engagements in the United States. The Board left the whole matter to Elton, who took the issue to the Toronto Musicians' Association, who agreed with the Board's original decision to let the musicians go. The six players presented their own appeal to the Toronto Musicians' Association, but this was turned down; the union maintained that according to TSO contracts players must fulfil all out-of-town commitments. However it was not the players who had refused to go to Detroit, but rather the government of the United States that had denied them entry. Many agreed with the action taken by the Amsterdam Concertgebouw, which had cancelled an extensive tour of the United States because several of their members had been denied entry. MacMillan has been described as being rather quiet about the situation, but in correspondence he stated that he fully concurred with the Board's decision. There was no doubt where MacMillan stood, and it indicated a certain insensitivity toward the musicians. Although MacMillan believed in democracy and the freedoms it stood for, he had been instrumental in depriving these six musicians of their democratic rights.

The six musicians affected were violinist Steven Staryk, double bass players Ruth (Ross) Budd, Abe Mannheim, and William Kuinka, flutist Dirk Keetbaas, and violinist John Moscow. (Perhaps the only problem the U.S. government had with John was his family name.) Public opinion was split over the Board's and MacMillan's action, but many felt that the U.S. authorities did not have the right to dictate who could play in the TSO and that the TSO should have taken the same action as the Concertgebouw. Had this position been taken, the Toronto Symphony Orchestra might have avoided criticism both in Canada and internationally. Instead, this saga remains, and every time the orchestra celebrates an important anniversary, the media resurrects this unfortunate episode from the past.

The season, however, did include many outstanding concerts. On 1–2 January 1952 the orchestra and the Toronto Mendelssohn Choir joined to present George Frideric Handel's *Messiah*. This particular performance was significant because it was recorded by Beaver Records on the then new LP 33⅓ system. The technicians and equipment for this occasion were hired from RCA Victor. The soloists were soprano Lois Marshall, contralto Mary Palmateer, tenor Jon Vickers, and bass James Milligan, with harpsichordist Greta Kraus. The recording was a great success; in two years Beaver Records Canada and RCA Bluebird Classics in the United States sold 45,000 copies.

Leopold Stokowski made his first visit to the orchestra on 19–20 February. The program included two of his symphonic transcriptions (five pieces by Henry Purcell and J.S. Bach's Passacaglia and Fugue in C minor), Edmund Rubbra's Symphony No. 5 in B flat major, Antonio Vivaldi's Concerto Grosso in D minor, and the Prelude and Love Death from Wagner's *Tristan und Isolde*. On 5–6 February Clifford Curzon was soloist for Beethoven's Piano Concerto No. 5 in E flat major ('Emperor'). The original program for this concert was altered in view of the recent death of King George VI. The first half (during which the audience was requested not to applaud) consisted of an orchestral arrangement of the Chorale Prelude *In Thee O Lord Do I Put My Trust* by Johann Sebastian Bach, followed by Beethoven's Symphony No. 3 in E flat major ('Eroica').

On 28 February, the orchestra was back in Maple Leaf Gardens to give a gala concert for the Toronto Police Association, conducted by Heinz Unger with baritone Todd Duncan and members of the National Ballet of Canada. The dancers performed the *pas de deux* from *Don Quixote* by Ludwig Minkus and the Polovetsian Dances from *Prince Igor* by Alexander Borodin. Finally, two young Canadian artists who were receiving public acclaim across North America were back to perform with the orchestra. Lois Marshall appeared in a subscription concert on 11 April 1952 and also sang with the orchestra in Detroit in November 1951. Glenn Gould was soloist for an all-Beethoven concert on 12 December.

Repercussions over the 'Symphony Six' controversy were still being felt. Numerous   **1952–1953**
meetings involving the six musicians were held with the Civil Liberties Association, the Toronto Board of Control, the TSO Board, and the Toronto Musicians' Association, but nothing changed. The Toronto Musicians' Association stood by its decision to

Violinist Blain Mathe

support the action taken the Board and MacMillan. Unfortunately, support for the six musicians was negated by the leadership of the Canadian Labour Congress, who washed their hands of the matter. Regretfully the musicians lost. The saga was ended but not forgotten.

The Board planned a series of three special concerts called the 'Biggest "Little Series"' to raise money for the orchestra's Sustaining Fund. The first concert, on 23 February, was a recital given by British pianist Clifford Curzon; his program consisted of works by Brahms, Liszt, and Schubert, along with Beethoven's Piano Sonata in C sharp minor, op. 27, no. 2 ('Moonlight'). On 11 March Victor de Sabata returned to conduct a varied program consisting of the Symphony No. 4 in E minor by Brahms, *Le tombeau de Couperin* by Maurice Ravel, and Ottorino Respighi's *The Pines of Rome*. The final concert of this series was given on 20 May by the Boston Symphony Orchestra conducted by Charles Munch in a program that included *Jeu de cartes* by Igor Stravinsky, *Prélude à l'après-midi d'un faune* by Claude Debussy, and the Symphony No. 4 in A major ('Italian') by Felix Mendelssohn. The series was budgeted to raise $6,000 but it fell a little short.

The main subscription series saw performances by prominent international artists. Yehudi Menuhin played the Mendelssohn Violin Concerto in E minor. Otto Klemperer, on his first visit to the TSO, conducted an all-Beethoven program including Symphony No. 6 in F major and Symphony No. 7 in A major. Isaac Stern was back once again, on this occasion performing the Violin Concerto in D minor by Sibelius. Rudolf Serkin came at the end of March to play the Mozart Piano Concerto in D minor, K 466. On 9 December the orchestra made a return visit to Detroit for a concert in the Masonic Auditorium, apparently with no visa problems. The program consisted of the *Academic Festival Overture* by Brahms, Modest Mussorgsky's *Pictures at an Exhibition*, and William Walton's Symphony No. 1. Financially, the season was comparatively successful, with a relatively small deficit of $9,000, but this was a substantial change from the previous season's surplus of $300.

W.G. Watson, who had been President of the Board for the past fourteen years, resigned as President, although he remained involved with the symphony as a Board member. His successor was Trevor Moore, brother of the eminent accompanist Gerald Moore. This would be the first of two terms Trevor Moore would serve as head of the TSO Board.

The deficit at the end of the 1952–3 season caused the Board some discomfort. E.H. Ely, a new Board member, outlined a campaign to raise $100,000 that he hoped would be completed by 15 December, but, by the time the Board met on 18 January only $57,000 had been raised. It was therefore suggested that the appeal should be extended to radio, television, and newspapers. By this time the Toronto City Council's annual donation to the orchestra was in the region of $5,000. (Since this money was placed in the overall Sustaining Fund, it is difficult to know the precise amount.) The Board also considered the possibility of a joint appeal for a provincial government grant to support several organizations who were facing similar financial problems – the National Ballet of Canada, the Canadian Opera Company, the Toronto Mendelssohn Choir, and the Art Gallery of Toronto.

The 1953–4 season presented its full share of outstanding international artists. On 20 October Mieczyslaw Horszowski made his Toronto debut with the orchestra in a performance of the Piano Concerto No. 4 in G major by Beethoven, and on 3–4 November Benno Moiseiwitsch played the *Rhapsody on a Theme of Paganini* by Rachmaninoff. Two weeks later Joseph Szigeti returned to play the Beethoven Violin Concerto in D major. On 5–6 January the outstanding young Austrian pianist Paul Badura-Skoda made his TSO debut with a performance of Béla Bartók's Piano Concerto No. 3. On 19–20 January Betty-Jean Hagen, a talented twenty-three-year-old Canadian violinist and recipient of many awards, gave an exciting interpretation of Édouard Lalo's *Symphonie espagnole*.

The Women's Committee, which had become a dynamic force in raising funds for the orchestra, entered into discussions on becoming incorporated. This meant that while they would still be part of the TSO organization, they would be totally responsible for their own operation. The last concert of the season was sponsored by the Women's Committee to raise money for the orchestra's Sustaining Fund. The guest artist was the celebrated clarinettist Benny Goodman, who played the Concertino for Clarinet and Orchestra by Carl Maria von Weber. The concert was an overwhelming success. Varsity Arena, with a seating capacity of more than 5,000, was sold out and the Sustaining Fund received over $3,000.

1954–1955   Finances were again the main topic at the beginning of the season. The accumulated deficit of $21,500 was aggravated by a demand by the musicians' union for a substantial increase in salary. In addition, Canada Packers, who had sponsored the Pops Concerts for a number of seasons, hinted that they might discontinue their support next season. This action could put an end to the Pops Concerts and consequently the broadcast revenue from the CBC. After two days of non-stop negotiations the union agreed to allow the renewal of the musicians' contracts at the same rates as last season. The Sustaining Fund also received a welcome injection of extra dollars when the grant from the Toronto City Council was increased by $3,000 to a total of $13,000. The Women's Committee also increased its fundraising activities and was able to raise a record amount of $45,000. If expenses were kept in line with the previous season, the projected deficit for the season would be $29,000.

The Board had another urgent situation to deal with during this season. On 14 January, Sir Ernest MacMillan sent a letter to Trevor Moore advising him that he wanted to retire at the end of the 1955–6 season. This would be his twenty-fifth season with the orchestra and he felt that the time had come for him to step down. MacMillan's resignation was accepted, and on 26 January the Board agreed to form a selection committee to find a suitable replacement. At the Board meeting on 7 April this committee reported that they had decided to recommend the appointment of Walter Susskind, the former conductor of the Scottish National Orchestra. The recommendation that Susskind be offered a three-season contract, effective November 1956, was approved unanimously.

Among the many international artists to appear with the orchestra during the 1954–5 season were soprano Irmgard Seefried, who was the soloist for the second Pops Concert, and Clifford Curzon, who returned to play the Piano Concerto No. 4 in G major by Beethoven. The Old Vic Theatre Company from London, England, engaged the TSO to play Mendelssohn's incidental music for performances of Shakespeare's *A Midsummer Night's Dream* on 14–16 December at Maple Leaf Gardens. The cast included Stanley Holloway, Moira Shearer, and Robert Helpmann, and the orchestra was conducted by Hugo Rignold, who was born in England but had spent much of his youth in Canada.

Maureen Forrester made her TSO debut on 14 January, singing two arias: 'Che faro senza Euridice' from *Orpheus ed Euridice* by Christoph Willibald Gluck and the well-known 'Amour, viens aider ma faiblesse' from *Samson et Dalila* by Camille Saint-Saëns. On 1 February Zino Francescatti played Tchaikovsky's Violin Concerto in D major in a concert that also included Vaughan Williams's *Sinfonia Antartica*. On 9 February the

Canadian Music Associates presented a concert of new Canadian music with MacMillan conducting the TSO. The program included compositions by Murray Adaskin, François Morel, Godfrey Ridout, Andrew Twa, Udo Kasemets, Adone Zecchi, and Robert Fleming. On 15–16 February, Boyd Neel, the founder of the famous Boyd Neel Orchestra in England, was the guest conductor. Andrés Segovia made his TSO debut on 15 March with a performance of the Concerto for Guitar and Orchestra in D major, op. 99, by Mario Castelnuovo-Tedesco. For the last concert of the subscription season, Yehudi Menuhin returned to play the Violin Concerto in E minor by Mendelssohn.

The twenty-fifth and final season for Sir Ernest MacMillan was one of exceptional diversity in terms of artists and programming. Walter Susskind, Music Director and Conductor Designate, made his North American debut with the TSO with two weeks of subscription concerts, a Secondary Schools Concert, and a Pops Concert. The program for the first pair of subscription concerts, presented on 22–3 November, included Beethoven's Piano Concerto No. 5 in E flat major ('Emperor') with Leon Fleisher as soloist and *Nocturne* by Canadian composer Harry Freedman. Freedman had joined the orchestra in 1946 as an oboist and English horn player. He remained with the TSO until 1970, and for his last season he was the orchestra's first composer-in-residence. For the second pair of concerts the following week Susskind was the soloist for Mozart's Piano Concerto in D minor, K 466, conducting from the keyboard. Vaughan Williams's *A London Symphony* completed the program. For the Pops Concert Susskind was joined by soprano Mary Simmons, who sang the aria 'Hear ye, Israel' from Mendelssohn's *Elijah*, as well as 'Voi lo sapete' from *Cavalleria rusticana* by Pietro Mascagni, and 'Pace, pace mio dio' from Verdi's *La forza del destino*. On 8–9 November Heinz Unger conducted a program that included two symphonies: Beethoven's Symphony No. 8 in F major and Tchaikovsky's Symphony No. 5 in E minor. During December the Sadler's Wells Ballet (now the Royal Ballet) from the Royal Opera House, Covent Garden, London, came to Toronto for three performances at Maple Leaf Gardens. Robert Irving conducted the Toronto Symphony Orchestra for these performances.

On 10 January the TSO was back once again in Detroit with a program that included *New York Profiles*, a suite for orchestra by the young American composer Norman Dello Joio. Canada was represented by Harry Freedman's *Nocturne*. Detroit audiences had been appreciative of the Toronto Symphony Orchestra, and on each visit the press lavished praise on the orchestra. During January, two distinguished

1955–1956

violinists were back: Isaac Stern on 17–18 January to play the Beethoven Violin Concerto in D major, and Jascha Heifetz on 31 January and 1 February for the Sibelius Violin Concerto in D minor.

On 7 February MacMillan conducted a choral concert with the combined forces of the Toronto Mendelssohn Choir and the TSO. The program consisted of two prominent choral works: Mozart's Mass in C minor, K427, with soloists Lois Marshall, Mary Morrison, Jon Vickers, and Donald Garrard, and Vaughan Williams's *Dona Nobis Pacem*, a cantata for soprano, baritone, and chorus, with soloists Lois Marshall and Donald Garrard.

On 21 February the orchestra once again went to Maple Leaf Gardens, this time for the annual Toronto Police Association concert. Paul Whiteman conducted an all-Gershwin gala that naturally included the ever-popular *Rhapsody in Blue*, a work that George Gershwin had written for Whiteman. Towards the end of this season, Pierre Monteux, who at eighty-one was still one the world's leading conductors, made his TSO debut on 13–14 March with a program that included two works by French composers: the *Ballade* for piano and orchestra by Gabriel Fauré, and the *Concertino for Piano and Orchestra* by Jean Françaix. Canadian pianist Raymond Dudley was the soloist for both works. Mozart's Symphony No. 39 in E flat major, K 543, Symphony No. 2 by Paul Creston, and Richard Strauss's *Till Eulenspiegels lustige Streiche* completed an outstanding concert. Two weeks later, Sir Thomas Beecham made a long-awaited return to conduct the orchestra. His program consisted of works by composers that he had championed in more than sixty years of conducting. The concert opened with *The Great Elopement Suite* – music by Handel, arranged by Beecham – followed by Mozart's Symphony No. 41 in C major, K 551 ('Jupiter'). Frederick Delius (on whose works Beecham was an authority) was represented with scenes from Act 2 of *Irmelin*. The Symphony No. 7 by Jean Sibelius rounded out the program; Beecham was fascinated with the music of Sibelius and recorded many of his works.

Sir Ernest MacMillan's final appearance as conductor of the TSO came in the pair of concerts on 10–11 April. The Toronto Mendelssohn Choir, soprano Mary Simmons, contralto Maureen Forrester, tenor Jon Vickers, and baritone James Milligan were all participants in a full evening of great music making. The concert opened with MacMillan's setting of the *Te Deum Laudamus*, which he had composed in 1936, followed by Tchaikovsky's symphonic fantasia *Francesca da Rimini*. *Schicksalslied* (Song of Destiny), a short choral work by Brahms, concluded the first half of the evening. The balance of the concert was given over to an exceptional performance of Beethoven's Symphony No. 9 in D minor. This impressive concert was a lasting tribute to a man who had dedicated so much of his career to promoting music in Toronto. Surprisingly, the music of Wagner was not included in this last concert.

Sir Ernest MacMillan was, from an orchestral standpoint, a good, if perhaps not great, conductor. He emphasized diversity in programming, and introduced new works to the orchestra's repertoire. There were, however, some missed opportunities that might have promoted the TSO as an international ensemble. The orchestra's occasional visits to Detroit and Michigan were the only efforts in this direction. MacMillan sometimes gave the impression that he was more concerned about his own reputation than that of the orchestra, and he may have been unaware that at times he alienated himself from the orchestra.

However, Sir Ernest will always be remembered for his determination to maintain the orchestra during the Second World War. In no way did he allow this orchestra to deteriorate, as had been the case during the First World War. His second and perhaps most important contribution was his dedication to music education for school children and young people. His personal concern and enthusiasm has carried on through the years, and music education is still a high priority within the TSO today. MacMillan was a member of the Canada Council from 1957 to 1963. In 1957, he was awarded the Richard Strauss medal (an honour little known outside of Europe) by the German Performing Rights Society in recognition of his outstanding dedication to the protection of copyright. MacMillan was also an accomplished composer and instrumentalist. Augustus Bridle, the music critic of the *Toronto Daily Star*, wrote this description of Sir Ernest: 'He is a keyboard virtuoso, soloizes on the organ, and plays piano-solo accompaniments so superbly that the singer or the violinist is not conscious that the audience may sometimes listen to the piano. As an organist he would have been among the world's greatest. At times he conducts an orchestra as though he were playing it on keyboard and pedals.'

In his later years Sir Ernest was recognized as one of Canada's elder statesmen, and was awarded Canada's highest civilian honour when he was made a Companion of the Order of Canada.

Walter Susskind

Tones that sound, and roar and storm about me until I have set them down in notes.

Although Walter Susskind was well known at the time in Britain and Europe, his North American presence consisted of his recent guest appearances with the TSO. Walter Susskind (1913–80) was born in Prague. He received his musical education at the Prague State Conservatory, where he studied piano with Karel Hoffmeister and composition with Josef Suk and Alois Hába, and at the German Academy of Music, where he studied conducting with George Szell. After his graduation, he became assistant conductor of the German Opera in Prague, and from 1933 to 1942 he was also the pianist with the Czech Trio. In 1938 he left Prague after his parents, who were unable to leave the country, had urged him not to remain in Czechoslovakia under the deteriorating conditions of the Nazi regime. He later learned that his mother had been interned at the same time as Karel Ančerl.

Susskind eventually settled in England, where he resumed his conducting career in 1941 and in 1946 became a British citizen. He held music director positions with the Carl Rosa Opera Company (1943–5), the Scottish National Orchestra (1946–52), and finally the Victoria Symphony Orchestra in Melbourne, Australia (1953–5). Walter Legge engaged Susskind to conduct the Philharmonia Orchestra for a 1945 recording of the Sibelius Violin Concerto with the French violinist Ginette Neveu. In 1950, when Jascha Heifetz joined the Philharmonia Orchestra for a recording session that included the Tchaikovsky and Walton violin concertos, Susskind was again chosen to conduct.

1956–1957

The TSO's 1956–7 season opened with enthusiasm and a sense that a new episode in the life of the orchestra was about to begin. The deficit had been drastically reduced and the number of subscriptions was the largest in the orchestra's history. Also, the Junior Auxiliary of the Women's Committee had raised funds to purchase new chairs for the orchestra, which were greatly appreciated by the musicians.

For Susskind's inaugural subscription concert Massey Hall was festooned with floral decorations, palms, and evergreens. When Susskind came on stage and stepped onto the podium the audience of 3,000 stood with the orchestra and applauded enthusiastically for several minutes. Susskind was noticeably touched by the warm-hearted reception. The superb program opened with two shorter works – the Overture to *Oberon* by Carl Maria von Weber and the *Symphonic Metamorphosis after Themes by Carl Maria von Weber* by Paul Hindemith. This was followed by Beethoven's Piano Concerto No. 2 in B flat major, with Glenn Gould as soloist, and the Symphony No. 9 in E minor ('From the New World') by Antonín Dvořák.

The new music director had assured both orchestra and audience that many more inspired concerts were in store. The following day Hugh Thomson of the *Toronto Daily Star* wrote, 'You could tell from the very opening of the first work of the Orchestra's agenda that Susskind was going to give quality performances.' The long-awaited new era had arrived.

On 6 November, Susskind conducted the Canadian premiere of Vaughan Williams's Symphony No. 8. Two weeks later Elisabeth Schwarzkopf, the internationally acclaimed soprano, was soloist for a performance of Richard Strauss's *Four Last Songs*. Sir Thomas Beecham returned with a less characteristic Beecham program that included Beethoven's Symphony No. 4 in B flat major and Dvořák's *The Golden Spinning Wheel*. In January Mischa Elman was the soloist for a performance of Mendelssohn's Violin Concerto in E minor, a work that he had also played in December 1912 with the former Toronto Symphony Orchestra under Frank Welsman.

On 6 February the Toronto Mendelssohn Choir joined the TSO for a performance of *La damnation de Faust* by Berlioz, with soloists Lois Marshall, Richard Cassilly, James Milligan, and Victor Braun. On 26–7 February, Boyd Neel was the guest conductor for a concert that featured four principals of the orchestra. Violinist Hyman Goodman and cellist Rowland Pack played the Double Concerto in A minor, op. 102, by Brahms. Then they were joined by violist Stanley Solomon and violinist Harold Sumberg for the quartet in *Introduction and Allegro* by Elgar. The season also included guest artists pianist Witold Malcuzynski on 12–13 March and violinist Nathan Milstein on 26–7 March.

At the beginning of Susskind's first season the musicians had been a little less than enthusiastic about his appointment. Many felt that the musicians had been 'sidelined' by the Board because they were not consulted. However, by the end of the season all ill feeling was dispelled as they realized the calibre of Susskind's dexterity and musicianship. Harry Freedman, oboist and Canadian composer, said that Susskind was unquestionably a superb musician. Susskind had also undertaken to conduct his full share of the Sunday afternoon Pops Concerts. The season was a financial success, closing with a small surplus of $2,400. Trevor Moore, who had completed his term as President of the Board, resigned at the end of this season.

1957–1958

Susskind was quick to realize that the TSO was an orchestra with immense potential and he was most anxious to develop it as a major international ensemble. To accomplish this he undertook some necessary adjustment within the orchestra ranks; four members were dismissed and three took retirement.

Thomas S. Johnson, the new President of the Board, met with officials of the recently formed Canada Council in Ottawa, and on his return reported that the TSO Association could look forward to a grant of approximately $25,000. The Canada Council grant was approved in November. In addition, the grant from the Toronto City Council was now $15,000. Some of this funding provided for the addition of three full-time musicians and an extra hour of rehearsal each week.

There was a feeling of anticipation that the upcoming season would be another year of superb performances. The opening subscription concert featured Denis Matthews, an English pianist noted for his brilliant interpretations of the Beethoven concertos. For his TSO debut he played Beethoven's Piano Concerto No. 4 in G major. On 30 October the orchestra played a special concert in Peterborough, Ontario, for that city's Rotary Club. The program included Mozart's Piano Concerto in A major, K488, with Walter Susskind as soloist, conducting from the keyboard. On 5–6 November mezzo-soprano Jennie Tourel made her TSO debut, singing two arias by Mozart and the *Lieder eines fahrenden Gesellen* (Songs of a Wayfarer) by Gustav Mahler. Tourel had also appeared the previous summer in Toronto in a concert with the Israel Philharmonic Orchestra conducted by Walter Susskind. Early in December Yehudi Menuhin returned to perform Beethoven's Violin Concerto in D major. On 10 December the orchestra returned to Detroit where Susskind again played the Mozart A major piano concerto and conducted from the keyboard. This work was also repeated for the first subscription concert in the new year. On 14–15 January Alexander Brailowsky was soloist for Rachmaninoff's Piano Concerto No. 2 in C minor. On 22 January, at a concert sponsored by the York Concert Society, Heinz Unger conducted an augmented orchestra of 102 musicians along with the Bach-Elgar Choir of Hamilton, Ontario, soprano Mary Simmons, and contralto Elizabeth Benson-Guy in the Canadian premiere of Mahler's Symphony No. 2 ('Resurrection'). For the Pops Concert on 26 January, Joan Hammond, one of the leading sopranos from the Covent Garden Opera, made her TSO debut in a program that included the Prelude and Liebestod from Wagner's opera *Tristan und Isolde*, and the 'Letter aria' from *Eugene Onegin* by Tchaikovsky. Heinz

Jack Benny rehearsing with the TSO before his Canadian debut on 12 November 1957

Unger returned on 11–12 February to conduct the Canadian premiere of *Phantastic Apparitions of a Theme by Hector Berlioz* by the German composer Walter Braunfels. The *Toronto Daily Star* contributed $3,000 toward the sponsorship of an all-Canadian concert on 5 March. However, the only Canadian work to be presented was Healey Willan's Symphony No. 2 in C minor. The remainder of the program consisted of Edvard Grieg's Piano Concerto in A minor with Patricia Parr as soloist, and the overture to Giuseppe Verdi's opera *La forza del destino*. For a Toronto Mendelssohn Choir concert with the TSO on 19 March, Susskind conducted a performance of Arthur Honegger's dramatic oratorio *Jeanne d'Arc au bûcher* (Joan of Arc at the Stake). The singing roles were performed by Ilona Kombrink, Irene Byatt, Alan Crofoot, Donald Young, and Donald Bartle, while the speaking roles of Joan of Arc and Brother Dominic were played by Vera Zorina and John Drainie respectively. Offstage voices included William Hutt, Frank Peddie, and Cynthia Michaelis.

The concerts on 25–6 March included the North American premiere of Walter Susskind's *Nine Slovak Sketches*. In his program note Susskind states, 'You may rightly wonder how a humble composition of my own found its way into a program otherwise devoted to the works of several great masters. In case it occurred to you that I simply forced the piece on the orchestra, your assumption was quite right. They had no choice in the matter.' The work was well received and demonstrated not only that Susskind was a competent composer but also that he had a sense of humour. For the last subscription concert of the season, soprano Irmgard Seefried made a welcome return to sing J.S. Bach's Cantata No. 202: *The Wedding* and three songs by Richard Strauss ('Morgen,' 'Wiegenlied,' and 'Ständchen').

Financially the season had been an outstanding success, probably due to the excellent programming and choice of guest artists. The accumulated deficit was only $1,265. In his report to the annual general meeting on 29 May 1958, manager Jack Elton said that the season had been one of continued progress.

1958–1959   During the summer of 1958 a complex situation arose regarding the relationship between the TSO and the CBC. The first issue was that the CBC wanted to reschedule the broadcasts of the CBC Symphony Orchestra to Sunday afternoons – the time slot allotted to the TSO Pops Concerts. Since all these concerts were broadcast live to air, this was a serious problem. If the CBC did not broadcast the Pops Concerts, the TSO would lose not only the broadcast revenue but also the financial support of the concert sponsors, and this would make the Pops Concerts financially unviable.

The CBC was also giving serious thought to developing the CBC Symphony Orchestra into a full-time ensemble with year-round contracts. This change would create serious difficulties for the TSO. Fifty per cent of the TSO musicians also played in the CBC Symphony Orchestra. Under the existing arrangement, musicians who played in both orchestras could supplement their twenty-six-week TSO contracts with additional engagements in the CBC Symphony Orchestra to create more continuous employment. If the CBC went ahead with their plan for a full-time orchestra, the TSO would lose most of its prime musicians. After a series of discussions between the TSO management, the CBC, and the musicians' union, the CBC decided to put their plan on hold, and both orchestras began preparations for their regular seasons. Meanwhile, in October the TSO received a Canada Council grant of $25,000 for the season.

The TSO season opened on 26 October with the first of twenty-six Sunday afternoon Pops Concerts sponsored by Canada Packers and broadcast live over the CBC trans-Canada network with Walter Susskind conducting. The program included *Moldau* from *Ma Vlast* by Bedřich Smetana to commemorate the fortieth anniversary of the founding of the Czechoslovakian Republic. For the first subscription concert on 28–9 October guest pianist Byron Janis played Rachmaninoff's Piano Concerto No. 3 in D minor. On 11–12 November Dietrich Fischer-Dieskau, the famous German

Sir Malcom Sargent

baritone was soloist for Cantata No. 56: *Ich will den Kreuzstab gerne tragen* by J.S. Bach and Mahler's *Kindertotenlieder*. On 19 November, the TSO was presented by International Artists in a concert devoted to arias from operas by Puccini and Verdi sung by soprano Frances Yeend and tenor Eugenio Fernandi.

During the week of 7 December the distinguished British conductor Sir Malcolm Sargent made his TSO debut. First he conducted a Pops Concert that included works by Frederick Delius and Edward Elgar as well as his own concert arrangement of Ottorino Respighi's *La boutique fantasque*. His program for the subscription concerts on 9–10 December consisted of Vaughan Williams's Overture to *The Wasps*, *The Walk to the Paradise Garden* by Frederick Delius, Elgar's *Enigma Variations*, and Brahms's Symphony No. 4 in E minor. True to form, on both occasions he came on stage with his traditional carnation boutonniere. A few days after Christmas Godfrey Ridout (who in later years became the program annotator for the TSO) conducted a Pops Concert that featured popular music from the light-hearted operettas by William S. Gilbert and Arthur Sullivan. This program was typical for Ridout. He had a great passion for England, and he loved the music of British composers.

The TSO had been invited to give a concert in the Buffalo Philharmonic Orchestra subscription series during the 1958–9 season at Kleinhans Music Hall. The program presented on 13–14 January included the *Fairy Tale Suite* by Josef Suk, *Divertimento for Strings* by Canadian composer Oskar Morawetz, and Symphony No. 2 by Dmitri Kabalevsky. The Buffalo press enthusiastically praised the TSO for its steady rich sound and well-proportioned string tone as well as the precision of the woodwind, brass, and percussion sections.

Boyd Neel, another notable English conductor, was invited back to the TSO on 1 February. Neel was already well known in the Canadian music scene, not only as the founder and conductor of the Boyd Neel Orchestra but also as the dean of the Faculty of Music at the University of Toronto and the Royal Conservatory of Music. On

11 February the Toronto Mendelssohn Choir joined forces with the TSO in a performance of Verdi's *Requiem*. On 25 February musicians from the TSO and the CBC Symphony Orchestra gave the Canadian premiere of Gustav Mahler's Symphony No. 5 for the York Concert Society with Dr Heinz Unger conducting. Before the concert Geoffrey Waddington presented Unger with the Mahler medal from the Bruckner Society of America, given in recognition of Unger's efforts on behalf of Mahler's music in Canada. Other recipients of the Mahler medal include Bruno Walter, Otto Klemperer, and Leonard Bernstein. The soloist for this memorable concert was Moura Lympany, who played the Beethoven Piano Concerto No. 4 in G major.

It was evident that Susskind's approach to concert presentation, program, content, and orchestral development was helping the TSO to become an ensemble of international stature. Within three years he had introduced twenty-seven new or seldom heard works, many of them Canadian premieres, and fourteen new works were planned for the upcoming season. In addition two Mahler Symphonies, No. 2 and No. 5, had their Canadian premieres under Heinz Unger, using some TSO musicians. Susskind possessed an indisputable high regard for the pre-eminent musicianship of the orchestra. It might be said that during this three-year period the TSO changed from a local orchestra into a Canadian orchestra of international prominence.

During this season, however, it seemed that the Board of Directors had lost track of the ongoing life of the orchestra. According to the Board records, the four meetings called between January and May 1959 were all cancelled owing to lack of a quorum. When a meeting was at last convened, the minutes reveal that the CBC had abandoned any ideas of organizing concerts or broadcasts that would interfere with TSO concerts. The accumulated deficit had reached $6,300 but Sir Ernest MacMillan magnanimously contributed $2,000 from his retirement grant. The minutes also report that the Ford Motor Company of Canada had agreed to co-sponsor the Pops Concerts for the 1959–60 season.

1959–1960   The first Board meeting of the season was once again cancelled owing to lack of a quorum. In exasperation President Thomas Johnson sent a letter to all members pointing out that it was difficult to carry out the business of the orchestra when Board members failed to attend meetings that were called.

The Canada Council had increased its grant by $5,000, for a total of $30,000, but due to the ever-increasing costs of maintaining the orchestra – now considered one of the major arts organizations in the country – the Board planned to make a separate presentation to the Canada Council for special financial consideration. The Board had hoped to be able to inaugurate the musicians' pension plan during the 1959–60 season, but this move was delayed owing to a lack of substantial funds. The musicians' union, however, asked the Board to reconsider this decision, since the plan had already been deferred once in 1958. The pension plan represented an important element in the upcoming contract negotiations. The Board knew it would be difficult to reach a new agreement without either a pension plan or a substantial salary increase. Many Board members still seemed oblivious to these serious issues, and several more meetings were cancelled owing to lack of a quorum. However, during a discussion held between those members who were in attendance and Jack Elton, the orchestra manager, Elton reported that he had made an initial offer to the union regarding the new contract for the 1960–1 and 1961–2 seasons: a two-year contract of twenty-five weeks per year, plus a salary increase of five dollars per week. The union wanted a contract for twenty-six weeks per year plus an increase of ten dollars per week. Since the current contract was for twenty-four weeks, under the union's proposal the orchestra would be able to give four or five additional concerts.

Walter Susskind attended the Board meeting on 31 March 1960 to review the status of the orchestra. He reported that the orchestra was improving slowly but steadily, and said that a weakness in the violin section could be remedied by the addition of one or two players from the CBC Symphony Orchestra – particularly Albert Pratz, the concertmaster. Susskind considered Pratz to be the finest violinist in Canada and definitely wanted him in the TSO. Susskind also requested an extra hour of rehearsal for the subscription concerts. It was reported that an amendment to the Lord's Day Act (Ontario) had received royal assent, and consequently the TSO was free to charge admission for Sunday concerts. Another problem to be dealt with was the decision by Ford Motor Company not to continue co-sponsorship with Canada Packers of the Pops Concerts. If another co-sponsor could not be found, the TSO would lose about $30,000 in broadcast revenue from the CBC.

Artistically the 1959–60 season maintained a high calibre. On 27–8 October Géza Anda played the *Piano Concerto for the Left Hand* by Maurice Ravel, and on 10–11 November Pierre Fournier gave a performance of the Elgar Cello Concerto in E minor. Myra Hess, a great friend of the TSO, returned to perform Beethoven's Piano Concerto No. 4 in G major in a special concert on 27 January. She had recently recovered from a mild heart attack and there were indications that certain engagements might be cancelled, but she apparently was determined to proceed with her North American tour. Guest conductors during the season included Bernard Heinze,

John Barbirolli, Boyd Neel, and Ernest MacMillan. The concerts on 2–3 February included the world premiere of Symphony No. 2 by Oskar Morawetz, a work that had been commissioned by the TSO under a grant from the Canada Council. The season closed with a small surplus of $547, made possible by an anonymous donation of $7,100.

1960–1961   Finding a new joint sponsor for the Pops Concerts was proving difficult. Finally the TSO decided to underwrite the first half of the season while Canada Packers supported the second. On 20 October the musicians' union accepted an offer from the TSO for $105.50 per week base pay for a twenty-five week season. Jack Elton met with the Canada Council in January 1961 to explore an increase in the grant. Members of the Council raised the point about integration of the CBC Symphony Orchestra and the TSO. The Council agreed that there was no need for two symphony orchestras in Toronto, and said that the TSO should arrange its schedule to accommodate CBC Symphony Orchestra requirements. This would mean that the TSO would be in a position to allow year-round employment to musicians.

Contract negotiations between the union and the TSO dragged on through the year; by the end of the season neither side had budged. At the annual meeting on 1 June 1960 T.S. Johnson was able to report only that the TSO management was standing firm. Financially the season ended with its largest accumulated deficit to date – $30,000 – due primarily to the costs of financing half of the Pops season. Manager Jack Elton had been dealing with media reports that were critical of the TSO management. When Johnson, who had suffered a heart attack and been advised to rest, announced his resignation, the Board decided that his replacement needed to have experience in handling labour relations. On 20 July 1961 the Board announced that they had persuaded Trevor Moore to return as president for the 1961–2 season. Moore was well qualified, and he had the expertise to cope with the situation.

Meanwhile the orchestra's high quality of performance was maintained through another season of great music. For the opening concert Louis Kentner played the *Concerto symphonique* by Ernest Bloch, a first performance by the TSO. On 30 November, the Toronto Mendelssohn Choir joined the orchestra for a performance of Carl Orff's *Carmina Burana*. A dress rehearsal of the work was also included in the Secondary Schools concert on 29 November. Glenn Gould returned on 6 December for the Canadian premiere of Arnold Schoenberg's *Piano Concerto*. In January the French conductor Pierre Monteux made his TSO conducting debut in a program that included the *Symphony 'Mathis der Maler'* by Paul Hindemith and Maurice Ravel's second suite from *Daphnis et Chloé*. However, because of illness, Dame Myra Hess was unable to fulfil her engagement for concerts on 7–8 February. Walter Susskind was re-engaged as Music Director and Conductor for the next three seasons.

The negotiations between the musicians' union and the TSO management had not proceeded satisfactorily for either side. Management made an offer of $105.50 per week for twenty-four weeks for the 1961–2 season and $110 per week for twenty-five weeks for the 1962–3 season. This final offer was to expire at 11 a.m. on 1 November 1961. If the offer was not accepted, the manager was authorized to cancel or postpone concerts scheduled for the first two weeks of the season. Walter Susskind, who was sympathetic toward the musicians' situation, said that he felt the musicians' demands were quite justified if they were to build an orchestra of the calibre that Toronto should have, but he also understood the Board's dilemma in raising finances. In this precarious situation it looked as if the future of the orchestra was in doubt, but on 15 November, after two weeks without concerts, an agreement was finally reached, giving the musicians an extra week in the 1962–3 season and a weekly base rate of $110. The orchestra was able to resume its concerts and fulfil an engagement with the Toronto Mendelssohn Choir for a performance of *La damnation de Faust* by Hector Berlioz.

1961–1962

The TSO season opened on 19 November with a Pops Concert featuring Joseph Rouleau, a great Canadian bass at the Royal Opera House, Covent Garden. The first subscription concerts on 22–3 November included guest artist Yehudi Menuhin playing the Violin Concerto No. 1 by Dmitri Shostakovich. Management, always aware of increasing expenses, placed a request in the program for the donation of a backstage rehearsal piano.

Jack Elton, who had been under a great deal of stress during the last two seasons, approached Walter Homburger regarding the possibility of his taking over the position of Managing Director for the orchestra. Homburger's expertise and knowledge as a concert impresario were well known, and Elton's suggestion was welcomed. Trevor Moore, Jack Elton, and Walter Homburger reached an agreement and the Board accepted their proposal that Walter Homburger become Managing Director on 1 February 1962. Jack Elton assumed the position of Assistant Managing Director.

On 13 February a performance of the *Sacred Service – Avodath an hakodesh* by Ernest Bloch was given by the Toronto Mendelssohn Choir and the TSO, conducted by Walter Susskind with Norman Summers as cantor and Rabbi Gunther Plaut as narrator.

The Toronto Symphony Orchestra in Massey Hall, Walter Susskind conducting

Daniel Barenboim was the soloist for the concert on 10 April, performing Beethoven's Piano Concerto No. 5 in E flat major ('Emperor'). The last concert of the season was a performance of J.S. Bach's *St Matthew Passion* at Convocation Hall, University of Toronto, with the Toronto Mendelssohn Choir, soprano Elizabeth Benson Guy, tenor John Boyden, baritone William Perry, and bass Robert Reid, all conducted by Sir Ernest MacMillan.

When Trevor Moore, having fulfilled his mandate as President of the Board, stepped down at the end of the season, he left the TSO in a more secure position. With a new Managing Director at the helm the ship was back on course. R. William Finlayson became the new President of the Board.

1962–1963   Walter Susskind's six seasons with the TSO were an unqualified success. He not only had raised the standard of the subscription concerts but that of the Sunday Pops series as well. He had also introduced a system of rotation for the string sections (with the exception of the first desks), a practice that was quite common in major symphony orchestras. Hyman Goodman, who was concertmaster during the Susskind years, described Susskind in a letter to the TSO Archives in 1990: 'He had a great sense of humour and could conjure up a speech in front of an audience that would be witty and intelligent. He had great knowledge of the scores, and was very responsive towards the requirements of soloists.'

The second pair of subscription concerts for the 1962–3 season included Vladimir Ashkenazy playing Rachmaninoff's Piano Concerto No. 3 in D minor. Three guest conductors were on the podium during the season: Sir Malcolm Sargent in January, and Thomas Schippers and Josef Krips in February. Teresa Stratas, who at the time was one of the youngest singers at the Metropolitan Opera, was guest soloist on 26–7 March. Five years previously, Walter Susskind had chosen her to sing Mimi in Giacomo Puccini's *La bohème* with the Canadian Opera Company – an engagement that launched her international career. The orchestra also went on a spring tour, giving concerts in Ann Arbor and Holland, Michigan, and Windsor, Ontario.

Negotiations were still continuing on the eventual integration of the TSO and the CBC Symphony Orchestra. Walter Susskind had met with CBC Music Director Geoffrey Waddington to discuss the matter and a basic agreement had been approved. The CBC apparently wanted to keep the negotiations private so no formal statement was made.

The 1963–4 season commenced with the introduction of Boris Brott as Assistant Conductor. Brott, the son of well-known Montreal musician and composer Alexander Brott, had at fourteen been awarded a scholarship to study with Igor Markevitch. During the previous TSO season he had made a brilliant debut with the orchestra in a special series featuring Canadian talent. Now, at twenty years of age, he was the youngest assistant conductor of a major orchestra in North America.

1963–1964

This was also to have been Susskind's last season as Music Director, but the Board asked him to remain for an additional year so that the search for his replacement could be completed, and Susskind agreed to stay.

To open the season John Browning played the *Piano Concerto* by Samuel Barber in a program that also included the Canadian premiere of Benjamin Britten's *Sinfonia da Requiem*. For the third pair of subscription concerts Susskind conducted the Canadian premiere of the Symphony No. 7 by American composer Walter Piston. Then, on 29 November, the orchestra departed on a seven-day tour of the eastern United States, which included their first performance in Carnegie Hall, as part of the International Festival of Visiting Orchestras series. The well-balanced program consisted of *Vier letzte Lieder* (Four Last Songs) by Richard Strauss with Lois Marshall as soloist, Harry Somers's *Movement for Orchestra*, Paul Hindemith's *Nobilissima visione*, and Dvořák's Symphony No. 7 in D minor, op. 70. The New York critics were full of praise: on 5 December 1963 a review in the *New York Times* said, 'It is a smooth, responsive, accurate ensemble' and gave high praise to the string and woodwind sections. The *New York Post* reviewer wrote, 'Its musical elegance and artistic maturity, however, revealed a classic, precise splendor that marked it as a formidable rival in the major league.'

The new year was heralded by the appearance of Seiji Ozawa, a young Japanese conductor who had been one of the New York Philharmonic Orchestra's assistant conductors. Leonard Bernstein had brought this young conductor to the attention of Walter Homburger. On this recommendation Ozawa was invited to conduct the TSO on 8–9 January. His program opened with *Requiem*, a work for string orchestra by Tōru Takemitsu, a composer whose music was well known to Ozawa. The program also included the Symphony No. 5 by Sergei Prokofiev and the Symphony No. 5 in E minor by Tchaikovsky. The response to Ozawa was so overwhelming and his impact so great that he was invited back to conduct a special concert on 4 March. For this concert Ozawa chose Beethoven's Symphony No. 1 in C major, to be followed by Gabriel Fauré's *Ballade*, op. 19, for piano and orchestra with Seiji Ozawa's wife, Kyoko Edo-Ozawa, as soloist. To complete the program Ozawa led the orchestra in a masterful performance of *Symphonie fantastique* by Berlioz.

A unique concert on 14 January was co-sponsored by the Canadian Accordion Teacher's Association and featured the classically trained Danish accordionist Mogens Ellegaard. At the time, many people were not accustomed to hearing classical music played on the accordian. Ellegaard had based his career on bringing the accordian and classical music together, and at this concert he performed an accordion concerto written for him by Niels Viggo Bentzon.

On 21–2 January David and Igor Oistrakh, the famous Russian violinists, were guest artists for an exciting evening of concertos. The concert opened with the Concerto in D minor for two violins and strings by J.S. Bach, performed by father and son. This was followed by the Mendelssohn Violin Concerto in E minor played by Igor and Beethoven's Violin Concerto in D major performed by David. On 25 March, the Toronto Mendelssohn Choir joined the TSO for a performance of Bach's Mass in B minor, conducted by Walter Susskind. The performance was a success, but during rehearsal the

Assistant Conductor Boris Brott, Concertmaster Hyman Goodman, and Music Director Walter Susskind in front of Carnegie Hall in New York, December 1963

Members of the TSO outside Carnegie Hall, December 1963

choir had a few problems. Susskind stopped the rehearsal and, with his typical humour said, 'We are supposed to be singing a Mass in B minor, but I think we are in a B major mess.' The rehearsal proceeded and all was well.

Following the last concert of the season the orchestra left for a two-week tour of the United States. In June it was announced that Seiji Ozawa had been appointed the new Music Director beginning with the 1965–6 season. The appointment was received with overwhelming approval by both the orchestra and the public. Ozawa had endeared himself to everyone. Financially the orchestra was in a sound position with a relatively small deficit of $17,000.

1964–1965   Susskind's last season was an eventful one. The disbanding of the CBC Symphony Orchestra left the TSO as the main orchestra in Toronto, and the TSO was to fulfil some engagements that had been planned for the CBC Symphony Orchestra, including the *Concerts of the Two Worlds* series. For smaller performances the CBC hired part of

CARNEGIE HALL / *72nd Season*

INTERNATIONAL FESTIVAL
OF VISITING ORCHESTRAS

Wednesday Evening, December 4, 1963, at 8:30 o'clock

THE CARNEGIE HALL CORPORATION
in association with   THE J. M. KAPLAN FUND, INC.

presents # The Toronto
Symphony Orchestra

Walter Susskind, *Music Director*
Boris Brott, *Assistant Conductor*
Lois Marshall, *Soprano*

THE STAR SPANGLED BANNER
GOD SAVE THE QUEEN

Hindemith   NOBILISSIMA VISIONE   (Suite from the Ballet,
also called "St. Francis")
Einleitung und Rondo
Marsch und Pastorale
Passacaglia

Somers   MOVEMENT FOR ORCHESTRA

Strauss   FOUR LAST SONGS
"Frühling"
"September"
"Beim Schlafangehen"
"Im Abendrot"
Soloist: **Miss Marshall**

INTERMISSION

Dvořák   SYMPHONY NO. 2 IN D MINOR, Op. 70
Allegro maestoso
Poco adagio
Scherzo: Vivace—Poco meno mosso
Finale: Allegro

Tour Direction: Columbia Artists Management, Inc.
Personal Direction: Judd, Ries & Dahlgren

Carnegie Hall Playbill, December 1963

Lois Marshall with the TSO at Carnegie Hall, December 1963

the TSO as the CBC Toronto Orchestra, but this ensemble was not often needed and after a short period was discontinued.

The orchestra was enlarged from eighty-three musicians to eighty-six. The new-comers – violinists Jean Todd and Myron Moskalyk, and double bass player Larry Pohjola – had all been members of the National Youth Orchestra of Canada. Susskind had founded the National Youth Orchestra of Great Britain and, on coming to Canada, was anxious to build a similar organization. In 1960 he initiated an orchestral workshop in Stratford, Ontario, which led directly to the founding of the National Youth Orchestra (NYO). Susskind was director of the NYO until 1964, and conducted the 1961 and 1963 sessions. He was also the conductor for the NYO's European tour in 1966. The NYO and other youth orchestras had an important impact on the TSO, as later chapters will show.

Also during the 1964–5 season, the Players Committee wrote a letter to the chairman of the Board of Trustees of Massey Hall asking them to resolve the acoustical problems on the stage of Massey Hall. Although the acoustics for the audience were considered good, the musicians on stage found it difficult to hear other sections of the orchestra, and these problems were definitely affecting the quality of performance. The Committee asked that the necessary renovations be completed before the beginning of the 1965–6 season.

The winter of 1965 brought several untimely deaths. In January Cameron McKay, the principal double bass of the orchestra, died suddenly. Then on 25 February Heinz Unger, a frequent guest conductor with TSO, passed away, shortly after completing a rehearsal with the orchestra. Two weeks previously, he had conducted the TSO in a performance of Mahler's Symphony No. 3 for broadcast on the CBC's *Sunday Night* series. The musicians had great respect for Unger, and remembered him for his original interpretation and expressive performance on the podium. Principal horn player Eugene Rittich admired his profound and philosophical understanding of music.

One highlight of the 1964–5 season was the orchestra's first television appearance. The show, produced by CFTO, was pre-taped on 25 March with Walter Susskind conducting. Artistically, the season was a great success. There were three guest conductors: Hans Schmidt-Isserstadt, founder of the Nordwest Deutsche Rundfunk Orchestra, István Kertész, music director of the Cologne Opera, and, of course, Seiji Ozawa. Guest artists included Hermann Prey, Nathan Milstein, Van Cliburn, Emil Gilels, Leonard Rose, and Daniel Barenboim. For his last choral concert of the season, Walter Susskind conducted a performance of Benjamin Britten's *War Requiem* with soloists soprano Lois Marshall, tenor Peter Pears (who had sung in the world premiere of the work at

Coventry Cathedral in 1962), and baritone Victor Braun. The Toronto Mendelssohn Choir rehearsed for the concert under their new conductor, Elmer Iseler.

Walter Susskind's final concert as Music Director of the TSO opened with his *Nine Slovak Sketches*. The soloist for this concert was Leonard Rose, who played Dvořák's Cello Concerto in B minor, and the program concluded with *Le sacre du printemps* by Stravinsky. Walter Susskind had made an important contribution to the overall development of the orchestra. With highly skilled musicianship he had placed the orchestra in the international sphere. The TSO was no longer just an orchestra somewhere in Canada. It is surprising that no attempt was made to secure a recording contract during his tenure since he had made a number of recordings with the Philharmonia Orchestra in England. There are only two recordings of the TSO under Susskind. One is of Gabriel Pierné's *Children's Crusade* with the Mendelssohn Choir, made in 1960 on the Beaver label. The other, made for Capitol in 1965, contains two Canadian works: Roger Matton's *Concerto for Two Pianos* (with duo-pianists Renée Morisset and Victor Bouchard), and Oskar Morawetz's Piano Concerto No. 1 (with pianist Anton Kuerti).

Seiji Ozawa and Karel Ančerl

Musicke, the Mosaique of the Air.

This chapter covers the orchestra under two different music directors. One was an enthusiastic, charismatic young man, who almost overnight had enthralled music critics across North America. The other was a mature elder statesman who was one of the predominant maestros of the European classical music scene. Neither stayed with the TSO for long. The younger conductor moved on to new challenges, while the more senior conductor unfortunately succumbed to a long and painful illness. Both men had a profound effect on the future of the TSO.

1965–1966

Seiji Ozawa received his early musical training in Japan, where he first studied piano but after a hand injury switched to conducting and composition. He moved to Paris where, in 1959, he was awarded first prize at the International Conductors' Competition at Besançon. Charles Munch, one of the judges, invited him to the Berkshire Music Center (Tanglewood), where he studied conducting with Munch and Pierre Monteux, and also received the Koussevitsky Memorial Scholarship. Ozawa next moved to Berlin, where he studied with Herbert von Karajan. While in Berlin, he met Leonard Bernstein, who offered him a position as assistant conductor with the New York Philharmonic. Ozawa held this job from 1961 to 1965, when he became the music director of the TSO. Bernstein personally introduced Ozawa to the TSO on the morning of his first rehearsal.

Ozawa's acceptance of the position as music director and conductor immediately heightened the enthusiasm of the TSO audiences. His previous guest appearances had generated much interest, which was reflected in a demand for subscription series tickets. In an interview with Sylvia Fraser of the bygone *Star Weekly* Ozawa said, 'They want to make music in Toronto – the audience and the musicians – and that is very important. I do not want to be a fancy director in a fancy house – a mere decoration. The Toronto Symphony is a good orchestra – the relationship between a conductor and an orchestra is a kind of marriage.' During his first season Ozawa conducted eleven of the fifteen pairs of subscription concerts. The orchestra had also been invited to England to represent Canada for the Commonwealth Arts Festival. The expenses of the tour were fully covered by the Canadian government and the Festival of Britain.

Before Toronto audiences saw Ozawa in his new position as Music Director of the TSO in Massey Hall, he and the orchestra, along with members of the National Ballet of Canada and the Canadian Opera Company, were invited to participate in a special concert on 14 September to celebrate the opening of the new Toronto City Hall. Thus the orchestra was first conducted by Ozawa along with George Crum, conductor for the National Ballet, and two conductors for the Canadian Opera Company, James Craig and Ernesto Barbini. The TSO entourage was then off to Britain to participate in the Commonwealth Arts Festival from 23 September to 1 October, followed by three concerts in France – two in Paris and one in Lyon. In Britain they gave concerts in Glasgow, Liverpool, London, and Cardiff. The tour repertoire included Tchaikovsky's Symphony No. 5 in E minor, Harry Somers's *Suite for Harp and Chamber Orchestra*, Prokofiev's *Romeo and Juliet*, and Berlioz's *Roman Carnival Overture*. In London Lois Marshall joined the orchestra for Maurice Ravel's *Shéhérazade*, and in Paris and Lyon she sang 'Ah perfido' from Beethoven's opera *Fidelio*. Judy Loman, principal harpist of TSO, was the soloist for Harry Somers's *Suite for Harp and Chamber Orchestra*. The tour was very successful. A critic for the *London Sunday Times* said the TSO presented 'orchestral virtuosity of the great international class,' and the *London Daily Express* commented that 'Toronto's orchestra has little to fear from European rivals.' French critics were equally ecstatic.

The concert in Cardiff took place in Llandaff Cathedral, where applause was not permitted. The musicians were somewhat perplexed, and had little idea of how their performance had been received – that is, until they came outside and found the audience applauding enthusiastically for what had been an outstanding concert. Another problem with Llandaff was the lack of heat. Cathedrals can be quite cool, especially on late September evenings – so cool that some musicians wore their coats.

The TSO returned to Toronto amid accolades and praise from all levels of government. On 12 October, following the opening night concert, Toronto mayor Phil Givens and the Toronto City Council hosted a magnificent reception at the new City Hall in honour of Seiji Ozawa and members of the orchestra. On the same occasion, Mayor Givens presented Sir Ernest MacMillan with the Civic Award of Merit, the highest honour bestowed by the City of Toronto, for his distinguished public service.

The tour had proved that the TSO had an international identity, and the orchestra revelled in the tributes lavished on their new Music Director. Isadore Dubinsky, one of the few musicians left from the von Kunits days, was apparently very moved by the overwhelming success of the tour.

For the opening subscription concert in Massey Hall, Seiji Ozawa chose an orchestral program: the *Royal Fireworks Music* by George Frideric Handel, the Symphony No. 1 in C minor by Georges Bizet, and the first TSO performance of Harry Freedman's *Chaconne*. At this time Freedman played oboe and English horn in the orchestra. The concert ended with Ravel's transcription of Modest Mussorgsky's *Pictures at an Exhibition*. The evening was an overwhelming success. The orchestra and Ozawa treated the Toronto audience to the brilliant playing that had enthralled the public and critics alike in Britain and France. Ozawa was also building his reputation as a superb conductor; Leonard Bernstein said of him, 'Seiji is a genius – and I don't throw the word around lightly.'

On 26–7 October, contralto Maureen Forrester and the Toronto Men Teachers' Choir gave a performance of Brahms's *Alto Rhapsody*. On 16 November Claudio Arrau played Beethoven's Piano Concerto No 4 in G major. Georg Solti, music director of the Royal Opera House, Covent Garden, made his TSO debut on 30 November in an orchestral program that included Robert Schumann's Symphony No. 4 in D minor and Béla Bartók's *Concerto for Orchestra*. Hermann Scherchen, another internationally acclaimed conductor, led the TSO in a concert that included Anton Bruckner's Symphony No. 2 in C minor. Lukas Foss, conductor of the Buffalo Philharmonic Orchestra, made his TSO debut on 28 December.

On 10 January, the orchestra departed on a short tour of eastern Ontario and Quebec that included an exchange subscription concert with the Montreal Symphony Orchestra. In return, the Montreal orchestra under Zubin Mehta gave a concert in Massey Hall that included *Lignes et points* by Canadian composer Pierre Mercure and *Ein Heldenleben* by Richard Strauss.

The 8 February concert featured the talented young violinist Itzhak Perlman, who had made his New York debut in 1963 and had instantly been engaged for performances with all the leading orchestras in North America. For his TSO debut, he played Prokofiev's Violin Concerto No. 2. On 1–2 March Jesse Kregal, who was in his second season as the TSO timpanist, performed the Canadian premiere of the *Concerto for Five Kettledrums* by Robert Parris with the composer in the audience. This work had been written for Kregal and was premiered by the National Symphony Orchestra in Washington the previous year. The following week both a guest conductor and a guest soloist

Georg Solti made his TSO debut in 1965, conducting works by Schumann and Bartók

made TSO debuts: André Previn conducted a program that included one of his own compositions – *Overture to a Comedy* – and John Ogdon, the British pianist who had won the Liverpool International Competition in 1959, was the soloist for Schumann's Piano Concerto in A minor.

During the 1965–6 season the orchestra welcomed seven new members: Corol McCartney, violin; Richard Armin, cello; Nancicarole Musser, double bass; Robert Aitken, principal flute; Norman Tobias, bassoon; Fredrick Rizner, horn; and Eugene

Violinists Agnes Roberts, Teresa Obercian, Corol McCartney

Watts, principal trombone. This season was also marked by the death of Harry Warlow. Warlow had been closely associated with the orchestra for twenty-seven years, mainly as public relations counsel. He was highly respected by both musicians and members of the orchestra association. Walter Homburger, who had now completed three years as Managing Director of the TSO, was chosen by *Maclean's* magazine as one of the outstanding Canadians for 1965. Edward Pickering, a vice-president of Simpson Sears, was elected president of the Board at the 1966 annual general meeting. Pickering, who was anxious to increase the size of the Board of Directors and reorganize its operations for greater efficiency, asked Board member Terence Wardrop to propose a plan of reorganization. Wardrop made extensive recommendations for a structured committee system and the by-laws of the TSO Association were also revised. The Board was increased from thirty to fifty-five members and directors were elected on a rotating basis. A fixed quorum of twenty-three would also eliminate the problem of meetings being cancelled because of the lack of a quorum. The financial situation was healthy. The CBC had increased their fees for remote broadcasts by $5,500 and Toronto City Council had raised its grant from

$37,500 to $43,500. Sales of subscription series also increased. The Ozawa charisma had taken hold of the symphony audiences and their enthusiasm had made a profound impression on the TSO. The overall deficit was now down to a manageable $35,500.

Artistically all things appeared to be going well, and generally speaking the organiza-tion of the orchestra was sound. However, several problems were appearing on the horizon. Neither the musicians nor Ozawa were happy with the continuing onstage acoustic problem at Massey Hall. Both Edward Pickering and Walter Homburger were aware of the difficulty, and principal trumpet Joseph Umbrico, chairman of the Players Committee, forwarded a letter expressing the musicians' serious concerns and request-ing the Board to take some action to rectify the problem. The Planning Committee of the Board recommended that a study should be undertaken. Homburger contacted William Severns, past Managing Director of the Los Angeles Philharmonic, who agreed to come to Toronto in November to conduct a study. The Severns report intimated that, in the long term, it would be better to plan for a new hall. In May 1967 the Board established a committee to study the requirements for and feasibility of a new concert hall, and what was needed to bring this about.

1966–1967

The orchestra entered the television arena with four broadcasts – three for CBC and one for CTV. In September 1966 there was a televised performance of Beethoven's Symphony No. 9 in D minor conducted by Seiji Ozawa, with Lois Marshall, Maureen Forrester, Leopold Simoneau, Donald Bell, the Festival Singers of Canada, and mem-bers of the Toronto Mendelssohn Choir. On 24 November a CTV program titled 'A Gift of Music' was taped for broadcast during the Christmas season, again with Ozawa conducting. A CBC program on 10 February consisted of two cello concertos played by Mstislav Rostropovich: the Cello Concerto No. 2 by Dmitri Shostakovich and the Cello Concerto in C major by Franz Joseph Haydn. Rostropovich's perform-ance of the Shostakovich concerto for the subscription series in Massey Hall earlier that week was the North American premiere of this work. For a CBC telecast on 17 May Igor Stravinsky conducted his *Oedipus Rex* with the Festival Singers of Canada, a choral ensemble he greatly admired.

Colin Davis, Niklaus Wyss, Rafael Kubelík, and Paul Kletzki were all guest conductors for the 1966–7 season. Guest artists included two world-renowned cel-lists: Mstislav Rostropovich and Jacqueline du Pré, who played the Cello Concerto No. 1 in A minor by Camille Saint-Saëns. Reri Grist, who was rapidly becoming an acclaimed opera star, made her TSO debut singing two concert arias by Mozart – *Mia*

Seiji Ozawa conducts the TSO for a CBC Television broadcast, 1967

speranza adorata, K 416, and *Vorrei spiegarvi*, K 418 – and Zerbinetta's recitative and aria from Richard Strauss's opera *Ariadne auf Naxos*. On 14 November entertainer Danny Kaye conducted the orchestra for a most hilarious and successful Pension Fund concert.

Within the orchestra ranks there were a number of changes. Three musicians joined the orchestra: Thomas Monohan became principal double bass, Barbara Bloomer joined the horn section, and John Wyre took over as timpanist. Departures at the close of the season included those of principal cellist Malcolm Tait, who resigned to become artist-in-residence at the University of New Brunswick; Niklaus Wyss, who vacated the position of Assistant Conductor; and Hyman Goodman, who resigned as concertmaster to seek sunshine and studio work in southern California. Apparently there had been some disagreements between Goodman and Ozawa. Goodman may have had difficulty accepting a young and charismatic conductor. Goodman later said, 'He was 28 and I was 53. He didn't like me and I've got a poor poker face. I figured the best thing to do

Danny Kaye conducting the TSO in rehearsal for a Pension Fund benefit concert, November 1966

was to get out of the orchestra.' During the season Ozawa had introduced a system in which the concertmaster shared his duties with associate concertmaster Isidor Desser and principal second violin Clifford Evens.

Touring was also part of the season. A ten-day tour of Florida was followed by a successful six-day tour of the eastern United States that included Washington and New York. Back in Canada the orchestra was invited by the Centennial Commission to participate in a series of concerts in Montreal during a festival of international artists and ensembles at Expo '67. The TSO's special concert in the Place des Arts was

Tom Monohan, principal double bass

conducted by Seiji Ozawa, with soprano Lois Marshall, who sang the *Vier letzte Lieder* (Four Last Songs) by Richard Strauss. The concert also included the world premiere of *Contrastes* by Canadian composer, teacher, and violinist Otto Joachim, a work which was commissioned by the Toronto Symphony Orchestra. Carl Nielsen's Symphony No. 5, op. 50, completed a program that had been made possible through a grant from the Centennial Commission. For a Centennial Project the TSO received a grant from IBM to make two recordings for Columbia Records. The first was a recording of *Symphonie fantastique* by Berlioz. The second was a selection of music by Canadian composers including *Two Sketches for String Orchestra* by Ernest MacMillan, *Images* by Harry Freedman, *Triptyque* by Pierre Mercure, and *L'étoile noire* by François Morel. Both recordings were distributed free of charge to 3,000 schools across Canada, courtesy of IBM.

This busy season also included two major administrative changes. First, the Toronto Symphony Orchestra changed its name to The Toronto Symphony (TS). The original name of the orchestra was reinstated some twenty-seven years later.

The second administrative change was the incorporation of the Toronto Symphony Foundation, an entirely separate organization from the TS Association. The Foundation's single purpose was to establish an endowment fund that would maintain continuing financial support for the orchestra. Many of the leading orchestras in the United States had adopted this approach as a result of reduced financial support from governments (which had fallen to an average of approximately 22 per cent of total revenues). However, until the mid-1980s, grants from federal, provincial, and municipal governments accounted for approximately 48 per cent of the overall TS budget. At the annual general meeting on 12 September 1967, Board President Edward Pickering reported that the Toronto Symphony Foundation had been established in order to create an endowment fund that would make an important contribution to orchestra revenues. Unfortunately, his statement was not taken seriously. Ten years later the

Endowment Fund still had less than a million dollars. The fact that government grants might well be drastically reduced was ignored by both Board and management, a complacent attitude that was seen in almost every major orchestra in Canada. Years later, when government funding was indeed sharply reduced, attempts were made to catch up. However, at the turn of the twenty-first century, while major orchestras in the United States had accumulated substantial endowment funds in the area of two hundred million dollars, the TS fund stood at about fifteen million.

The new contract for the musicians was possibly the most encouraging working agreement they had ever negotiated. The minimum weekly salary was increased from $130 to $180 per week, and the season was extended from thirty to forty-two weeks. There was also a clause whereby the management could contract the orchestra for additional services for radio, opera, and television and could schedule these services into the season. However the TS management was aware that these salaries were still low in comparison to those of other major orchestras in North America. The budget of $1,172,000 involved the largest operating deficit in the history of the orchestra, but there was also some relief. The Canada Council increased its grant to $200,000, while grants from the Ontario Arts Council and the Metropolitan Toronto Council were increased by $25,000 and $7,000 respectively. The Women's Committee had also raised $100,000. These increases assisted in closing the gap between expenses and earned income.

1967–1968

The concern over the formation of a government-sponsored permanent orchestra in Ottawa had partially dispersed. The National Arts Centre plan for a ninety-member symphony orchestra had been abandoned in favour of a chamber orchestra of forty-five musicians. However, a subsidy to maintain even a small orchestra in Ottawa could potentially divert approximately one million dollars of Canada Council funds, reducing the amount to be allocated to existing orchestras in Montreal and Toronto.

The TS opened its season with a tour of Ontario sponsored by the planning department of the Ontario Centennial Commission. Seiji Ozawa was conductor and the soloists were violinist Gerard Kantarjian, the new concertmaster, and world-renowned Canadian baritone Victor Braun. For the opening subscription concert, the women in the orchestra sported fashionable new black centennial concert dresses – the subject of an amusing photo call by the local press. This concert also included a performance of Otto Joachim's *Contrastes*, which the orchestra had premiered in Montreal in May 1967. An announcement in the program for the 17–18 October concert indicated that, following the practice of other orchestras in Canada and Great Britain, the national anthem would be played only at the beginning and end of each season and on special occasions when royalty was in attendance. Karel Ančerl, the music director of the Czech Philharmonic Orchestra, made his TS debut on 21 November with a program that included works by two well-known Czech composers: the concert overture *Othello* by Antonín Dvořák and two movements, *Š árka* and *Tábor*, from *Ma Vlast* by Bedřich Smetana. Walter Susskind returned to the podium on 23 January 1968 for a concert that demonstrated three aspects of his career: he conducted the orchestra; he was the soloist in Leoš Janáček's *Concertino for Piano*; and the program included his orchestral transcription of Sergei Prokofiev's piano work *Visions fugitives*. Susskind is not well known as a composer, but Janice Susskind, recalling her late husband, said that he composed constantly. One of his works, written in Toronto, is a concerto for timpani and orchestra, which unfortunately was never performed by the TS.

Per Bastiana Tai-Yang Chen, a new composition by Luigi Nono that had been commissioned by the TS under a grant from the Centennial Commission, had its world premiere on 31 October. The work was scored for magnetic tape and instruments. John Beckwith's program note stated, 'It is a fifteen-minute work, composed on fifteen large graph-paper pages – one minute per page. The tape part is here indicated by special graphic notations so that its gestures can be followed.' Verdi's *Rigoletto* was chosen for a concert performance on 11 and 13 January with a cast that featured Reri Grist, George Shirley, and Louis Quilico, along with the newly formed Toronto Symphony Chorus, whose choral director was Lloyd Bradshaw. Meanwhile, with opera in mind, serious negotiations were under way with the Canadian Opera Company to engage the TS for the six-week opera season from mid-September to mid-October. The last concert of the 'Jazz and the Symphony' series on 27 April featured guest artist Benny Goodman. The program opened with J.S. Bach's Brandenburg Concerto No. 1 in F major, BWV 1046, followed by Weber's Clarinet Concerto No. 2 with Goodman as soloist. The second half of the concert was devoted to Benny Goodman and his sextet for an evening where jazz and the classics were blended with masterful skill.

The unexpected news in February that Seiji Ozawa was resigning at the end of the 1968–9 season to take up the position of music director and conductor of the San Francisco Symphony stunned both musicians and audience. Unfortunately the news was given to the media by the San Francisco Symphony before checking with the TS Board on the timing of joint announcements. This situation put the TS Board in the embarrassing situation of calling a press conference to confirm Ozawa's resignation.

Under Ozawa's leadership the high quality of the orchestra had become known internationally. In view of such recognition, it is difficult to understand why no attempt appears to have been made to retain Ozawa at any cost. In his statement to the Board concerning Ozawa's decision to leave, managing director Walter Homburger reported that Ozawa felt that after four years with the TS the musicians would have acquired all the knowledge he could impart and that the time had come for a change.

The selection committee that was formed wasted no time in searching for a new conductor. Homburger submitted names that might be considered, but indicated that not all would be available. After some discussion it became obvious that Karel Ančerl, the conductor of the Czech Philharmonic Orchestra, might be free and should be approached. Homburger went to Zurich, and after lengthy discussions with Ančerl, advised the selection committee that Ančerl was willing to accept the position. The full Board discussed and endorsed the appointment of Karel Ančerl as Music Director and Conductor of the TS with a contract for three seasons commencing with the 1969–70 season.

January 1968 marked the death of Vincent Massey, who had been President of the Board from 1931 to 1934. Massey had been instrumental in governing the orchestra in its early days and he was also the first Canadian to be appointed Governor General of Canada. At the end of the 1967–8 season, Jack Elton, the assistant managing director and a long-time member of the administration, decided to retire. Elton had given many years of devoted service and had shown exemplary management skills in his time with the orchestra.

The 1968–9 season opened with an expectation that it would be a memorable one. The orchestra was now the accompanying ensemble for the Canadian Opera Company season from September to mid-October at the O'Keefe Centre. The operas were *Aida* by Giuseppe Verdi, *La Bohème* and *Tosca* by Giacomo Puccini, *Salome* by Richard Strauss, and *Louis Riel* by Canadian composer Harry Somers. The conductors were Ernesto Barbini, Victor Feldbrill, and Samuel Krachmalnick from the New York City Center Opera. Both Herman Geiger-Torel (the general director of the Canadian Opera Company) and Walter Homburger were happy with the collaboration.

Three TS tours were planned for the season: two to the eastern United States, and one to Japan. The first U.S. tour, which took the orchestra to Burlington (Vermont) and Boston, was combined with visits to Montreal and Ottawa; the second tour included New York and Philadelphia. In addition, two recordings scheduled with RCA

1968–1969

Victor introduced Ozawa to the international recording industry. These recordings featured four compositions by Tōru Takemitsu – *Asterism*, *November Steps*, *Green (November Steps II)*, and *Requiem for Strings* – and Olivier Messiaen's *Turangalîla symphonie*. Kazuyoshi Akiyama had made his North American debut with the TS during the 1967–8 season, and was appointed Assistant Conductor. His conducting duties for the current season included student concerts and out-of-town engagements as well as several subscription concerts.

The zenith of Ozawa's tenure was undoubtedly the tour to his homeland. There were three concerts in Osaka, one in Nagoya, and four in Tokyo. All were successful and greatly appreciated by Japanese audiences. The musicians had an exciting time, enjoying not only the concerts but also the sights and sounds of Japan and their experiences with Japanese culture and customs.

On 25–6 February 1969 Eliahu Inbal made his Canadian debut as a guest conductor with a program that included Arthur Honegger's Symphony No. 2 (*Symphonie pour cordes*) for string orchestra with solo trumpet. Charles Munch was to have conducted this concert but had cancelled because of an illness that eventually caused his death in 1968. The performance of Honegger's symphony was dedicated to his memory. Josef Krips, conductor of the San Francisco Symphony, conducted an all-Brahms concert on 28–9 Jan-uary with guest soloist Masuko Ushioda playing the Violin Concerto in D major. On 4–5 March, two young musicians gave one of the most anticipated concerts of the season: conductor Daniel Barenboim and Jacqueline du Pré (the remarkable young English cellist who was acclaimed by New York critics as the first lady in music) in an impressive performance of the Elgar Cello Concerto in E minor. Other prominent guest artists included pianists Lorin Hollander, Byron Janis, and Peter Serkin. There were two major choral works in Ozawa's final season with the TS. On 25–6 March he conducted a performance of *La damnation de Faust* with the Toronto Symphony Chorus and soprano Lois Marshall, tenor John McCollum, bass Ezio Flagello, and baritone Leonid Skirko. On 6–7 May the Toronto Symphony Chorus and Orchestra, joined by soprano Helen Boatwright and baritone Tom Krause, combined for a performance of *Ein deutsches Requiem* (A German Requiem) by Brahms. On 10 May Duke Ellington and his orchestra were guest artists for a concert in the 'Jazz and the Symphony' series.

The final concert for Seiji Ozawa as Music Director and Conductor of the TS in Toronto took place on 14 May. The program consisted of *Three Places in New England* by Charles Ives, Mozart's Piano Concerto No. 23 in A major, K 488, with pianist John Browning, Johann Strauss's overture to *Der Zigeunerbaron* (The Gypsy Baron), and the suite from Richard Strauss's *Der Rosenkavalier*. Ozawa's last engagement with the TS was

Cellist Jacqueline du Pré

Karel Ančerl (1908–1973)

a concert for the opening of the National Arts Centre in Ottawa on 6 June. According to Jacob Siskind of the *Montreal Star*, there was 'a smash bang performance of Tchaikovsky's Symphony No. 4 that shot the audience from its seats liked popped corn even before the last drum rolls had stormed to an end.' Then it was time to say goodbye. It is interesting to speculate that if Ozawa, at age fifteen, had not broken both forefingers in an accident during a football match, he might still be a pianist rather than an internationally acclaimed conductor.

During this season, Terence Wardrop, a Board member with great enthusiasm and concern for the day-to-day operations and future plans of the orchestra, presented two important proposals to the Board. The first concerned the Co-ordinated Arts Services, an organization founded in Toronto under the sponsorship of the Canada Council and the Ontario Arts Council for the purpose of helping arts organizations to decrease expenses by eliminating duplication of operating procedures. The TS joined this plan, along with a number of other groups, including the Canadian Opera Company and the National Ballet of Canada. The Co-ordinated Arts Services took over subscription services for all member organizations and was to become an important element in all facets of the TS administration.

Wardrop's second proposal came from the planning committee, of which he was chairman. This proposal was for a summer home for the TS at Niagara-on-the-Lake, in conjunction with the Shaw Festival. Performance facilities were to be built on land allocated by the Department of Northern Affairs, and both the federal and provincial governments seemed enthusiastic about the project. Wardrop requested a moral commitment from the Board so that planning could go ahead, but the motion that was finally made, seconded, and carried contained too many conditions and exceptions. The plan dissolved, and an opportunity to lengthen the concert season, give the orchestra a permanent summer home, and create a new summer audience was lost.

The arrival of Karel Ančerl as Music Director and Conductor was an auspicious event. Karel Ančerl (1908–73) had been conducting since the age of twenty-three. He studied composition and conducting at the Prague Conservatory, and composed numerous works, including a suite for string orchestra in quarter-tones. He was a member of Hermann Scherchen's conducting class in Strasbourg and later became his assistant, and he also studied conducting with Václav Talich in Prague. In 1933 he began a career as conductor for the theatre and for Prague radio. During the war years he was imprisoned at Auschwitz, where his parents, wife, and child were put to death.

After the war, Ančerl returned to Prague, where he eventually remarried and held conducting appointments with the Prague Opera (1945–8) and the Czech Radio Symphony Orchestra (1947–50). In October 1950 he was appointed artistic director of the Czech Philharmonic Orchestra, a position he held until 1968. The Russian invasion of Czechoslovakia that occurred while Ančerl was guest conducting in North America prevented him from returning to his orchestra, and he decided to make his home in North America. At first the TS musicians were not unanimously excited about Ančerl's appointment, but after a few weeks both players and Board realized their good fortune in attracting one of the world's most respected conductors. He had built the Czech Philharmonic into one of Europe's most accomplished orchestras, and was obviously also aiming high for the TS.

For his first concerts, on 14 and 15 October, Ančerl chose Bedřich Smetana's symphonic poem *Wallenstein's Camp*, Schumann's Piano Concerto in A minor with Rudolf Firkusny as the soloist, and Dvořák's Symphony No. 6 in D major. On 4 and 5 November British soprano Heather Harper made her Canadian debut in a performance of the *Vier letzte Lieder* (Four Last Songs) by Richard Strauss. In the same concert Ančerl conducted the orchestra in its first performance of Mahler's Symphony No. 5.

1969–1970

Leontyne Price

November saw Ančerl's first choral concerts with the TS: three outstanding performances of Britten's *War Requiem* with soprano Lois Marshall, tenor Gerald English, baritone Victor Braun, the Toronto Mendelssohn Choir, and the Canadian Children's Opera Chorus. Percussionist Paul Caston recalled the excitement of the performance and how Ančerl kept the various forces under tight control while still allowing the music to speak for itself.

Ančerl told a story about his early attempts at English pronunciation. In Australia he was rehearsing the Melbourne Symphony Orchestra and Chorus in Dvořák's *Stabat Mater*. The chorus had not been well trained and were breathing unevenly. Ančerl stopped them in despair and said, 'Ladies and gentleman, please! Hold your breasts!'

Guest conductors for the 1969–70 season included Rafael Fruhbeck de Burgos, Lawrence Foster, David Oistrakh, and Seiji Ozawa, who returned for a Pension Fund concert with soloist Leontyne Price. Ozawa also conducted two subscription series concerts during his two-week return. The one on 24–5 March included the *Grande messe des morts* (Requiem) by Hector Berlioz with tenor Anastasios Vrenios and the Toronto Mendelssohn Choir, performed in memory of the late Charles Munch. Ančerl conducted two concerts that revealed his strong Czechoslovakian roots. The program for 28–9 April included the Symphony in D major by the Czech composer Jan Václav Voříšek. On 5–6 May violinist Josef Suk played the *Fantasie for Violin* written by his grandfather, also named Josef Suk. At the end of the subscription season Ančerl conducted the Canadian premiere of Dvořák's *Requiem* with the Toronto Mendelssohn Choir and soprano Edith Mathis, mezzo-soprano Lili Chookasian, tenor Peter Schreier, and bass Franz Mazura as soloists.

In addition to the regular season, Walter Homburger had negotiated a three-week Beethoven Festival to be held at the O'Keefe Centre from 1 to 19 June, with Ančerl conducting a stunning line-up of twelve concerts. Pianist Joseph Kalichstein, violinist Lorand Fenyves, and cellist Peter Schenkman performed the Triple Concerto in

C major, op. 56. Vladimir Ashkenazy played the Piano Concerto No. 3 in C minor. At the third concert André Watts played the Piano Concerto No. 4 in G major, and during the second week Josef Suk returned for the Violin Concerto in D major. The third week included a performance of the Piano Concerto No. 5 in E flat major ('Emperor') with Alfred Brendel as soloist. The final concert presented the Symphony No. 8 in F major and the Symphony No. 9 in C minor with the Toronto Mendelssohn Choir and soloists soprano Clarice Carson, mezzo-soprano Huguette Tourangeau, tenor Wilmer Neufeld, and bass Thomas Paul. Artistically and financially the festival was a success, in spite of initially slow ticket sales.

Meanwhile, the Toronto Mendelssohn Choir was celebrating its seventy-fifth anniversary season. In addition to exceptional concerts in the TS season, the choir presented two concerts of their own with the support of the TS. The anniversary concert on 14 January was a performance Handel's *Israel in Egypt*. J.S. Bach's *St Matthew Passion* was presented in February.

Artistically, the Toronto Symphony presented a season of outstanding concerts, including performances of seventeen works by Canadian composers. Financially, the picture was not so bright. On 18 March, at a special meeting called to address the dire financial situation, Frank McEachren, the chairman of the Board, said that every cloud had a silver lining, but as far as the orchestra was concerned, the reverse was true. The silver lining was on the outside, outlining the enormity and blackness of the cloud. There was an overall deficit of $185,000 and a forecasted deficit of $320,000 by the end of the season. In addition, negotiations with the musicians' union for a new contract were about to take place. The situation was extremely serious and unless a solution was found it was quite possible that the orchestra would fold. A crisis committee, consisting of two members of the Board, the chairman of the Women's Committee, two members of the Players Committee, the president of the musicians' union, and the president of the TS, was established and given two months to present a plan to the Board. Ontario Premier John Robarts met with the committee and promised to see what could be done to re-evaluate the province's financial support. At the same time the crisis committee was also negotiating with the Canada Council and Metropolitan Toronto. Gradually the financial black cloud began to lighten. The provincial government announced a one-time debt-reduction grant of $162,780 and also increased the 1970–1 grant by $70,000 over the previous year. The Canada Council increased their annual grant to $320,000 and gave an additional $30,000 to be applied directly to the deficit. The Metropolitan Toronto grant of $50,000 for the 1970–1 season remained unchanged from the previous year.

J. Allan Wood of the Toronto Musicians' Association, TSO Director Mel Kenny, double bass player Ruth Budd, and TSO President Frank McEachren at the signing of the new Master Agreement

A one-year contract agreement with the musicians' union had been reached with an overall pay increase of 6.35 per cent plus an increase in vacation pay from two weeks to three. Four new members joined the orchestra ranks. Albert Pratz returned after three years as concertmaster of the Buffalo Philharmonic Orchestra. Pratz was last in Toronto six years earlier as concertmaster of the CBC Symphony Orchestra, and prior to that had played in the NBC Symphony Orchestra under Arturo Toscanini. The other newcomers were violinist Eugene Kowalski, who came from the Winnipeg Symphony Orchestra, violinist Janice McRae, who for the past seven years had been a member of the Rochester Philharmonic Orchestra, and William Findlay, who had been principal cellist of the National Ballet Orchestra.

1970–1971   The previous season had confirmed Karel Ančerl's skill in interpretation, conducting technique, and development of the orchestra. Even the sceptics (and there were a few)

had been convinced that the TS had a distinguished conductor, and Ančerl's second season was awaited with anticipation and enthusiasm. When Gerard Kantarjian, who had been concertmaster for the past two seasons, resigned to pursue a career in chamber music, Albert Pratz was appointed to the position in an acting capacity until 1 January, when he officially assumed the position on the recommendation of Maestro Ančerl, who had been pleased with his work. Both Susskind and Ozawa had admired Pratz's playing and had wanted him as concertmaster. The orchestra's annual engagement with the Canadian Opera Company for its fall season continued, but Ančerl was never pleased with the arrangement. He felt that the orchestra's standards deteriorated during its six-week stint as a pit orchestra.

For the opening concert for the season Emil Gilels played the Piano Concerto No. 5 in E flat major ('Emperor') by Beethoven in a program that also included the Symphony No. 6 in B minor ('Pathétique') by Tchaikovsky and Mendelssohn's overture to *The Fair Melusina*. Other artists of international prominence who performed with the orchestra before the Christmas break included pianist Alicia de Larrocha, cellist Jacqueline du Pré, and singers Maureen Forrester, Reri Grist, Stuart Burrows, and Simon Estes. An all-Brahms concert on 11 December featured violinist Ida Haendal in the Violin Concerto in D major, along with the Symphony No. 3 in F major. During the rehearsal of the symphony Ančerl commented that the end of the last movement was the only Wagnerian moment in all of Brahms.

At the beginning of the new year, Karel Ančerl went on a European tour to fulfil guest conducting engagements, including a successful concert with the Israel Philharmonic Orchestra, but while in Israel, he fell ill. After extensive tests it was determined that he was suffering from a recurrence of a chronic illness. On the recommendation of doctors he entered hospital in Stuttgart for treatment and further tests. While Ančerl was recuperating, Homburger flew to Stuttgart to meet with him. They discussed a three-year contract extension, to which Ančerl agreed. This ensured that Ančerl would be with the orchestra until the end of the 1974–5 season.

In January, Walter Susskind returned as guest conductor for a program that included the Canadian premiere of his *Capriccio Concertante*. In February James Levine, the assistant conductor of the Cleveland Orchestra, conducted a pair of concerts with guest artist Yehudi Menuhin performing Mozart's Violin Concerto No. 5 in A major, K 219, and took the orchestra through its paces in a colourful performance of *Symphonie fantastique* by Berlioz. Also in February, Czech conductor Martin Turnovsky, who had received his musical training in Prague under the guidance of Ančerl, was guest conductor. When Ančerl was unable to conduct a pair of subscription concerts in April,

Karel Ančerl, Victor Feldbrill, Greta Kraus, Geza Anda, and Denis Langelier at the 1970 Piano Competition

because of illness, Victor Feldbrill took over at short notice. Toward the end of the season, the Toronto Mendelssohn Choir joined the TS for a performance of Krzysztof Penderecki's choral work *Passio et mors domini nostri Jesu Christi secundum Lucam* (*The St Luke Passion*) conducted by Elmer Iseler. Karel Ančerl attended the performance, and at the end of the work was overheard commenting to his wife, 'Mein Gott! Two hours without an *allegro*.'

With the main season completed, the orchestra embarked on its first summer season in the newly built Ontario Place, a cultural and amusement park situated on reclaimed land in the Toronto harbour. These concerts were sponsored by the Ontario government through the Ontario Arts Council as part of a program to present the performing arts to the public at the extremely low price of three dollars, the price of admission to the park. The fifteen TS concerts in the series were well received and attended by more than 100,000 people, who were able to listen to music on a relaxed summer's evening. At one concert, there were over 12,000 in the audience. The conducting duties were shared by Karel Ančerl, Walter Susskind, Seiji Ozawa, Boris Brott, Boyd Neel, and Victor Feldbrill. Minds and thoughts were now focused on the upcoming season, the fiftieth anniversary of the Toronto Symphony.

The fiftieth anniversary season represented a time of reflection upon the many dedi-cated people who over the years had made the orchestra possible: the musicians who had served with dedication and professionalism, even when monetary returns were low; the Board of directors and their committees who continually lobbied governments, corporations, and individuals to support a high-quality orchestra that was rapidly becoming internationally recognized; the Women's Committee with its long, successful history of raising substantial revenues; and finally the audiences who loyally bought subscriptions and individual tickets. All had contributed to the success of the Toronto Symphony in its first fifty years.

Frank McEachren, the chairman of the Board, announced the formation of the Associates of the Toronto Symphony, a new support group that was intended to permit younger people interested in the orchestra and its activities to take part in fund-raising projects while simultaneously providing a social milieu for its members. The Associates soon became active and in April announced two 'Pre-Concert Discussions' led by Canadian composers: the first with Harry Somers on *Stereophony* and the second with Oskar Morawetz on *From the Diary of Anne Frank.*

Special projects for the year included the creation of a medallion to commemorate the anniversary season. The issue consisted of 150 medals in gold, priced at $262.50, and 850 in silver, priced at $52.50, but unfortunately the response did not generate the expected revenue. In addition, Rothmans of Pall Mall Canada contributed funding for the production of a book by Arnold Edinborough entitled *The First Fifty.* This publica-tion provided an informative history of the orchestra, but it gave the appearance of having been hastily produced. On 26 October, the orchestra presented the world premiere of Harry Freedman's *Graphic I: 'Out of silence…,'* a work commissioned by the TS for the opening of its fiftieth season.

In December 1971, the Board gave approval for a 1974 European tour. This represented a substantial financial undertaking. The anticipated revenue of $150,000 from the federal government plus $100,000 in tour fees left an estimated deficit of $50,000 to be funded by sponsorships.

While the TS anniversary was toasted by various personalities, a wide range of music from the world's foremost composers – an essential ingredient to this momentous occasion – was performed. A large percentage of the conducting was undertaken by Maestro Ančerl, augmented by visits from James Levine, Seiji Ozawa, Roger Wagner, Arthur Fiedler, Walter Susskind, and André Kostelanetz. The guest artists for the season – including Elly Ameling, Vladimir Ashkenazy, Barry Tuckwell, Mstislav

Rostropovich, Lois Marshall, and Itzhak Perlman – also reflected the high status that TS had attained in its first fifty years.

A wealth of choral concerts presented a number of works not often performed. On 7–8 December Elmer Iseler was guest conductor for a program that consisted of Roger Matton's *Te Deum* (composed in 1967), Arnold Schoenberg's *Friede auf Erden* (Peace on Earth), and Arthur Honegger's *Une cantate de Noël*. Baritone Louis Quilico and the Toronto Mendelssohn Choir participated in all three works and the Canadian Children's Opera Chorus joined in for Honegger's cantata. The work of Honegger was again featured on 1–2 February with a performance of his dramatic oratorio *Jean d'Arc au bûcher* (Joan of Arc at the Stake). Performers included soloists Denise Pelletier, Jean-Louis Roux, Claude Corbeil, Gerald English, Lynne Cantlon, Patricia Harton, and Nicole Lorange, along with the Toronto Mendelssohn Choir and the Canadian Children's Opera Chorus, all conducted by Ančerl. A third choral work was presented on 22–3 February in a program of two Berlioz works: the *Symphonie fantastique* and its choral sequel, *Lélio*. The supporting artists were actor Colin Fox, tenor John Mitchinson, and baritone Peter Barcza, along with the Toronto Mendelssohn Choir. The season closed on 23, 24, and 26 May with Verdi's *Requiem*, conducted by Ančerl with soprano Elinor Ross, contralto Lili Chookasian, tenor John Alexander, bass Bonaldo Giaiotti, and the Toronto Mendelssohn Choir.

Following the success of the Beethoven Festival at the O'Keefe Centre in June 1971, a Brahms Festival for this season was given in the same venue. The three-week event featured all of Brahms's symphonies and concertos. There was also a performance of *Ein deutsches Requiem* (A German Requiem) with soprano Lynne Cantlon and baritone Victor Braun, and Maureen Forrester sang the *Vier ernste Gesänge* (Four Serious Songs), op. 121, and the *Alto Rhapsody*. All the concerts were conducted by Karel Ančerl.

The annual performances of Handel's *Messiah* by the TS and the Toronto Mendelssohn Choir over this Christmas season were in the hands of guest conductor Roger Wagner. On January 25 Czech pianist Jan Panenka made his Canadian debut with a performance of the Piano Concerto No. 3 by Bohuslav Martinů. Ančerl opened the concerts on 21–2 March with the world premiere of *Reflections for Orchestra* by Czech composer Tomas Svoboda. The season also included Van Cliburn playing Beethoven's Piano Concerto No. 5 in E flat major ('Emperor'). The program for 23 April, a repeat of the orchestra's first concert, given on 23 April 1923, included Tchaikovsky's Symphony No. 5 in E minor, a work that apparently was not one of Ančerl's favourites. During rehearsal, a bassoonist made an error and Ančerl stopped the orchestra to correct him. The bassoonist replied, 'It must be a mistake in the part.' Ančerl asked him to correct the mistake and play it the way he had asked, but the bassoonist did not give up so easily. 'I thought you must have marked the parts yourself,' he explained, 'so I played it the way it is in the music.' Ančerl calmly put down his baton and said, 'The last time I performed this music was thirty-five years ago.'

The anniversary euphoria carried over into the summer season at Ontario Place. Ančerl conducted two concerts, and guest conductors included Seiji Ozawa, Arthur Fiedler, Walter Susskind, and André Kostelanetz. There were also several personnel changes within the orchestra. New string players included violinist Richard Roberts, who became associate concertmaster, double bass player Edward Tait, violinist Carol Lieberman, and cellist Audrey King. Additions to the wind and brass section included Harry Sargous, who was installed as principal oboe, flutist Marjorie Yates, French horn players John Cahill and George Stimpson, and trombonist Frank Harmantas. An exciting and memorable season, which also included visits to New York, Washington, and Ottawa, had come to an end. It had not always been easy, but this anniversary year was an *annis mirabilis* and everyone turned with confidence to the next fifty seasons.

A new word was working its way into the TS vocabulary: lottery. During the last season, Co-ordinated Arts Services had set up a plan to hold a lottery that would provide financial assistance for arts organizations. In the first Lottario, held during the 1971–2 season, $70,000 was turned over to the Toronto Symphony Trust Fund, and it was hoped that this season the amount would increase.

1972–1973

At the end of the last season Karel Ančerl had made a request to increase the size of the orchestra to ninety-eight musicians over the next three years. This proposal was accepted in principle, providing the budget could sustain the additional salaries. New faces for the 1972–3 season included violinists Ronald Gorevic, Terry Moore, and Winston Webber, oboist Frank Morphy, French horn players Brad Warnaar and Richard Cohen, double bass player John Gowen, and percussionist Paul Caston. One of the nine musicians leaving the orchestra was violinist Isadore Dubinsky, who had been a member of the TSO since the first concert in 1923.

The 1972–3 season seemed to be plagued with illness. When Emil Gilels had to cancel his scheduled performance he was replaced by Lorin Hollander, who played the Saint-Saëns Piano Concerto No. 5 in F major. Rudolf Serkin was replaced by John Browning, who performed the originally programmed Brahms Piano Concerto No. 2 in B flat major. Albert Pratz, the concertmaster, who was unable to play the Violin

Karel Ančerl

Concerto in A minor by Alexander Glazunov, was replaced by Anton Kuerti, who performed the Mendelssohn Piano Concerto No. 1 in G minor. Illness also prevented Karel Ančerl from conducting the opening pair of subscription concerts on 24–5 October, so Victor Feldbrill, who had been conducting in England and Italy, stepped onto the podium.

Late on the evening of 2 November, Ančerl was taken ill with a recurrence of hepatitis, an infection that he had contracted during his years in German concentration camps during the Second World War. His doctors advised him not to resume conducting. Donald Johanos, associate conductor of the Pittsburgh Symphony Orchestra, stepped in at short notice for an unplanned debut with the TS, as did pianist Eugene Istomin. *Ma Vlast* by Smetana was withdrawn from the program and replaced with Haydn's Symphony No. 8 in G major ('Le soir'). The remainder of the program consisted of Stravinsky's suite from his ballet *L'oiseau de feu* (The Firebird), Chopin's Piano Concerto No. 2 in F minor with Istomin as soloist, and Dvořák's *Scherzo capriccioso*. Sergiu Comissiona also made his TS debut appearance along with violinist György Pauk. Seiji Ozawa returned for an outstanding interpretation of Berlioz's *Roméo et Juliette* with mezzo-soprano Rosalind Elias, tenor George Shirley, baritone Victor Braun, and the Toronto Mendelssohn Choir.

When Sir Ernest MacMillan died on 6 May 1973 the orchestra mourned the loss of its long-time dedicated conductor and friend. In mid-May Karel Ančerl announced that ill health prevented him from extending his contract beyond the end of the 1974–5 season. In the meantime the Board had resolved that Victor Feldbrill should be appointed as Associate Conductor on the understanding that this appointment did not indicate that he would become Music Director upon Ančerl's retirement.

Six weeks later, on 3 July, Karel Ančerl died at the age of sixty-five. For many years the maestro had suffered from hepatitis complicated by diabetes, but his death came as a shock to the Toronto Symphony and the musical community worldwide. The sense of loss felt by so many people was an indication of the extraordinary human qualities he possessed. His attempts to make the TS an ensemble of international distinction resulted in new standards of performance, and he instilled individual musicians with that same sense of achievement. As William Littler, music critic for the *Toronto Star*, wrote, 'Ančerl had a very high level of musicianship, he tuned the Orchestra.' At the end of the fiftieth anniversary season the orchestra had come to the end of an era, which ended sadly and suddenly on 3 July 1973. Hanna Ančerl kept the urn containing Karel's ashes in the Ančerl home, and after her death in 1986 the remains of Karel and Hanna were returned to Czechoslovakia for interment in Prague at the Slavin cemetery, where many distinguished Czechs are buried.

Victor Feldbrill, Resident Conductor

Music is an agreeable harmony for the honour of God and the permissable delights of the soul.

JOHANN SEBASTIAN BACH

1973–1975

The *Concise Oxford Dictionary* describes 'intermezzo' as 'a short connecting instrumental movement in an opera or other musical work.' In 1973 the Toronto Symphony Orchestra had reached a point that could be identified as the end of Act 1. This 'intermezzo' chapter records how the TS dealt with the situation that had been suddenly thrust upon them, and how it prepared for the beginning of the next act. The death of Karel Ančerl, which had stunned the music community in Toronto, across Canada, and abroad, placed the TS in a situation that required decisive managerial action. The 1973–4 season had been planned and publicized and contracts had been signed for the European tour. After consultations with the Board, Walter Homburger immediately left for Europe to attempt to resolve three important matters. The first was to find a suitable conductor who could undertake a European tour with a possibly unfamiliar orchestra and approve any program changes for the tour. The second matter was to find conductors that might be available to take on some of the upcoming Toronto concerts that had been allotted to Ančerl. The third, and most important matter in the long term, was to consult other orchestra managers about a possible future music director and conductor to succeed Ančerl.

Homburger solved the first problem with little delay. Kazimierz Kord, a prominent Polish conductor, agreed to undertake the European tour. The second matter required more negotiation. Homburger was particularly keen to meet a talented young German conductor who had given outstanding concerts in East Germany and had recently been allowed to cross into West Germany. Hearing that Klaus Tennstedt was conducting in Kiel, Homburger made a quick side trip to hear the concert. He was impressed with what he saw and heard, and after the concert he asked Tennstedt if he would come to Toronto to conduct the TS. Tennstedt accepted, and on 14–15 May 1974 he led the orchestra in an all-Beethoven program. This concert, his North American debut, was an important step in his conducting career.

The third concern was to sound out managers in Britain and Europe on suggestions as to who might be suitable and available to fulfil the position of TS Music Director and

John Chong and Victor Feldbrill at the 1972 Student Composer Competition

Conductor. One name discussed in orchestra circles was that of a young English conductor. Andrew Davis had emerged rather dramatically on the London music scene in November 1970 when, at short notice, he took over a BBC Symphony Orchestra performance of Leoš Janáček's *Glagolitic Mass* at the Royal Festival Hall. The reviews were full of praise and Davis was described as Britain's most promising conductor. Homburger met with Davis and arranged for him to guest conduct the TS on 7–8 May 1974.

In August 1974 the Board wisely appointed Victor Feldbrill as Resident Conductor. Feldbrill had worked closely with Ančerl and was well attuned to his orchestral goals and overall strategy. He also had a long and dedicated association with the TS. At the

Victor Feldbrill, TS Resident Conductor

time Feldbrill was responsible for the new series of Pops Concerts as well as the Student's and Young People's Concerts, and he was co-ordinator of the Public Schools Concerts. Extra duties in his new appointment included providing artistic advice on programming for future seasons and conducting some of the main series of concerts.

Board members were aware of the warm leadership qualities and vast musical knowledge Ančerl had brought to the orchestra. At the annual general meeting, James W. Westaway, recently appointed President of the Board, commended the orchestra's high standard of performance and also the efforts of Walter Homburger at such a crucial time. He described Homburger as the most competent orchestra manager in Canada and possibly in North America, internationally respected among managers, conductors, and artists, and said that those who knew Homburger's work would quickly recognize that he represented the orchestra's best hope of finding a new conductor.

Financially, the orchestra was in good shape at the end of the 1972–3 season, and subscription sales for the 1973–4 season had not dropped despite expectations of a possible decrease in the wake of Ančerl's death. In spite of a projected deficit of $25,000, the season ended with a surplus of $1,800. During the year, a Canada Council analysis of revenues of major symphony orchestras in Canada revealed that the TS covered 50 per cent of its expenses through box office revenues – the highest of any orchestra in the country. The average for other orchestras was 43 per cent.

Guest conductors who were invited during these two intermezzo seasons included Pierre Hétu, Walter Susskind, James Levine, Andrew Davis, Stanislaw Skrowaczewski, Aldo Ceccato, Václav Neumann, Pinchas Zuckerman, Edo de Waart, Eduardo Mata, and Erich Leinsdorf. Some conductors stayed for two or three weeks. The opening concert for the 1973–4 season was conducted by Pierre Hétu, with Garrick Ohlsson playing the Brahms Piano Concerto No. 2 in B flat major. Hétu also included *Fantasmes* by Canadian composer André Prévost in his debut concert. Walter Susskind's program

TS guest conductor Václav Neumann

presented Bedřich Smetana's *Ma Vlast* – an appropriate choice and a tribute to one of his fellow countrymen. Kazimierz Kord made his debut with the TS on 5 February and conducted two more concerts the following week. His program included some of the repertoire for the upcoming European tour. For James Levine's concerts on 19–20 February, two guest artists made their TS debuts: soprano Jessye Norman and baritone John Shirley-Quirk sang Mahler's *Lieder aus Des Knaben Wunderhorn* in a performance that critics described as sensational. For his Canadian (and TS) debut, Andrew Davis conducted a performance of Janáček's *Glagolitic Mass*, with the Toronto Mendelssohn Choir, soprano Lois Marshall, contralto Eleanor James, tenor Kenneth Riegel, and baritone Michael Devlin. Pinchas Zukerman, who had appeared with the TS as violinist, returned as conductor and was also soloist for the Mozart Serenade in D major, K 250 ('Haffner'). Zukerman's program also included Hindemith's *Concerto for Trumpet and Bassoon* with soloists Joseph Umbrico, trumpet, and Nicholas Kilburn, bassoon. In his TS debut, Edo de Waart included Srul Irving Glick's *Lamentations for String Quartet and Orchestra* (*Sinfonia concertante No. 2*) with the principals of the string

Jessye Norman

sections playing the solo quartet parts: violinists Alfred Pratz and Julian Kolkowski, violist Stanley Solomon, and cellist Peter Schenkman.

On 24 March 1974 the orchestra embarked on a long tour that took them to many of the leading concert venues in Europe, including Antwerp, Frankfurt, Nuremberg, Stuttgart, Vienna, Munich, and Bonn. The tour began on 13 March 1974 with a concert at the Royal Festival Hall in London. The Royal Philharmonic Society, which presented this concert, had been formed in 1813 with the aim of encouraging the appreciation of music. This role was fulfilled by promoting concerts, commissioning new works, and awarding honours for outstanding achievement in creativity and performance. The TS concert was the first time the Society had presented a Canadian orchestra. In Vienna, there were gasps as the orchestra took their positions on the stage of the Musikverein – at that time the Vienna Philharmonic Orchestra had no female musicians. The twenty-two women musicians, three of whom were double bass players, proved an interesting topic of discussion for the Vienna audience.

Much of the programming for this tour had to be changed. The European tour originally planned by Ančerl did not involve soloists. Evidently Ančerl felt that the orchestra could hold its own before European audiences, and European concert managements obviously considered Ančerl's distinguished reputation sufficient to ensure successful concerts. However, Ančerl's death had changed this thinking, and some organizers requested that soloists be included in the programs for the tour. Consequently, when Homburger was in Europe, one of his tasks had been to procure soloists to perform with the orchestra, and to gain approval from the various concert organizations for the altered programming.

In the end, seven artists were contracted. Because of the short notice, no single artist was available for the complete tour, so various artists were contracted for concerts that fit within their individual schedules. Thus Radu Lupu played the Schumann Piano

Andrew Davis at Massey Hall

Music, in the best sense, does not require novelty; nay, the older it is, and the more we are accustomed to it, the greater its effect.

JOHANN WOLFGANG VON GOETHE

'One day, whilst I was at King's College, Cambridge, a friend of mine asked if I would conduct a small group for a performance of a Haydn divertimento. From then on I knew that conducting was the career in music that I would follow,' Andrew Davis said in an interview with the author.[1] After this first experience, Davis conducted three contrasting works for the Cambridge University Musical Society: *Five Pieces for Orchestra*, op. 16, by Arnold Schoenberg, Alban Berg's *Violin Concerto*, and *Harold in Italy* by Hector Berlioz.

Andrew Davis began playing the piano at the age of six. He had little or no interest in sports, and concentrated instead on music, with his parents' encouragement. At Watford Grammar School he sang treble in the school choir and was conscripted to conduct an orchestra that included some of his teachers. He also studied organ and in 1963, on the strength of his commitment, won an organ scholarship to King's College, Cambridge. There he discovered the harpsichord and was encouraged to play the instrument by the late Thurston Dart. In 1967 he accepted another scholarship, to study conducting at the Accademia di Santa Cecilia in Rome under Franco Ferrara. After his return to England in 1970, he was associate conductor of the BBC Scottish Symphony Orchestra for two years. He was also principal guest conductor for the Royal Liverpool Philharmonic Orchestra from 1974 to 1977. Davis had also been busy in the London recording studios, not only conducting the Philharmonia Orchestra and London Philharmonic Orchestra, but also playing harpsichord with smaller ensembles such as the Academy of St Martin-in-the-Fields.

1975–1976

The 1975–6 season opened on 18 October with a Young People's Concert conducted by Victor Feldbrill with Doug McCullough as narrator for *Tubby the Tuba at the Circus*. This season of Young People's Concerts was ambitious. Feldbrill conducted four concerts with guests, including Bob McGrath and the Sesame Kids, the Paula Moreno Spanish Dance Company, and David Amram and the Modern Fables Company. Andrew

Andrew Davis and Isaac Stern in rehearsal, February 1977

Davis opened the subscription season on 21 October with Stravinsky's *Petrushka* and the Symphony No. 3 in E flat major ('Eroica') by Beethoven. It was a full house and patrons were not disappointed with what they heard and saw. Critics and audience alike were convinced that the TS had made a wise choice in Andrew Davis. The concert was repeated two days later in Hamilton at the Great Hall of Hamilton Place.

Davis had plans to conduct the complete cycle of Mahler symphonies. On 4–5 November, he programmed the Symphony No. 1 along with *Jeux vénitiens* by Witold Lutosławski and Johann Nepomuk Hummel's Trumpet Concerto played by Maurice André, who was making his Toronto debut. Davis believed in the importance of presenting the broadest possible musical spectrum and this program was no exception.

Davis was also enthusiastic about the works of Edward Elgar. Edward Greenfield of the *Guardian* had written, 'What is quite clear is that Davis is an Elgarian to his fingertips. Davis seems to have a natural feeling for Elgarian ebb and flow.' In early December, Elgar's *Dream of Gerontius* was presented with the Toronto Mendelssohn Choir, mezzo-soprano Alfreda Hodgson, tenor Anthony Rolfe Johnson, and baritone Douglas Lawrence. From the opening notes of the Prelude to the final Amen Davis was in full command and demonstrated his ability to blend orchestra and voices with finesse. This was the first time Davis worked with Elmer Iseler and the Toronto Mendelssohn Choir, and over the years they developed a close relationship that resulted in the presentation of many outstanding choral concerts.

On 24 May 1976 Andrew Davis and the TS set off on a twelve-day tour of eastern Canada with concerts in Quebec City, Fredericton, St John's, Moncton, Charlottetown, Wolfville, Halifax, and Saint John. The two soloists for the tour were principal cellist Daniel Domb, for performances of Schumann's Cello Concerto in A minor, and principal bassoonist Christopher Weait, who played Mozart's Bassoon Concerto in B flat major, K 191. There had been doubts about the advisability of this tour, but in his report to the Board, Walter Homburger described the enthusiastic responses of capacity audiences along with excellent reviews for the performances of both Maestro Davis and the orchestra. Financially the tour was also a success, owing in part to the assistance given by the Touring Office of the Canada Council.

During February Davis participated as both conductor and guest artist in Manuel de Falla's *Concerto for Harpsichord*, a work that displayed Davis's musical dexterity and erudition. The balance of the program consisted of the Concerto Grosso in B flat major, op. 3, no. 1, by Handel, J.S. Bach's Brandenberg Concerto No. 5 in D major, BWV 1050, and Stravinsky's *Pulcinella* with soloists Janet Stubbs, John Martens, and Gary Relyea.

Andrew Davis had wisely restrained himself from overloading TS programming with music by British composers. However, for the final concert of the Ontario Place summer season, he 'let his hair down' with an all-English program consisting of Elgar's *Pomp and Circumstance March No. 5* and the *Enigma Variations*, Gustav Holst's *The Planets*, and the 'Intermezzo and Serenade' from *Hassan* by Frederick Delius.

In February 1976 the Co-ordinated Arts Services announced an archival program for member organizations. They would provide a qualified professional archivist to train volunteer archivists of cultural organizations. It was at this juncture that the author became involved with the TS. The orchestra's archives were sadly depleted and much had been destroyed when a water main burst and flooded the basement of Massey Hall. Regretfully no one within the organization realized that many of the valuable documents could have been dried and saved. However, all was not lost. A complete set of bound programs found in a disused cupboard in the offices at 215 Victoria Street provided a helpful historical resource.

At the annual general meeting of the Board in October 1975 James Westaway completed his term as President. The new President elected at this meeting was one of the younger members of the Board. From the time he joined the Board in 1961, Terence Wardrop had devoted himself to the future of the orchestra. He had served with dedication on subcommittees and had given valuable guidance on many legal matters. Wardrop was an excellent choice for President when a young music director was taking over the podium. The enthusiasm of Davis and Wardrop, combined with the managerial experience of Walter Homburger, made for a successful opening to the orchestra's 'second act.'

The season opened on a high note. A recording contract with Columbia Records, made possible by a special financial contribution from the Women's Committee, had been signed and plans for a tour to China in the 1977–8 season were proceeding satisfactorily. The Beethoven Festival, also planned for the following season, had received the support of a sponsor for half of the concerts, and it was likely that other sponsors would be found. Andrew Davis, Klaus Tennstedt, and Erich Leinsdorf had all been engaged as conductors for the Festival.

The partnership between the TS and the Canadian Opera Company had finally been terminated. Financially, the arrangement had worked well for both Symphony and Opera, but severe financial problems had forced the Canadian Opera Company to curtail their season. The Canadian Opera Company decided it would be more

1976–1977

TS guest conductor Klaus Tennstedt

profitable if they could spread their productions over the fall and winter rather than presenting a concentrated season in the early fall. This meant that the Toronto Symphony would not be available as a pit orchestra, since their season was scheduled from September to June.

The site for the 'new Massey Hall' was resolved in late July 1976. The TS had not been directly involved in this decision; the main participants were the trustees of Massey Hall, Marathon Realty, the Toronto Historical Board, and the City of Toronto. Indirect participation of the TS, however, served to clarify the main purpose of the new hall, and did much to counter opposition to the use of the hall as a primary residence for the Toronto Symphony and the Toronto Mendelssohn Choir. Indeed, it was upsetting for the managements of both symphony and choir to confront a rather callous attitude on the part of municipal officials toward the existence and survival of their organizations, and a lack of awareness of the value of the concerts they provided. This problem was neither new nor specific to Toronto. In 1922, Bernard Shaw commented to Edward Elgar on 'the indifference of a country where the capacity and tastes of youth and sporting coster-mongers are the measure of metropolitan culture.' In a report to the Board in October 1976, Wardrop said he did not believe that the municipality of Metropolitan Toronto understood fully the contribution made by the performing arts to the life of the community. However, federal, provincial, and municipal governments, through their respective arts councils, did continue to give valuable financial assistance.

Once again the need for a substantial endowment fund became evident, as various levels of government reviewed their budgets and expressed doubts about maintaining current levels of support. On 13 April, the Board approved a plan for individuals or corporations to endow chairs of principal players. Such endowments had long been in operation with orchestras in the United States. However, the TS plan did not succeed as well as it might have. By 1999, only five chairs had been endowed – three

TS guest conductor Erich Leinsdorf

by that ever-faithful group, the Women's Committee.

Andrew Davis suggested that a principal guest conductor be appointed for four to six weeks of each season and recommended that Klaus Tennstedt be approached. In the long term the appointment of a principal guest conductor could have been a financial advantage because it would be more economical than contracting the services of four to six different guest conductors, but the suggestion was put on the back burner. At the end of the season, Victor Feldbrill resigned his position as Resident Conductor, noting that this position had become unnecessary since the orchestra now had a Music Director resident in Toronto. However, Feldbrill remained as conductor of the Toronto Symphony Youth Orchestra and was also invited to guest conduct the TS in the Light Classics Series, a project he had launched in 1974.

Andrew Davis continued his plan to conduct all the Mahler symphonies. Symphony No. 3 was given on 7–8 December with contralto Maureen Forrester, the women of the Toronto Mendelssohn Choir, and the choristers of St Michael's Cathedral Choir School. The performance on 7 December was dedicated to Benjamin Britten, who had died on 4 December. Mahler's Symphony No. 4 was performed on 17–18 May with soprano Susan Davenny Wyner in her TS debut.

On 29–30 March, Albert Pratz, the concertmaster of the TS, had a forty-year-old dream come true when he played Max Bruch's Violin Concerto No. 3 in D minor, op. 58, for the first time. Pratz had first seen the concerto when he was a student in London in the 1930s, and had been trying to obtain a copy ever since. Finally in Vienna, when the TS was on its 1974 European tour, he asked a friend to look in Dopplinger's, a well-known music store. To Pratz's surprise his friend returned with the violin and piano parts, and the orchestral parts turned up at the CBC about a year later.

The major choral contribution to the season, performed on 10, 11, and 13 May, was *Roméo et Juliette*, Hector Berlioz's dramatic symphony, with the Toronto Mendelssohn Choir, contralto Florence Quivar (her Canadian debut), tenor Leo Goeke, and baritone James Morris. On 12, 13, and 15 April Mstislav Rostropovich made his Canadian conducting debut with the TS in a solid Russian program that opened with Mikhail Glinka's lively overture to his opera *Ruslan and Lyudmila*. This was followed by Dmitri Shostakovich's Symphony No. 9 and Tchaikovsky's Symphony No. 4 in F minor.

The Ontario Place concerts for the summer of 1977 sparkled with an interesting mix of guest conductors. Walter Susskind returned for the two opening concerts, although unfortunately his second concert was rained out. Klaus Tennstedt, James Conlon, André Kostelanetz, Erich Kunzel, and Franz Allers also conducted, and Andrew Davis closed the season with Mahler's Symphony No. 1.

1977–1978

The highlight of the 1977–8 season was the historic three-week tour to Japan and China. The TS was the first Canadian orchestra to be invited to enter China after the Cultural Revolution. This tour, the most ambitious and exciting to date, was financed by the Canada Council and the Department of External Affairs as well as by corporate sponsorships. The only other symphony orchestra from North America to have played in the People's Republic of China was the Philadelphia Orchestra in 1974. On 21 January 1978 the Toronto Symphony and two soloists, Maureen Forrester and Louis Lortie, flew from Toronto to Tokyo, where they stayed for five days, giving two concerts: one in the Bunka Kaikan Hall and the other in the NKH Hall. On 28 January, they flew to Beijing to play three concerts. On 3 February they moved on to Shanghai for two concerts, and the tour ended with two performances in Canton. The concerts in China were almost as political as they were artistic. A short time earlier Western music, particularly Beethoven and Schubert, was considered to be a corrupting bourgeois influence, but there had been a sudden switch in official policy. In December 1976, when representatives from Ottawa and the TS visited Beijing to make final arrangements for the tour, they found the Chinese officials most cooperative. The symphony submitted four full programs and asked the Chinese authorities to choose two: those chosen had Beethoven in one and Tchaikovsky in the other. Of the three concerts given in Beijing, one included Tchaikovsky's Symphony No. 4 and songs from Mahler's *Des Knaben Wunderhorn* sung by Maureen Forrester, and the other, Beethoven's Symphony No. 5 in C minor and Liszt's Piano Concerto No. 1 in E flat major, with Louis Lortie as soloist. The final concert in Beijing, given in the Capital Gymnasium before an audience of 18,000, featured both of the guest artists on the tour. Maureen Forrester, who was not originally scheduled to sing, became one of the hits of the evening. The audience was particularly delighted when she sang a Chinese encore.

Louis Lortie was also a favourite, and at the end of the Liszt concerto, he seemed overcome by the tremendous ovation he received. Li Teh-lun, the principal conductor of the Beijing Capital Orchestra, asked Andrew Davis to conduct the Capital Orchestra in rehearsal, as they were preparing a Beethoven symphony for the first time. Davis agreed to do so, and invited Li Teh-lun to conduct a TS rehearsal.

The *People's Daily* reported that the first night the TS performed in Beijing was forty years to the day since Dr Norman Bethune came from Canada to China. 'We wanted to pay back in friendship our moral debt to Dr Bethune.' While in the Beijing area, the orchestra visited the Great Wall of China. Peering down from one of the guard towers percussionist Daniel Ruddick said, 'Wouldn't it be funny if thousands of Mongol hordes came riding over those hills?' 'There would be a lot of openings in the orchestra next year,' retorted fellow percussionist Don Kuehn.

When the orchestra arrived in Shanghai they were greeted at the airport by the clashing cymbals and booming drums of the Shanghai Ballet Orchestra. The hotel assigned to the orchestra reminded Andrew Davis of the Adelphi in Liverpool with its baronial English architecture. The entire serving staff lined the main staircase to applaud the musicians as they arrived. At a reception after one of the concerts, Wang Yi-ping, vice chairman of Shanghai's Municipal Revolutionary Committee, toasted the TS, not with a typical Communist slogan, but with the venerable English toast, 'Bottoms up.'

The last concert of the tour was given in Canton. The TS had become one of the hottest tickets in China and demand in Canton was so great that, unknown to the players, local authorities had arranged a public Wednesday morning get-together for members of the TS and the Kwang-chow (Canton) Philharmonic Society. That audience heard more than they expected. Not only did the Chinese players play traditional pieces, they also played Western chamber music with members of the TS, and Andrew Davis conducted the premiere of a piece he had written at breakfast! The entire orchestra appeared on the evening program, playing music by Brahms, Morel, Liszt, and Mahler. The Chinese officials, who were much taken by Maureen Forrester, asked if she would sing again. Because of some last-minute confusion caused by Canton Television, the stagehands had neglected to set enough chairs in the violin section for the Lizst piano concerto. Unruffled, violinists Andrea Hansen and Sigmund Steinberg propped themselves on an instrument case in the wings and started playing along. Harpist Judy Loman asked, 'Where's your music?' 'You think we can't play it from memory by now?' answered Steinberg. Following the concert, Arthur Menzies, the Canadian ambassador, thanked the orchestra for accomplishing what no amount of diplomatic hospitality

The TS travellers at the Great Wall in China, with TS President Terence Wardrop in centre, February 1978

could have hoped to do. The Chinese officials were overjoyed and hailed the tour as a complete success.

Recalling her personal impressions in the *Globe and Mail*, Maureen Forrester later said, 'It was an incredibly interesting and fascinating tour. I have never travelled anywhere where everybody was so co-operative. Peking had the best food, mostly because we ended up in a hotel where the chef loved musicians.' Forrester, who was contracted to sing at only five concerts, finished up singing at all ten.

The orchestra returned exhausted, but nothing could dampen their enthusiasm for a most exciting and rewarding tour. External Affairs Minister Donald Jamieson, who accompanied the orchestra on parts of the tour in both Japan and China, was also appreciative of their success. CBC television produced an excellent documentary of the tour, entitled 'Music East, Music West,' directed by Norman Campbell.

The TS on stage at the Capital Gymnasium in Beijing, 1978

Members of the TS meet with Chinese musicians, 1978

Meanwhile TS audiences had not been deprived of concerts: the Buffalo Philharmonic Orchestra, conducted by Michael Tilson Thomas, was engaged to play for the first week of the TS's absence. Their program included Béla Bartók's suite *The Miraculous Mandarin* (a touch of China?) and Tchaikovsky's Symphony No. 5 in E minor. The Cleveland Orchestra, conducted by Lorin Maazel in his Toronto debut, filled in for two subscription concerts in the second week, playing Schumann's Symphony No. 2 in C major and Brahms's Symphony No. 1 in C minor.

Prior to the regular subscription season, the orchestra presented a highly successful six-week Beethoven Festival with conductors Erich Leinsdorf, Klaus Tennstedt, and Andrew Davis. Their different conducting styles and interpretations of Beethoven's music added much interest. With a 97 per cent capacity, it was the most successful festival the TS had produced.

Nicholas Fiore, the principal flute, retired at the end of the 1977–8 season. Bass trombonist Murray Ginsberg, who was having a lip problem, would retire at the end of the 1978–9 season. In his memoirs, Murray describes his audition with Walter Susskind when he joined the orchestra. He played a number of pieces to demonstrate his qualifications. 'That's all very charming,' Walter Susskind said. 'Now,' he continued, 'can you play the Bolero?' 'No,' I replied. 'Good,' Susskind responded with a twinkle in his eye, 'You've got the job.'[2] When Albert Pratz announced that he also intended to retire at the end of the 1978–9 season, it was hoped that a Canadian could be found to fill the position of concertmaster. Steven Staryk was a prime choice, but the conditions under which he would agree to take the position were not in the best interests of the orchestra. A leading member entitled by contract to be absent from a number of concerts of his choosing would have a bad effect on the morale of other orchestra personnel. Andrew Davis recommended that Staryk not be offered the position, but since Walter Homburger indicated that there were no other Canadians who could be considered, Davis suggested that the Board consider hiring the assistant concertmaster from one of the major orchestras who had expressed interest in the position.

While the issue of a new concertmaster was under discussion Davis informed Terence Wardrop and Walter Homburger that he would not be renewing his contract at the end of the 1979–80 season. Davis explained that he was not accepting a post with another orchestra but wanted to explore freelance opportunities, including opera. At this time, four major North American orchestras were searching for music directors, and a few months earlier, Davis had turned down an offer from one of them. After discussions with Homburger, Davis agreed to stay for the 1980–1 season, which was to be the opening season of the new hall. The TS was not prepared to lose Andrew Davis.

Within three years the orchestra had advanced considerably on the international scene. A major recording contract with Columbia Masterworks, additional tours, and the high quality of musicianship within the orchestra eventually convinced Davis to stay; he remained in Toronto for a further ten years.

During the summer of 1978, on the recommendation of Davis, the Board completed negotiations with Moshe Murvitz, assistant concertmaster of the Israel Philharmonic Orchestra, who accepted the position of concertmaster of the TS on a two-year contract beginning with the 1979–80 season. Two important administrative positions were also vacant. Michael Aze and Stephen Adler had resigned their positions as Orchestra Manager and Director of Public Relations respectively. Jack Mills became the new Orchestra Manager and Douglas Allen was appointed to take over public relations.

1978–1979

On 12 September ground-breaking ceremonies took place for the 'new Massey Hall' on the south-west corner of King Street West and Simcoe Street and construction of the superstructure began the following spring. The new concert facility was to have state-of-the-art acoustical qualities, but as later narrative will reveal, this promise was not fully realized. The new permanent home for the Toronto Symphony and the Toronto Mendelssohn Choir would cost $42 million, of which some $15 million was raised by donations from the public.

A number of musicians had left at the end of the 1977–8 season, and a number of new faces appeared. Jeanne Baxtresser, former principal flutist of the Montreal Symphony Orchestra, took up the equivalent position in the TS. Patricia Krueger, the percussionist and keyboard musician whose talents had been heard as an extra on frequent occasions, joined the orchestra on a full-time basis. Other new faces included double bass player Peter Madgett, who had been principal bassist with the Hamilton Philharmonic Orchestra, and three violinists: Yoon Chang, James Wallenberg, and Arkady Yanivker.

In mid-November 1978 the orchestra, with pianist Arthur Ozolins, made a one-week tour that included concerts in Ottawa, at Carnegie Hall in New York, at Brooklyn College in Brooklyn, and at the Kennedy Center in Washington, DC. For repertoire Davis chose Beethoven's *Leonore Overture No. 2*, Brahms's Symphony No. 1 in C minor, Prokofiev's Piano Concerto No. 2, and Schubert's Symphony No. 9 in C major ('Great'). The orchestra received wide acclaim in both New York and Washington. Theodore W. Libbey Jr of the *Washington Star* stated, 'The "Great" C major Symphony of Schubert was given a performance which made last week's effort by the

Aaron Copland conducted the TS on 10 August 1979 at Ontario Place

Philadelphia Orchestra look uninspired at best, and coarse by comparison with the Canadians' classy treatment.'

From 22 April to 10 May the orchestra was on tour in western Canada and on the west coast of the United States. They began in Calgary and Edmonton in Alberta, then moved on to Saskatchewan and British Columbia. In California concerts were given in Pasadena, Long Beach, Fresno, and Santa Barbara. The two soloists for the tour were harpist Judy Loman and cellist Daniel Domb. For her performance of Handel's Harp Concerto in B flat major, op. 4, no. 6, Loman used the edition prepared by the great harpist Carlos Salzedo with a cadenza by Marcel Grandjany. Daniel Domb played the Saint-Saëns Cello Concerto No. 1 in A minor.

The tour was not without mishaps. Concertmaster Albert Pratz suffered an angina attack; although he was able to play the last concert, on his return to Toronto doctors advised him not to perform for three months. Associate concertmaster Jascha Milkis also suffered an angina attack. Violinist Jan Whyte was taken ill and had to return to Toronto for surgery, cellist Rafael Furer had an emergency dental problem, and violinist Georgina Roberts had to rush back to Toronto owing to the sudden death of her husband.

To round out this eventful season, two internationally acclaimed singers made TS debuts. On 16–17 January, mezzo-soprano Dame Janet Baker gave exquisite performances of the scena and aria 'Ah Perfido' from Beethoven's opera *Fidelio* and the five *Wesendonck Lieder* by Richard Wagner. For the Pension Fund concert on 28 May, tenor Luciano Pavarotti sang arias from several popular Italian operas. Both artists charmed audiences in unforgettable concerts. On 3 April, cellist Yo-Yo Ma made his TS debut playing the Elgar Cello Concerto in E minor with Victor Feldbrill conducting. About twelve measures into the work, one of the strings on his cello snapped. Ma rushed off stage and returned within a minute with a new string in place. Feldbrill turned to the audience and said, 'I think we will start from the beginning once again,' and Yo-Yo Ma, with a big smile on his face, fully agreed.

The new hall was slowly becoming a reality and enthusiasm for it was growing. Orchestra musicians began to express thoughts and feelings about both halls – old and new. Bassist Jane McAdam said, 'What I look forward to most is not having to carry my bass up and down stairs to the basement storage. Just try doing that in a long dress with a purse on one arm!' French horn player Fredrick Rizner commented, 'I don't think I'll really miss the old hall too much. A new hall will certainly give a lift in every way. It may give us a better sense of identity as an orchestra.' The Seat Endowment Committee of Roy Thomson Hall was constituted to encourage patrons to endow seats in the new hall with a donation of $1,000. These endowed seats were identified by small metal plaques bearing the names of donors or of individuals or organizations they wished to honour. The concept took hold rapidly and by February 1979, 400 of the 2800 seats had been endowed. A number of seats were endowed in honour of former members of the orchestra such as violist Sydney Levy, who was an orchestra member from 1932 to 1970. The children at one Toronto school raised enough money through their school concert for a seat in the new hall. The Women's Committee magnanimously offered to purchase a new Steinway concert grand piano for the orchestra, to be installed in the new hall. A decision was made to purchase from Steinway in Hamburg and Vladimir Ashkenazy generously offered to select the instrument. After a long and thorough examination Ashkenazy chose a piano, which duly arrived from Hamburg in the late summer. This piano remained in Roy Thomson Hall until 1999, when a replacement was required. This time the order was placed with Steinway's New York office and Emanuel Ax selected the instrument.

Opera was a growing interest for Andrew Davis. He had been conducting at Glyndebourne, the English summer home for opera, since 1973, and now he had engagements booked for Covent Garden and the Paris Opera. The first operatic component of the TS season was the January presentation of Berlioz's 'legende dramatique,' *La damnation de Faust*. Davis mustered a distinguished group of artists: mezzo-soprano Maria Ewing, tenor Robert Tear, bass-baritone José van Dam, and bass Christopher Cameron, along with the St Michael's Cathedral Choir School and the Toronto Mendelssohn Choir. On 31 January and 1 February, Davis conducted a full-length concert performance of Tchaikovsky's *Eugene Onegin* with a cast that would have been the envy of any opera house: Lois Marshall, Elisabeth Söderström, Marianna

Yo-Yo Ma

Paunova, Nicolai Gedda, Pierre Boutet, Richard Stilwell, Don Garrard, and Christopher Cameron, along with the Toronto Mendelssohn Choir, all singing superbly in Russian. A second program on 22–4 April presented the Prelude and first act of Wagner's *Die Walküre* with three internationally acclaimed Wagner interpreters: Jessye Norman, Manfred Jung, and Aage Haugland. This performance was taken to Carnegie Hall on 26 April, where it received high praise from critics.

The season also had its full share of guest artists and conductors making TS debuts. In January James Galway played Carl Reinecke's Flute Concerto in D major. On the second night of the program, before he began the concerto, Galway countered a lukewarm review with the announcement, 'Apparently one critic in this city doesn't like good music.' For his debut Lazar Berman played Tchaikovsky's Piano Concerto No. 1 in B flat minor and Brahms's Piano Concerto No. 1 in D minor. First-time guest conductors included Charles Dutoit, Simon Rattle, Riccardo Chailly, Kurt Sanderling (who was also making his Canadian debut), and Raymond Leppard (who conducted the traditional *Messiah* performances). The Ontario Place summer season featured conductor Calvin Simmons, dancers Karen Kain and Frank Augustyn from the National Ballet of Canada, pianist Robert Kortgaard (winner of the 1979 Canadian Music Competition), and pop composer Marvin Hamlisch.

Tuesday, 25 March 1980, marked the death of Walter Susskind in California at the age of sixty-six. The concert on 8 April was dedicated to him, and the orchestra played the *Slavonic Dance No. 10* in E minor by Antonín Dvořák in his memory. At the end of the 1979–80 season Moshe Murvitz, who had come from the Israel Philharmonic Orchestra to take up the position of concertmaster, decided to return to Israel. Although his contract was for two years, the conditions did not meet his requirements as concertmaster. The announcement that the new hall would not be ready for the planned opening in September 1981 and that a new opening date had been set for September 1982 was no surprise – visual evidence indicated that another year of construction would be required.

In February 1980 the Canada Council sent letters to all major Canadian orchestras outlining decisions regarding future funding. One decision was that operational grants would not be available to orchestras whose operational deficit was 30 per cent or more of their total budget. Another controversial ruling concerned a Canadian music quota system: one out of every ten works played had to be a Canadian composition. If orchestras chose to perform additional Canadian works, they would be eligible to apply for additional project funding which they might well need if a shortfall were anticipated.

Jessye Norman performed in Act I of *Die Walküre* with the TS, April 1980

Finally, the Toronto Symphony Youth Orchestra participated in the Canadian Festival of Youth Orchestras at the Banff Centre, where the TSYO performed under guest conductor Nicholas Braithwaite. After the festival Ermanno Florio and David Zafer conducted the TSYO for an extra concert in Lethbridge, Alberta, which resulted in a *Lethbridge Herald* headline: 'Youth orchestra program provides spellbinding evening.'

The TS began the 1980–1 season in a sound financial position: a deficit of $92,000 against an operating budget of just over $5 million presented no cause for concern. Concert attendance continued to grow and the orchestra now enjoyed one of the largest subscription audiences in North America. The attendance at Ontario Place during the previous summer had reached a total of 108,000 (12,000 higher than the previous summer), much to the delight of the Ontario Place management, who readily invited the orchestra back for the summer of 1981.

To open the season the orchestra played a new composition by Canadian composer Norman Symonds: *The Gift of Thanksgiving*, commissioned by Imperial Oil. The music reflects the tradition of Thanksgiving as seen by newcomers to this North American custom. The orchestra also welcomed five new members to its ranks: clarinettist Joaquin Valdepeñas, originally from Mexico, violinists Hyung-Sun Paik from Los Angeles and Mark Skazinetsky from Kitchener, violist Pamela Inkman from the Vancouver Symphony Orchestra, and cellist Marie Gélinas, a new graduate from the Juilliard School of Music.

The Toronto Symphony Youth Orchestra seemed to steal much of the limelight during this season. In March 1981, as part of an exchange program with the Montreal Civic Youth Orchestra, the TYSO travelled to Montreal. In addition to workshops and masterclasses, the orchestra played concerts in Montreal and Trois-Rivières. Ermanno Florio shared conducting duties with string conductor David Zafer, woodwind coach Christopher Weait, and brass coach Eugene Rittich for a formidable repertoire consisting of Igor Stravinsky's *Symphonies of Wind Instruments*, Edvard Grieg's *Holberg Suite*, Beethoven's Symphony No. 8 in F major, and Nikolai Rimsky-Korsakov's *Capriccio espagnole*. The Youth Orchestra was well received. A review in the Trois-Rivières *La Nouvelleste* stated, 'The Toronto Symphony Youth Orchestra: Astonishing! ... Such a concert proves that it is possible to attain excellent results even with musicians who have not yet reached professional status.'[3] The TSYO played two run-out concerts to complete their season – one in the Scarborough Town Centre and one at the Guelph Spring Festival. In the eight years since its inauguration, the Youth Orchestra's high

1980–1981

level of performance had been maintained by a faculty composed of musicians from the TS and enhanced by masterclasses given by guest soloists performing with the TS.

The third concert of the TS season presented Haydn's Symphony No. 94 in G major ('Suprise') along with contralto Maureen Forrester and tenor Siegfried Jerusalem singing Mahler's *Das Lied von der Erde*. The following week Davis conducted the North American premiere of Sir Michael Tippett's *Triple Concerto for Violin, Viola and Cello* played by violonist Steven Staryk, violist Rivka Golani-Erdesz, and cellist Daniel Domb. In November Erich Leinsdorf conducted a program of music by Richard Strauss with soprano Gianna Rolandi, who was making her TS debut. Andrew Davis's Metropolitan Opera debut in February 1981, conducting Richard Strauss's *Salome*, was an instant hit with audience and press alike.

During October, a short tour in the United States took the orchestra to Kalamazoo and Ann Arbor, Michigan, Oxford and Columbus, Ohio, and Huntington, West Virginia. During the season, the TS sponsored a joint performance with the Canton Acrobats in the O'Keefe Centre – a highly successful project that earned $45,000 for the orchestra. Also, the Board approved plans for an extensive tour of England and Europe during March 1983, including concerts in London, Manchester, Birmingham, and Leeds, four concerts in Germany, and two in Vienna. John Wyre, who had been principal timpanist for the past eight years, announced that he would be resigning at the end of the season in order to spend more time with the percussion ensemble Nexus, which was rapidly gaining popularity and was about to undertake its first European tour.

With the opening date for the new hall established, there were a number of issues to be resolved between the boards of the hall and the TS. One important issue was the rental fee, which had not yet been agreed upon. Another was the use of the rehearsal hall; it was to have the same dimensions as the stage, but indications were that it might fall short of serving the function for which it was intended. In an April 1981 update Alan Marchment, Chairman of the TS Board, described a proposal that the Hall and Symphony board members be members of both boards. Marchment said that this was not possible and could lead to conflict of interest situations. He also emphasized the importance of both boards being open to each other's problems and working together to resolve them as quickly as possible. To that end, a joint committee of three members from each board was formed.

1981–1982   The 1981–2 season turned out to be a historic one. The farewell to Massey Hall, which had been the orchestra's home since 1922, gave rise to mixed emotions. The cramped

Maureen Forrester and Andrew Davis in rehearsal with the TS, September 1980

conditions backstage had become a way of life: a table tennis game provided a relaxing break for musicians and the card table in a smaller adjacent room seemed to be a focal point for string players, including the concertmaster. In the library, where scores and parts were stacked to the ceiling, a ladder was sometimes used to procure music. The green room was not a room but an area adorned by portraits, one of which was of Sir Ernest MacMillan. As a concert hall, Massey Hall was acoutistically kind to the audience but not to the musicians, who had difficulty in hearing other sections, although for recitals it seemed a perfect venue. Audiences also had mixed feelings about the upcoming change, and many were sad that this was to be the last season in the 'Old Lady of Shuter Street.' However, the new hall had its appeal. According to descriptions, not one of the 2,800 comfortable seats would be more than 107 feet from centre stage and there were no pillars to block sight lines. The expansive lobby area would afford easy access to all seating areas and provide adequate space for a relaxing intermission, in contrast to the crush of concert-goers in the small lounge at Massey Hall.

Artistically, the TS decided that its last season at Massey Hall should be commemorative in nature. Seven conductors, including Günther Herbig, Neeme Järvi, Walter Weller, and Jiří Bělohlávek, made their TS debuts. Soprano Kathleen Battle,

Andrew Davis and Walter Homburger,
June 1982

pianist Ken Noda, violinist Shlomo Mintz, and oboist Heinz Holliger also appeared with the orchestra for the first time. In addition, artists who had been guests on numerous occasions came back for this farewell season. On 20 and 21 October, Davis conducted Mahler's Symphony No. 9, the second-last step in his project to perform all of the Mahler symphonies with the TS. On 18 and 19 May he also conducted performances of Sir Michael Tippett's *The Vision of Saint Augustine* with bass-baritone John Shirley-Quirk and the Toronto Mendelssohn Choir.

While the season was proceeding some acrimony developed in the boardrooms of both the new hall and the TS. The main issue involved a decision by Walter Homburger to offer International Artists (a concert series sponsored by his company, Walter Homburger Ltd.) for sale to the TS. The Board, realizing that the TS would require additional revenue to cover the higher costs of the new hall, accepted Homburger's offer. Meanwhile, the board of the new hall announced plans to present their own concerts; they had visions of obtaining International Artists as a basis for their own series. Individuals who were members of both boards were faced with a conflict of interest, and about six Board members of the TS resigned so that they could continue to serve on the board of the new hall.

Other difficult issues to be negotiated included the rental fee, not only for the auditorium but also for administrative space. At one point the board of the new hall altered the rental figure, which in turn made it difficult for the TS Board to finalize a budget for the new season. It seemed that neither board was fully briefed on the many intricacies involved with relocating to the new hall.

In January 1982 the new hall was officially named Roy Thomson Hall, in appreciation to Kenneth Thomson for a donation of four million dollars for maintenance of the hall. This decision was a disappointment to the concert-going public who felt that the

Farewell to Massey Hall, June 1982

hall might have been named after a prominent Canadian musician such as Glenn Gould.

The gala closing concert given in Massey Hall on 4 June 1982 included music from the Toronto Symphony Orchestra's first performance on 23 April 1923. Andrew Davis shared the podium with guest conductors Erich Kunzel and Elmer Iseler. The Toronto Mendelssohn Choir, who had been tenants of Massey Hall since 1894, sang the Hallelujah chorus from Handel's *Messiah*. Erich Kunzel conducted the *Slavonic Dance No. 1* by Dvořák. One highlight of the evening was the performance of *A Farewell Tribute to the Grand Old Lady of Shuter Street* by composer Johnny Cowell, a member of the trumpet section, commissioned by the Toronto Symphony to commemorate the occasion. In his program note Cowell wrote, 'Some time ago the idea came to me that I would like to write a farewell tribute to the Grand Old Lady of Shuter Street before the Toronto Symphony Orchestra moved out of Massey Hall ... What I finally wrote was my own personal feelings about a place where I have spent a good deal of my life.'[4] Erich Kunzel conducted the orchestra in this world premiere performance. The concert ended with Tchaikovsky's Symphony No. 5 in E minor, conducted by Andrew Davis. After the concert, the audience, many of whom were dressed in fashions of the 1920s, made their way to Roy Thomson Hall for a walk through the new facility and a glass of champagne on stage, followed by a late-night supper across the street at the restaurant Ed's Warehouse. This momentous evening of nostalgia mingled with exuberance was both a fitting tribute to the old and a celebration of the new.

Andrew Davis at Roy Thomson Hall

Such sweet compulsion doth in music lie.

JOHN MILTON

1982–1983

On Sunday, 12 September, a special 'Hard Hat' concert was presented – a preview of the gala concert to be given the following day as a thank-you to everyone who had been involved in the construction of the hall. At noon on Monday, 13 September 1982, the section of Simcoe Street from King Street to Front Street was closed to traffic for the official opening of Roy Thomson Hall. Dignitaries representing the federal, provincial, and municipal governments were in attendance, along with representatives of the boards of Roy Thomson Hall, the Toronto Symphony, and the Toronto Mendelssohn Choir. After the customary speeches had been made, Edward A. Pickering, President of the Board of Governors of Roy Thomson Hall, cut the ribbon. Seventeen years of planning, consultation, and building had come to fruition. The new home for the Toronto Symphony and the Toronto Mendelssohn Choir was open!

An important occasion should have a fanfare, and Andrew Davis had spent part of the previous summer reading through fifty-two anonymous scores that had been submitted to a fanfare competition. The winner of the competition would receive a commission grant provided by the Ontario Arts Council, and the fanfare would be played at the opening gala concert. The anonymous work that Davis chose was *Fanfare* by Raymond Luedeke, scored for twelve valveless trumpets, orchestra, and organ. Ray, the associate principal clarinettist of the TS, said that when Andrew Davis telephoned him and said 'I have something to tell you,' his immediate thought was that his position in the orchestra was finished, since he had not yet been given tenure. When Davis told him that his composition had won the fanfare contest, Ray was amazed and relieved.

The gala concert, broadcast across Canada by the CBC, was given in the presence of Edward Schreyer, the Governor General of Canada, and his wife, Lily. The concert opened with Luedeke's *Fanfare*, followed by a choral work – William Walton's *Belshazzar's Feast*, with baritone Victor Braun and the Toronto Mendelssohn Choir. The organ of the new hall, built by Gabriel Kney, was featured in Francis Poulenc's Organ Concerto in G minor, performed by organist Hugh McLean. Davis and McLean had been organ scholars at King's College Chapel, Cambridge. The Mendelssohn Choir also sang two

Dame Janet Baker

unaccompanied Canadian works: R. Murray Schafer's *Sun*, and Sir Ernest MacMillan's arrangement of the French Canadian folk song *Blanche comme la neige*. The second suite from Maurice Ravel's *Daphnis et Chloé* brought a colourful and exciting day to a close.

The orchestra's first subscription concert in Roy Thomson Hall, on 22 September, was also a gala affair. Andrew Davis conducted Mahler's Symphony No. 2 in C minor, with contralto Maureen Forrester, soprano Lilian Sukis (in her TS debut), and the Toronto Mendelssohn Choir. This was also Steven Staryk's first season as concertmaster. Staryk had first joined the orchestra as a teenager in 1950 and was one of the six musicians who were refused admission to the United States for the TSO's concert in Detroit in 1951. The 'Symphony Six' left the orchestra when their contracts were not renewed. In 1956 Staryk went to London, England, where his outstanding musicianship was quickly recognized. He was chosen by Sir Thomas Beecham as concertmaster of the Royal Philharmonic Orchestra, the youngest musician to ever hold that post. In 1960, on the recommendation of Rafael Kubelík, Staryk accepted the post of concertmaster of the Concertgebouw Orchestra in Amsterdam and while with this orchestra he worked with Eugen Jochum, Bernard Haitink, and George Szell. In 1963 he became concertmaster of the Chicago Symphony Orchestra. Staryk had held three concertmaster positions by the age of thirty-five.

Meanwhile, there were a number of technical and administrative problems to be resolved. One of these was the scale of fees charged by Roy Thomson Hall for various services including corkage, waiters, and lobby space, and for day-to-day operations, including artists' rooms, security, the rehearsal hall, and air conditioning. Also, box office difficulties had necessitated a separate TS box office. The problems between the TS and Roy Thomson Hall were becoming public knowledge and the boards of both organizations issued a press release explaining that these 'growing pains' were being dealt with expeditiously.

Andrew Davis and Yehudi Menuhin, February 1982

The artistic presentation for the season was enhanced by two innovations. One was the introduction of Evening Overtures – forty-five-minute concerts given at 6:45 p.m., before the main concert, featuring members of the orchestra in performances of chamber music. On many occasions, Andrew Davis performed as a pianist or harpsichordist. The second innovation was the Great Performers Series. This series was actually a continuation of Walter Homburger's International Artists Series. Artists featured in this opening season included Dame Janet Baker, Itzhak Perlman, Yo-Yo Ma, Annie Fischer, Yehudi Menuhin, and Jessye Norman, along with two visiting orchestras: the Scottish National Orchestra, conducted by Sir Alexander Gibson, and the Minnesota Orchestra, conducted by Neville Marriner.

To crown this historical and momentous season, the orchestra embarked on an extremely successful European tour. With visits to seventeen cities in six different countries, it was the longest tour undertaken by a Canadian orchestra. The two soloists for the tour were pianist André Laplante and the orchestra's principal flute, Jeanne Baxtresser. The tour repertoire included Beethoven's Symphony No. 6 in F major, Dvořák's Symphony No. 7 in D minor, Mahler's Symphony No. 5, excerpts from Prokofiev's first and second *Romeo and Juliet* suites, Carl Philipp Emanuel Bach's Flute

Concerto in D minor, Mendelssohn's Piano Concerto No. 1 in G minor, and Prokofiev's Piano Concerto No. 2.

On 25 February the orchestra left Toronto for Manchester. The program for the first concert, presented on Sunday, 27 February, in the Free Trade Hall, home of the Halle Orchestra, included Laplante playing the Mendelssohn Concerto. According to Michael Kennedy in the *Daily Telegraph*, 'the orchestra had captured the Manchester audience which gave it a rip-roaring ovation.' After the concert there was a reception for the orchestra in Manchester's richly adorned city hall. On Sunday morning several musicians made their way to Manchester Cathedral, where, after the service, associate librarian Errol Gay was invited by the cathedral organist to play the organ. For the concert in Leeds, given in the city hall, Jeanne Baxtresser was soloist for the C.P.E. Bach flute concerto. Mahler's Symphony No. 5 made up the balance of the program. The concert in Birmingham was held in the Town Hall, home of the City of Birmingham Symphony Orchestra since its inception in 1921, and was broadcast on BBC Radio 3. Following the concert there was a reception at the Council House, hosted by the lord mayor of Birmingham, who also invited the orchestra to a breakfast reception in the city hall the following morning. These social occasions reflected the Birmingham city council's support for the arts.

From London there was a 'run-out' concert at the Hexagon Theatre in Reading. The two London concerts in the Festival Hall were a fitting conclusion to the English portion of the tour, and the London press was full of praise. Edward Greenfield of the *Guardian* wrote that the orchestra 'has consistently established its claims as a strong characterful team,' and Nicholas Kenyon of *The Times* said, 'the Toronto Symphony Orchestra is a splendid orchestra.' While in London, Andrew Davis entertained the orchestra with dinner at a restaurant in one of the old warehouses that still stand alongside what was the St Katherine's Dock. The extensive advance press in England heralded the arrival of the orchestra, and indeed much of the success of the tour in England was due to the organizational skills of Belle Shenkman, a champion of Canadian artists in Britain.

The first concert on the continent was at the Théâtre musical de Paris (Chatelet) with Barbara Hendriks as soloist in four songs by Gustav Mahler. Then it was on to Frankfurt, Hanover, Bonn, and into Holland. The concert in Amsterdam was at the Concertgebouw, where Steven Staryk had been concertmaster. Back in Germany there were two more concerts – one in Leverkusen and one in Stuttgart – before moving on to Switzerland for performances in Zurich, Geneva, and Lausanne. During the fourth week of the tour the orchestra was in Vienna and Prague. This was the orchestra's second visit to the Austrian capital. On their first visit, they had amazed Viennese audiences not only with their performance, but also with the number of female members in the ensemble. In Prague, Karel Ančerl was on the minds of everyone. The two concerts there were dedicated to his memory, and the musicians were visibly moved by a large portrait of the late maestro. Sweeping her hand across a picture of the Czech Philharmonic Orchestra, French horn player Barbara Bloomer remarked, 'Now I know why he could never understand women in the orchestra. Look – not one.' She was right. That orchestra was an all-male ensemble. The TS was the first visiting orchestra to be included in the Czech Philharmonic subscription series and the audience was overjoyed by the two concerts.

The tour was a success with rave reviews everywhere. On 26 March the orchestra returned home, weary but satisfied that they had proved to England and Europe that they were a top-notch ensemble.

On 2 May Dr Armand Hammer celebrated his eighty-fifth birthday with the Toronto Symphony at a rehearsal conducted by Seiji Ozawa. Following a reception and dinner party he presented the TS with a cheque for $140,000. At the end of the season five long-time members of the orchestra retired: violinists Jose Sera and Berul Sugarman, double bass player Sam Davis, trumpeter George Anderson, and clarinettist Bernard Temoin. Berul Sugarman had been a member since 1925. And finally, the Executive Committee of the Board agreed that two musicians should be nominated to join the Board on an annual basis.

1983–1984

The season opened with continuing controversy between hall and orchestra over the rental agreement. The TS administration had investigated rental costs incurred by other North American orchestras and learned that their rent at Roy Thomson Hall was the highest – it was even higher than the New York Philharmonic's fee for Avery Fisher Hall. Since the Roy Thomson Hall board had imposed a fifty-cent surcharge on each ticket to cover future maintenance costs, it was becoming increasingly difficult to maintain reasonable ticket prices for TS concerts. In hindsight, it might have been better if the hall had been planned with the TS as a one-third owner of the project. Such an arrangement could be justified, since the TS performs more than a hundred concerts each year, and these concerts also generate spin-off financial income from sources such as parking, refreshment services, and the music store.

Andrew Davis agreed to a further one-year extension of his contract through the 1986–7 season. This meant that the artistic direction, including tours, could be planned

Andrew Davis and Elmer Iseler

well ahead. One possible tour under investigation for 1986 included participation in the Edinburgh International Festival and the BBC Promenade Concerts at the Royal Albert Hall in London.

The season opened with Deryck Cooke's reconstruction of the Symphony No. 10 in F sharp major by Gustav Mahler. With this performance, Davis fulfilled his objective of conducting all the Mahler symphonies with the TS. For the first concert of the Great Performers Series, Andrew Davis joined flutist Jeanne Baxtresser and clarinettist Joaquin Valdepeñas as pianist in works by Camille Saint-Saëns, Francis Poulenc, Johannes Brahms, Sergei Prokofiev, Leonard Bernstein, and Franz Doppler. Andrew Davis's fascination with opera and his interest in Richard Strauss were combined on 17 and 19 November in a concert version of Strauss's opera *Der Rosenkavalier* with a cast worthy of a leading opera house: sopranos Mechthild Gessendorf, Barbara Hendricks, and Roxolana Roslak, mezzo-sopranos Patricia Kern and Cynthia Clarey, tenors Barry Stilwell and Vinson Cole, baritone Derek Hammond-Stroud, and bass-baritone Richard Best, along with the Elmer Iseler Singers. On 11, 12, and 14 January Davis conducted performances of Berlioz's *L'enfance du Christ*, with mezzo-soprano Catherine Robbin, tenor Jerry Hadley, baritone Gary Relyea, bass-baritone Ingemar Korjus, and the Toronto Mendelssohn Choir.

It has always been difficult to produce the correct tone of bells in the 'Dies irae' section of Berlioz's *Symphonie fantastique* using ordinary tubular bells. In 1983 the TS decided to purchase two bronze alloy bells. These were cast specifically for the orchestra at the Royal Bell Foundry in Aarle-Rixtel, Holland. The D bell weighs 119 pounds, and the G bell 198 pounds. The new bells had their debut in a performance of *Symphonie fantastique* on 8 February 1984.

Davis's third choral contribution to this season was the first Toronto Symphony performance of Sir Edward Elgar's oratorio *The Kingdom* on 16–17 May with soprano Margaret Marshall, contralto Alfreda Hodgson, tenor Kenneth Riegel, bass-baritone John Cheek, and the Toronto Mendelssohn Choir. On 19 and 20 May the Toronto Symphony and the Toronto Mendelssohn Choir gave two concerts at Carnegie Hall in New York. The first was a repeat of Elgar's *The Kingdom* and the second was a performance of Beethoven's Symphony No. 9 in D minor with soprano Esther Hinds, mezzo-soprano Gabrielle Lavigne, tenor Jon Frederic West, and baritone Victor Braun.

Three guest orchestras participated in the TS subscription series. On 17 and 18 February the Philharmonia Orchestra from London, England, performed two concerts in the Great Performers Series, with Vladimir Ashkenazy as conductor and soloist. On 14 and 15 March the Stuttgart Chamber Orchestra with conductor Karl Münchinger gave concerts in the regular subscription series. Later in March the Czech Philharmonic Orchestra with conductor Václav Neumann also fulfilled concerts in the subscription series. Neumann was back in Toronto in mid-April to conduct the TS, and again in May for two more subscription series concerts, in addition to guest conducting the Toronto Symphony Youth Orchestra.

During the Toronto International Festival in June 1984 performances took place at various venues. The Toronto Symphony Youth Orchestra and the Toronto Mendelssohn Youth Choir gave a concert in the MacMillan Theatre, University of Toronto, on 11 June. On 19 and 21 June the senior groups of these organizations gave two performances of Hector Berlioz's *Roméo et Juliette* conducted by Andrew Davis, with mezzo-soprano Florence Quivar, tenor Marc DuBois, and bass James Morris.

In addition to an already busy season, the American Symphony Orchestra League and the Association of Canadian Orchestras held a joint conference in Toronto. This was the first time the two national orchestra organizations had combined their annual conferences, and also the first time the American Symphony Orchestra League had held a conference outside the United States. The Toronto Symphony was the host organization for this gathering, held at the Royal York Hotel on 5–9 June 1984. A large display devoted to the TS archives proved to be one of the main attractions, with many representatives examining the material closely and asking questions. In addition, on 6, 7, and 8 June the TS, as host orchestra, gave special concerts for the delegates at Roy Thomson Hall, with violinist Ida Haendel as guest soloist.

The Ontario Place season included several interesting events. The concert on 10 July was dedicated to Estonian and Finnish music. It was conducted by Neeme Järvi, with guest artist Ida Haendel, who played the Sibelius Violin Concerto in D minor, and the Estonian Choirs of Toronto, who sang Arvo Part's choral work *Frates*. Andrew Davis conducted the last three concerts of the Ontario Place season. Two evenings were devoted to ballet with guest artists Karen Kain and Frank Augustyn, principal dancers with the National Ballet of Canada. The final concert was a performance of Beethoven's Symphony No. 9 in D minor with soprano Frances Ginzer, mezzo-soprano Sandra Graham, tenor John Absalom, baritone Gary Relyea, and the Toronto Mendelssohn Choir. So ended another glorious season of music by Lake Ontario.

With the advantage of a fully air-conditioned concert hall, the TS also presented a summer season of concerts in Roy Thomson Hall, a venture that would not have been possible in Massey Hall. The music covered a wide spectrum, from a romantic evening of Viennese selections by Franz Lehár and the Strauss family conducted by Franz Allers, to a traditional Beethoven night conducted by Andrew Davis. In between there was a 'Pops and the Beatles' concert conducted by Eric Knight, an evening of music from Czechoslovakia and Hungary with Victor Feldbrill on the podium, one of Erich Kunzel's 'Best of Broadway' concerts, and 'A Night of Gilbert and Sullivan' in which Andrew Davis both sang and conducted.

1984–1985

At the opening of the season the TS was invited to perform for two high-profile events. On 14 September, Pope John Paul II visited Toronto to light the flame in the Peace Garden at Nathan Phillips Square. At Nathan Phillips Square, the orchestra was joined by the Toronto Mendelssohn Choir and soprano Joanne Kolomyjec, mezzo-soprano Sandra Graham, tenor Mark DuBois, and bass Christopher Cameron. The program consisted of two excerpts from Handel's *Messiah*, Elgar's *Pomp and Circumstance March No. 1*, the first movement from Brahms's Symphony No. 1 in C minor, and the overture to Beethoven's opera *Fidelio*. The second event was a gala concert on 1 October 1984 at Roy Thomson Hall with Queen Elizabeth II and the Duke of Edinburgh in attendance.

Andrew Davis and Alfred Brendel in rehearsal with the TS, May 1984

Artists included Guido Basso, Corey Cerovsek, Evelyn Hart, Frank Augustyn, Catherine McKinnon, Jon Kimura Parker, and Marie-Josée Simard. The CBC televised this concert nationally, with Veronica Tennant acting as host.

The opening concert of the regular season included a performance of Brandenburg Concerto No. 1 in F major, BWV 1046, to commemorate the 300th anniversary of the birth of Johann Sebastian Bach. Andrew Davis is known for his many accomplishments in music, but he is rarely thought of as a composer. On 24–5 October, he conducted the orchestra and the Toronto Children's Chorus in the world premiere of his *Chansons innocentes*, about which he said, 'I have tried to write a short work that will be challenging and fun for the singers (one hopes, for listeners too!) and that, at the same time, explores the visionary worlds of perception that seem to be much closer to children than to us when we "grow up."'[1] The text of the work consists of poems by e.e. cummings, Thomas Nash, and William Blake.

On 24 November composer Godfrey Ridout, who for many years had written program notes for the TS, passed away. His interesting and informative notes had helped audiences to better understand classical music. He enjoyed this writing because it allowed him to make the world of music more accessible to others.

The concert on 14 November introduced English conductor Jeffrey Tate (for his TS and North American orchestral debut) and pianist Brigitte Engerer (for her TS debut). Engerer was soloist for the Piano Concerto No. 2 in G minor by Saint-Saëns, and Tate conducted the *Leonore Overture No. 3* by Beethoven and the Symphony No. 1 in B flat major by Schumann. Helmuth Rilling, who ranks as one of the foremost choral conductors in the world, made his TS debut on 30 January, conducting the TS and the Toronto Mendelssohn Choir in a performance of J.S. Bach's *St John Passion*. The guest artists were soprano Costanza Cuccaro, mezzo-soprano Linn Maxwell, tenor Aldo Baldin, bass-baritone Wolfgang Schone (all of whom were making TS debuts), and bass-baritone Gary Relyea. The orchestra was augmented by Patricia Krueger on harpsichord, Mary Cyr on viola da gamba, and George Brough on organ.

At 2:00 p.m. on Sunday 17 March, the TS gave a special Maintenance Fund concert in Maple Leaf Gardens. The distinguished guest artist was tenor Luciano Pavarotti. Many people in the audience had travelled long distances to hear this famous tenor. There was an outburst of applause after every aria, but nothing outshone the cheers that followed Pavarotti's encore, 'Nessun dorma' from *Turandot* by Puccini. Wynton Marsalis made his TS debut on 27 and 29 March playing the Trumpet Concerto in E flat by Johann Nepomuk Hummel. While in Toronto Marsalis participated in a TS education presentation at Etobicoke Collegiate, giving advice and demonstrating the art of trumpet playing to an enthusiastic student audience, and also gave a master class for the brass section of the Toronto Symphony Youth Orchestra.

The end of the 1984–5 season witnessed the departure of two musicians who had served twenty years with the orchestra. Christopher Weait, co-principal bassoon, took a position as professor of bassoon at Ohio State University, and French horn player Barbara Bloomer left to focus on her teaching career in Toronto. During July and August the orchestra made its usual appearances at Ontario Place, where for many seasons it had delighted audiences with well-known classics in the open air on summer evenings.

The summer of 1985 was one of great excitement for the Toronto Symphony Youth Orchestra, which had had been invited to participate in the International Festival of Youth Orchestras to be held in Aberdeen, Scotland. Youth orchestras from around the world were invited to participate and perform. Conductor Ermanno Florio and string conductor David Zafer shared conducting duties, and the TSYO's challenging program set a high standard of performance for the festival: Weber's overture to his opera *Oberon*, *Passacaglia on a Bach Chorale* by Canadian composer Oskar Morawetz, the

Luciano Pavarotti, March 1985

Concerto Grosso No. 1 by Ernest Bloch, and finally, the Symphony No. 5 by Sergei Prokofiev.

After the performance in Aberdeen, the TSYO moved on to Stirling, where they repeated their concert program in Dunblane Cathedral. In addition, the TSYO had been chosen to participate in the opening concert in Hazlehead Park. This festive event included Tchaikovsky's *1812 Overture*, complete with fireworks, massed pipes and drums, and the Concert Chorus of the University of the Philippines. The International Festivals of Youth Orchestras, which are now held frequently, prove the value of supporting student performance in orchestras, choirs, and dance ensembles. BBC Promenade Concerts now include youth orchestras from all parts of the world, paying tribute to the importance of youth within the cultural scene.

A short excursion to Holland began with a reception hosted by the mayor of Amsterdam, followed by concerts in Den Bosch, and in Haarlem at the Concertgebouw. Back in Britain, there were two final performances. The first, on 9 August, was a lunch-hour concert on the north lawn of Lincoln's Inn – the 'hallowed' ground of the legal profession. The second concert, in Holland Park, was part of the London Youth Festival. The TSYO was the only non-British youth orchestra to be invited. According to the *Times* and *Daily Telegraph*, the TSYO concerts were a great success and represented an example of the high quality of performance possible from youth orchestras. They returned to Toronto on 13 August tired but proud of their achievements.

This season opened with a number of diverse concerns. The musicians' contract was up for negotiation, Andrew Davis announced that he would not renew his contract at the end of the 1987–8 season, and managing director Walter Homburger announced his intention to retire at the end of the 1985–6 season. On the artistic side, the orchestra was about to undertake its fourth European tour, an expedition that included two 'firsts' for a Canadian orchestra (performances at the Edinburgh International Festival and the 'Proms'), and had signed a recording contract with EMI.

1985–1986

With an important European tour about to be finalized, it was necessary to arrive at an amicable contract agreement within a reasonable time period. Negotiations ended with a salary raise for the musicians of 3.6 per cent, and the addition of a category for five to nine years of service in the seniority pay scale. However, a three-year contract, which would have given management the stability needed for scheduling, was not achieved. Negotiations were due to reconvene within six months, at which time outstanding issues were to be addressed and resolved.

Conductor Ermanno Florio and string conductor David Zafer with the Toronto Symphony Youth Orchestra, 1985

TSYO woodwind section

TSO percussionists Patricia Krueger and Daniel Ruddick

Andrew Davis's announcement that he was leaving the TS was not altogether a surprise. It was well known that he wanted to move on. However, he was proud of the TS, and his departure was not going to be easy. Walter Homburger, who had announced his retirement, had spent a quarter of a century 'at the helm' of the orchestra. The Board knew of the personal wishes of both these men, but regretted to see Davis and Homburger leave.

In September assistant general manager Wray Armstrong met with representatives of EMI/Angel to review a draft contract for future recordings, including a recording of *The Planets* by Holst during the current season. There were also plans for a recording of *Messiah* and piano concertos featuring Alexander Toradze. The acoustics of Roy Thomson Hall were a major concern. Davis met with Ed Pickering to discuss what could be done to improve the situation and in early October Pickering announced that acoustician Theodore Schultz had invited P.A. de Lange to review the acoustics of the hall. This was undoubtedly a result of Davis's meeting with Schultz and of the announcement that EMI/Angel would not use Roy Thomson Hall for recording purposes because it was not up to their standards. Consequently the TS recorded Holst's *The Planets* at the Centre in the Square in Kitchener. The recording was released in May 1986.

The major event of this season was the European tour, one of the most important in the orchestra's history. The orchestra had been invited to participate in the Edinburgh International Festival and was the first Canadian orchestra to do so. The Edinburgh International Festival was founded in 1947. The creation of an interna-

Rehearsal of Stravinsky's *Oedipus Rex* as part of the Edinburgh Festival, 1986

tional festival so soon after the end of the Second World War immediately caught the attention of music organizations worldwide and the festival was soon recognized as an important celebration of music and the arts. The founders of the festival believed that the programs should be of the highest possible quality and presented by the best artists in the world. The original intention that the festival should enliven and enrich the culture of Britain and Europe is closely reflected and maintained in its current aims and objectives.

The Toronto Symphony gave two concerts in Edinburgh's Usher Hall. The first opened with Berlioz's *Le corsaire ouverture*, after which the orchestra was joined by Ivo Pogorelich for the Tchaikovsky Piano Concerto No. 1 in B flat minor. The concert concluded with the Symphony No. 5 by Sergei Prokofiev. The second concert consisted of two compositions by Stravinsky. Contralto Alfreda Hodgson, tenors Robert Tear and Maldwyn Davies, baritone Anthony Michaels-More, bass-baritone Stafford Dean, and narrator John Neville, along with the Edinburgh International Festival Chorus, gave an outstanding performance of *Oedipus Rex*. Then the TS repeated a production of *L'histoire du soldat* (The Soldier's Tale) that had been first presented at Roy Thomson Hall in April 1983. Stravinsky said the work should be read, played, and danced, in that order. The cast included narrator John Neville, with Jeff Hyslop as the

TS in rehearsal on tour

devil, and two leading dancers from the National Ballet of Canada – Karen Kain and Peter Ottmann (who replaced Frank Augustyn on the tour owing to Augustyn's illness). The seven musicians in the small onstage orchestra were violinist José-Luis Garcia, bassist Thomas Monohan, clarinettist Joaquin Valdepeñas, bassoonist David McGill, trumpeter Larry Weeks, trombonist Gordon Sweeney, and percussionist David Kent. It was a brilliant evening that the festival audience would long remember.

Next morning it was on to the 'fair city' of Dublin. There was an amusing incident at the Edinburgh airport. The tour manager had announced that the flight would leave from embarkation point three and made her way there, accompanied by two others, in spite of an airport announcement specifying embarkation point twelve. The personnel manager, this writer, and the rest of the orchestra found their way to the correct location, where indeed there was a charter aircraft waiting to take the orchestra to Dublin. However, the flight was delayed for about twenty-five minutes before airport authorities found the three missing people. Perhaps it is wise to beware of tour managers while on tours!

The orchestra's first visit to the Emerald Isle was a short one. The concert that evening was held in the National Concert Hall with the Canadian ambassador, Dennis McDermott, in attendance. The program consisted of Tchaikovsky's Piano Concerto

Toronto Star music critic William Littler on tour with the Toronto Symphony

No. 1 in B flat minor with guest artist Ivo Pogorelich followed by Mahler's Symphony No. 9. The next morning the orchestra flew to London for a much anticipated appearance at the Henry Wood Promenade Concerts in the Royal Albert Hall.

The Promenade Concerts began on 10 August 1895 in the Queen's Hall. Robert Newman, the organizer of the concerts, appointed the twenty-six-year-old Henry Wood as permanent conductor. In 1927, when the Proms faced financial difficulties, the BBC agreed to take over this internationally recognized festival of music. The Toronto Symphony was the first Canadian orchestra invited to take part in the Proms. This was also a special occasion for Andrew Davis, who had conducted at the Proms since 1971, appearing with the BBC Symphony, the London Philharmonic Orchestra, and the Philharmonia Orchestra. Now he was bringing to the Proms a Canadian orchestra that was capable of maintaining the high standard of the Henry Wood Promenade Concerts.

The last stop in Britain was Cardiff, for the orchestra's second visit to Wales. Cardiff now possessed a new concert hall with extremely good acoustics. St David's Hall is modern in design with seating pods similar to those in Roy Thomson Hall, but with a more classic appearance, not unlike the seating arrangement in the Berlin Philharmonie. Ironically, the superb acoustics in Cardiff are due in part to the Canadian pine used for the interior finish of the hall (not Canadian concrete!). The evening before the concert in St David's Hall, Davis hosted a special party for the orchestra in the banquet hall of Cardiff Castle, a magnificent room with a high timber-vaulted ceiling, ornamented with the heraldic devices tracing the Bute ancestry. A delicious meal was followed by entertainment highlighted by the superb singing of a Welsh ladies' choir.

The TS program in Cardiff consisted of *Le corsaire ouverture* by Berlioz, Beethoven's Piano Concerto No 2 in B flat major played by Louis Lortie, and Ravel's orchestration of Mussorgsky's *Pictures at an Exhibition*. A saxophonist was required for this last work, and Andrew Davis had the right musician in mind. Much to the delight of the

Trumpeter Johnny Cowell serenading passers-by from his hotel room in Brussels

On-flight negotiations en route to Helskini. From left to right: TSO Board President Tom Beck, managers Wray Armstrong and Walter Homburger, and Board member David Howard

Andrew Davis and Brian MacDonald (seated) with Karen Kain, Frank Augustyn, and Jeff Hyslop, from the April 1983 production of Stravinsky's *L'histoire du soldat* (The Soldier's Tale)

orchestra – especially the clarinet section – Jack Brymer, the internationally renowned clarinettist, was invited to play the saxophone part. At the time, Brymer was writing a book about orchestras in which he had played. He was impressed with the TS, and devoted several pages to the orchestra. Reflecting on his forty minutes in the orchestra ranks, he wrote:

> In 1986 I was asked to join them for a concert they were giving in Cardiff, on a big European tour, and at times I could hardly believe I was not in one of our British orchestras – and it wasn't merely the language, or the fact that their conductor for the past twelve years had been one of our own young stars, Andrew Davis. There was something in their approach to the whole business of orchestral playing which was familiar, comfortable and satisfactory. This is the case of course with most of the world's orchestras, but particularly with them.

On 4 September the orchestra left for Bonn. After breakfast, buses conveyed all the personnel to Cardiff Airport – or so they should have. This author, not continuing the journey to Europe, returned to the hotel after seeing the coaches depart, to be greeted by the Board chairman with, 'Thank goodness you are here. I thought that everybody had left.' The author replied, 'The coaches have just departed.' The chairman and his wife rushed to the door to get a taxi, and apparently reached the airport before the coaches.

After their first concert on the continent at the Beethovenhalle in Bonn, the orchestra travelled on to Belgium to participate in the Flanders Festival. The TS gave one Festival concert at the Koninklijke Opera in Ghent, and a second at the Filharmonische Verenniging in Brussels. Copenhagen was the next destination for a concert in the famous Tivoli Gardens. From Denmark, the orchestra took a flight across the Baltic Sea to Finland for two concerts in Helsinki, then to Sweden for three concerts: one each in Stockholm, Malmo, and Goteborg. It was unfortunate that this Scandinavian odyssey did not include at least one concert in Norway. While the orchestra was on tour, the negotiations for a three-year contract were finalized and the musicians held a meeting in Helsinki in order to accept the terms offered by the Board. The final concert of the tour was given in Paris at the Salle Pleyel. Maria-João Pires was guest artist for a performance of Mozart's Piano Concerto No. 23 in A major, K 488. Then it was time to return to Toronto. The weary musicians knew that they had completed a most successful tour of Europe.

On all tours there are occasions when the unexpected occurs. In this case the first incident happened on the outgoing flight to Scotland. The tour schedule stated that dinner would be served, but 'dinner' turned out to be a cheese roll wrapped in cellophane! Part way through the same flight, violinist Peter Daminoff said he thought he could smell something smouldering, and one of the cabin crew noticed the same smell. After a thorough examination, the flight crew assured everyone that there was no need to worry and that they would take care of the situation. They did just that – they turned off the heat! Prestwick airport is not one of the world's most picturesque airports, but it was a welcome sight next morning. At the hotel in Amsterdam, one of the cellists decided to use the guest laundering facilities, but not being familiar with European-style washing machines he threw his clothes, complete with detergent, into a drier. After making enquires about the lack of water, he was introduced to a washer, where he added more detergent. He was apparently next seen with suds up to his waist.

One of the most spectacular TS concerts of the 1985–6 season at Roy Thomson Hall took place on 7 and 9 May. Andrew Davis conducted a concert performance of Richard Strauss's one-act opera *Daphne* with members of the Toronto Mendelssohn Choir and a cast that would have enhanced any of the world's opera houses: Catherine Malfitano, Ortrun Wenkel, Chris Merritt, Jon Fredric West, Victor Braun, Joanne Kolomyjec, Keith Olsen, Christopher Cameron, and John Fanning. Young People's Concerts were also of keen interest to Andrew Davis, and on 18 January he conducted an interesting program with the Toronto Children's Chorus. Engelbert Humperdinck's prelude to *Hansel and Gretel* was followed by 'Oh, Had I Jubal's Lyre' from Handel's oratorio *Joshua*, sung by the chorus, conducted by the choir's music director Jean Ashworth Bartle with Andrew Davis at the organ. The concert ended with Andrew Davis's *Chansons innocentes*. Davis was full of admiration for this choir and undoubtedly enjoyed this concert as much as the young audience.

1986–1987

The euphoria of the last season continued in the minds of the Board and musicians as the new season opened. In his report to the annual general meeting Thomas Beck, President of the Board, spoke of the well-received European tour, and added that the Board and musicians had reached a most satisfactory three-year settlement.

This was the last season under the management of Walter Homburger. Homburger, who arrived in Canada in 1940, came from a family with a rich musical tradition, but he never studied music himself. Homburger was head of his own International Artists Concert Agency, which he established in 1947, and in 1962 he had also become Managing Director of the TS. He was one of North America's leading arts administrators and his admirable relationship with artists' managements in North America extended to Britain and Europe. His musical vision was accompanied by his shrewd business sense, and consequently he was able to negotiate contracts with many of the world's leading artists. The fruits of his labours would be celebrated in the final concert of the season, commemorating his twenty-fifth and last season as managing director.

The first TS recording with EMI – Holst's *The Planets* – was successfully launched and the second recording – Handel's *Messiah* – was to be recorded in December at the Centre in the Square in Kitchener. Andrew Davis, after researching various previous recordings, decided to use an arrangement similar to that of a recording made by Sir Thomas Beecham in 1960 (which incidentally included Canadian tenor Jon Vickers). Performers included soprano Kathleen Battle, mezzo-soprano Florence Quivar, tenor John Aler, and bass Samuel Ramey, along with the Toronto Mendelssohn Choir. The recording was a success, not only because of the excellent choice of artists, but also because it was a welcome change from the traditional version presented year after year. More than ten years later the TS recording was still highly praised and the orchestra received reasonable royalties each year. In the meantime *The Planets* recording won the 1985 Juno award for the best classical recording.

Two key members of the administrative staff terminated their contracts: Harvey Chusid, Director of Marketing, and Hubert Meyer, the Personnel Manager, who had played tuba with the orchestra since 1957. Also, Steven Staryk was suffering from a problem with his arm and was not able to rejoin the orchestra until after Christmas. This problem had also prevented him from participating in the orchestra's European tour. Gerald Jarvis, who had filled his place, remained as concertmaster until Staryk's return.

The end of the season deficit of $1,075,000 may seem high but was not unworkable given an overall budget of $13 million. Wray Armstrong, the assistant managing director, announced that the Chrysler Corporation was interested in an arrangement with the TS (similar to the one it had with Roy Thomson Hall) whereby Chrysler supplied cars with small company insignia on the doors for business use. Discussions between the management of Roy Thomson Hall and the TS continued, and although some points of contention were cleared up there were no indications that the two organizations had resolved their major differences. It was becoming more and more evident that problems of varying importance were perhaps there to stay.

The last subscription season under Homburger's management reflected his expertise in program planning. Guest conductors included Kurt Sanderling, Sir Neville Marriner, Semyon Bychkov, and Pinchas Zukerman. The Great Performers Series

Kurt Sanderling and Murray Perahia, November 1986

graced the stage of Roy Thomson Hall with fourteen concerts by some of the greatest names in music: pianists Alicia de Larrocha, Bella Davidovich, Ivo Pogorelich, and Louis Lortie; opera stars Leontyne Price and Samuel Ramey; violinists Itzhak Perlman and Nadja Salerno-Sonnenberg; and chamber music ensembles such as the Stuttgart Chamber Orchestra, the Salzburg Musici, and the Sinfonietta of Israel.

Meanwhile preparations for the Great Gathering gala concert – a tribute to Walter Homburger – were proceeding. Funds raised for the concert were likely to reach $3 million, with additional financial support from the government of Ontario and the CBC. Publicity for the event included articles in the *Toronto Star*, the *Sunday Sun*, the *Globe and Mail*, the *New York Times*, and the *Financial Post*. The Great Gathering held on 9 March 1987 was an evening that would be long remembered. It was a sensational gala in every way. Celebrities, devoted subscription patrons, three hundred young musicians from across the province (financed by the Ministry of Citizenship and Culture), members of the TSYO, Ontario residents of the National Youth Orchestra, diploma students from the Royal Conservatory of Music, and a student representing each school board in Ontario – all witnessed this gathering of some of the world's greatest artists. The conducting was shared by Seiji Ozawa, Andrew Davis, Victor

Isaac Stern, Murray Perahia, Yo-Yo Ma, and Pinchas Zuckerman rehearse for the Great Gathering, March 1987

Feldbrill, and Elmer Iseler. Performers included cellists Yo-Yo Ma and Mstislav Rostropovich, flutist Jean-Pierre Rampal, violinists Isaac Stern, Pinchas Zukerman, and Midori, pianists Murray Perahia and Louis Lortie, contralto Maureen Forrester, and the Toronto Mendelssohn Choir.

The final work on the program was the overture to Johann Strauss's opera *Die Fledermaus*, with Isaac Stern as concertmaster, Yo-Yo Ma as principal cello, Pinchas Zukerman as principal viola, Jean-Pierre Rampal as principal flute, and a percussion section augmented with Maureen Forrester, Seiji Ozawa, Mstislav Rostropovich, Victor Feldbrill, and Elmer Iseler. The program finally ended with a momentous finale at 1:00 a.m. and the entire concert was broadcast live by CBC-TV across Canada. This event raised $1,150,000 for Toronto Symphony endowment fund.

Walter Homburger had provided excellent leadership to the orchestra for a quarter

Mstislav Rostropovich and Seiji Ozawa, March 1987 – The Great Gathering

century. In his final report to the annual meeting in October 1986 the traditional summary of the past season's accomplishments was cast aside in favour of reminiscences about behind-the-scenes adventures that the Board never got to hear about. Homburger recalled some of his memorable experiences:

We always try to meet our artists at the airport, or, in former days at Union Station. One day I went to the airport to meet Arthur Rubinstein. The plane arrived, everyone was out of customs, but no Rubinstein. I called his hotel to find him happily installed for six hours, what happened? He had woken up early in Chicago, decided

TSO Managing Director Walter Homburger and Assistant Managing Director Wray Armstrong

to take an early flight and forgotten he was going to be met. You go to meet an artist, whom you have not previously been acquainted, you have a photograph supplied by the agent, so I go to meet the famed Guiomar Novães, I look for a woman about 5ft 6 with loose hair, I miss her; she is 4ft 10 with upswept hair. Many years ago Andrés Segovia wanted some soda water at 2:00 a.m. He couldn't rouse anyone so he went in his pyjamas and bathrobe to the front desk to get some. A pianist rehearses on the piano he has selected, then just before the concert he decides to use the other one in the hall but of course it hasn't been tuned. One of the many happy recollections was the after-concert party when at 2:00 a.m. after a lot of celebrating Rostropovich took out his cello and played an unaccompanied suite by Bach as beautiful as I have ever heard.

Walter Homburger proposed that Wray Armstrong be appointed Managing Director at the beginning of the season and this was approved by the Board. Armstrong had been Homburger's assistant for five years and had been well trained in the difficult and demanding aspects of managing a symphony orchestra. It was obvious that Armstrong,   **1987–1988**

Principal Second Violin Julian Kolkowski models hats in Inuvik

a younger man, would use different methods to tackle day-to-day challenges and problems. Although his outlook on the orchestral scene was the same as that of his predecessor, he took a somewhat broader view.

The 1987–8 season was the culmination of Andrew Davis's tenure as Music Director. After thirteen years with the TS he would be returning to England to take the highly prestigious positions of principal conductor for the BBC Symphony Orchestra and music director of the Glyndebourne Opera, organizations he had been closely associated with for many years. The programs for his last season reflected many of his achievements with the TS.

The season opened with the orchestra about to depart on a Canadian tour. With Davis, the TS had undertaken tours to the west and the east of Canada. This tour would take them north to the shores of the Beaufort Sea. The Canadian Odyssey encompassed the far reaches of the Yukon and Northwest Territories as well as parts of Northern Ontario and Western Canada. The orchestra gave thirteen full symphonic concerts and twenty-seven chamber concerts, in which musicians formed small groups for educational performances in more remote communities. The first three concerts took place in Northern Ontario: North Bay, Sudbury, and Sault-Ste-Marie (where the Governor General of Canada, Jeanne Sauvé, was in attendance). The pinnacle of the tour was Inuvik, where the orchestra gave two concerts. The first, held in the Sir Alexander Mackenzie School auditorium on Saturday, 19 September, consisted of short popular orchestral pieces including Berlioz's *Roman Carnival Overture*, Haydn's Trumpet Concerto, Emmanuel Chabrier's *España*, and excerpts from Mussorgsky's *Pictures at an Exhibition*. Canadian compositions were represented by Godfrey Ridout's *Fanfare* and Weinzweig's 'Barn Dance' from his suite *Red Ear of Corn*. After the intermission, the Inuvik Delta Drummers and Dancers gave a colourful performance in music and dance. On the following day there was a chamber concert in the unique Igloo Church, while small groups of musicians dispersed to other parts of the region to give education concerts in Fort McPherson, Aklavik, and Tuktoyaktuk.

The TS had an extraordinary ice hockey team, the Flying Fortes. When the

Mario Duschenes conducts a sold-out Student Concert at the hockey arena in Sault Ste. Marie as part of the Orchestra's Canadian Odyssey Tour

orchestra visited a place where ice hockey is played, a game was planned with a resident team. In Inuvik everyone assumed that the ice would be in good condition for a game with a local team, but there had been a warm fall, so the event became a street hockey match. It must be noted that the TS team maintained its outstanding no-win record. Another interesting feature of the visit to Inuvik was the cuisine, including fish cooked in the true Arctic tradition.

The time spent in the Arctic resulted in additional visits by TS members and the Toronto Symphony Youth Orchestra. Rhombus Media, in cooperation with the CBC, produced an excellent film of the tour entitled 'Music in the Midnight Sun,' which was broadcast on the CBC television network. Television services in other countries also became interested in this extraordinary tour, and have programmed the film on their respective networks. Newspapers such as the *Globe and Mail*, the *Toronto Star*, the *Chicago Tribune*, and the *New York Times*, as well as the CBC national news, also covered portions of the tour.

In mid-November 1987 the Board announced that Günther Herbig had been appointed Artistic Adviser for a one-year term. This appointment was immediately recognized by the media and other personnel related to the orchestra as an indication

The TSO Flying Fortes prepare for a big game in Inuvik

Music Director Andrew Davis drops the puck at the face-off between Toronto and Finland

Violist Stanley Solomon instructs a young student in Tuktoyaktuk, September 1987

that Herbig would eventually become the new Music Director. Armstrong had initially contacted two conductors about the position: Mariss Jansons was not available since he had just completed negotiations for another position, and Kurt Sanderling replied that he was too old and instead recommended Herbig. Armstrong met with Herbig in Detroit (where he was the music director of the Detroit Symphony) and again in Israel. After much planning and discussion Herbig agreed to come to the TS.

Meanwhile, some important changes were taking place within the orchestral ranks. Jascha Milkis was promoted to second concertmaster and Steven Dann, a Canadian violist who had previously been principal violist with the Amsterdam Concertgebouw and the Vancouver Symphony Orchestra, signed a contract to become principal violist with the TS. The search for a concertmaster was still proceeding, with no immediate solution in sight.

The future of the Ontario Place summer season was also in doubt. Ontario Place had requested more 'pops orientated' programs but wisely the orchestra responded by asserting that they had no interest in backing up rock stars, and that they intended to continue presenting classical music. (It should be remembered that when Ontario Place opened, the provincial government stated that it was a place for all people, which presumably includes those who enjoy the classical music repertoire.)

Principal flutist Nora Shulman with students from Detah, Northwest Territories, September 1987

Double bass player Ruth Budd shares 'good vibrations' with students, Canadian Odyssey tour, September 1987

In February 1988 the orchestra once again travelled west to take part in the Olympic Arts Festival in Alberta. The first concert, given in the Jack Singer Concert Hall in Calgary, featured Canadian artists Leslie Newman on flute, and Jennifer Swartz on harp, playing Mozart's Concerto for Flute and Harp in C major, K 299. At the time both young musicians were students in Toronto and were TSYO alumni. The program concluded with Richard Strauss's *Ein Heldenleben*, with Steven Staryk playing solo violin. A second concert at the University of Lethbridge Theatre and a third in Banff at the Banff Centre repeated the same program: *Klee Wyck* by Canadian composer Harry Freedman, the Cello Concerto in A minor by Schumann with Canadian cellist Shauna Rolston, and Brahms's Symphony No. 1 in C minor. For this tour the orchestra received a grant of $225,000 from the Department of Communications.

A direct result of the recent Canadian Odyssey tour was the founding of 'Strings Across the Sky,' the brainchild of TS violinist Andrea Hansen. In the spring of 1988, Hansen, along with fellow TS musicians Patricia Krueger (percussion and keyboard) and Ronald Laurie (cello), returned to the Arctic with a donation of nine violins for children and videos of violin lessons by Andrea Hansen. These musicians realized the desire of people in Inuvik, especially youth, for an opportunity to develop a deeper musical knowledge and to learn to play classical music, and they saw an opportunity to strengthen relations with the nation's northernmost citizens. Hansen, Krueger, and Laurie left for the Arctic on 12 March, supported by funding from the Secretary of State of Canada, Imperial Oil, and private donations. The TS Youth and Education Committee later studied the feasibility of having the Toronto Symphony Youth Orchestra follow the senior orchestra's footsteps to the North. This project was presented to the Board and received approval on 2 June, and the tour took place in May 1989.

Long-range planning is a necessary ingredient in the life of any symphony orchestra, but at the Board meeting in February it appeared that this planning was about to assume greater importance. The Ontario Arts Council was involved in a long-range plan that would cap grant increases to the five major arts organizations in the province (the Canadian Opera Company, the National Ballet of Canada, the Shaw Festival, the Stratford Festival, and the Toronto Symphony) and would allow discretion as to individual allocation of funds. For the TS this announcement came at a difficult time. Serious thought was being given to a permanent summer home and plans also included additional touring to enhance the orchestra's international image.

The concerts for Andrew Davis's last season reflected the enthusiasm and enjoyment he had in working with the TS. Gustav Mahler, a favoured composer, was represented on 7 and 8 October with the Symphony No. 2 in C minor ('Resurrection'),

Andrew Davis's final concert as Music Director of the TS, April 1988. He is being presented with a Canadian-made canoe by TS Board Presidents.

with soprano Joanne Kolomyjec, contralto Maureen Forrester, and the Toronto Mendelssohn Choir. For the concerts on 3, 4, and 6 February 1988 Davis chose Edward Elgar's *The Dream of Gerontius*, with mezzo-soprano Alfreda Hodgson, tenor Keith Lewis, bass Stafford Dean, and the Toronto Mendelssohn Choir. Four performances of Mahler's Symphony No. 8 brought together more soloists and choirs that Davis had worked with: Faye Robinson, Mary Lou Fallis, Alfreda Hodgson, Gary Relyea, Phyllis Bryn-Julson, Janis Taylor, Artur Korn, Timothy Jenkins, the Vancouver Bach Choir, the Toronto Children's Chorus, the Toronto Boy's Choir, and the Toronto Mendelssohn Choir with its conductor, Elmer Iseler. Davis had experienced wonderful co-operation with the Mendelssohn Choir and Elmer Iseler, and their kindred affinity for choral music had given Toronto many memorable choral performances.

On 31 October and 1 November, Andrew Davis was at Carnegie Hall for the last time as Music Director of the TS. The first concert included Mendelssohn's Violin Concerto in E minor with Itzhak Perlman as well as Stravinsky's *Le sacre du printemps* (The Rite of Spring). Jon Vickers, who was to have been the guest artist for the second concert, was taken ill at short notice. Fortunately, Itzhak Perlman agreed to fill Jon Vickers's portion on the program by playing Beethoven's Violin Concerto in D major. On 10 and 11 February pianist Mitsuko Uchida and violinist Steven Staryk (former concertmaster of the TS) were soloists. Mitsuko Uchida played Arnold Schoenberg's *Piano Concerto* and Steven Staryk played the solo violin for *Ein Heldenleben* by Richard Strauss. Andrew Davis also participated in an Evening Overture chamber concert and conducted the TSYO during the season.

In his association with the TS, Davis had presented many different musical styles and interpretations. He was confident in the position he had undertaken. In an early interview, he said, 'Age doesn't enter into it. An orchestra can form an opinion of a new conductor within a quarter of an hour, and if he can prove his abilities, they will accept him.' Trumpeter Johnny Cowell said, 'We all knew very early that Davis was the one. The talent was there at the first rehearsal.' At rehearsals, Davis shunned the tantrums of the old-style podium lions who used to rant and roar to achieve their musical goals. He used humour as his preferred approach. At difficult rehearsals he could be heard to say, 'I might as well save my breath to cool my porridge.' During his tenure, Davis's efforts for and dedication to the orchestra had transformed it from 'just another symphony orchestra' to a virtuoso ensemble. Fortunately, the orchestra was not going to lose him entirely – he signed a contract to remain as conductor laureate, and would consequently return every season to conduct one or two programs.

The season end also saw the retirement of four long-serving members of the orchestra: Stanley Solomon, principal viola emeritus, left after forty-one years, clarinettist John Fetherston after thirty-two years, cellist George Horvath after thirty years, and violinist Stanley Kolt after twenty-one years. It is always sad to see long-time members depart because they have contributed so much talent and expertise to the orchestra. Past members of an orchestra are also a fountain of knowledge, with their recollections and reminiscences of people and events. Finally, principal bassoonist David McGill left to take the same position with the Cleveland Orchestra.

The Board of Directors closed the season with two important decisions. First, in a rather unorthodox move, they approved the appointment of Günther Herbig in a series of steps: as Artistic Director for the 1988–9 season, Music Director designate for the 1989–90 season, and Music Director for the 1990–1 and 1991–2 seasons. Second, on Maestro Herbig's recommendation, they appointed Jacques Israelievitch, the concertmaster of the St Louis Symphony Orchestra, to the same position with the TS, beginning with the 1988–9 season.

Günther Herbig

Music is the arithmetic of sounds as optics is the geometry of light.

CLAUDE DEBUSSY

Günther Herbig made his debut with the TS in February 1982 with an inspired performance of Bruckner's Symphony No. 8. Herbig was born in Ústí nad Labem, Czechoslovakia, in 1931. He began his music study at the age of nine with lessons in piano, cello, and flute, and in the early 1950s studied conducting at the Musikhochschule in Weimar with Hermann Abendroth. Later he also studied with Hermann Scherchen, Arvids Jansons, and Herbert von Karajan. He held conducting positions at the Deutsches Nationaltheatre (Weimar, 1957–62) and the Hans-Otto-Theatre (Potsdam, 1962–6), the (East) Berlin Symphony Orchestra (1966–72 and 1977–83), and the Dresden Philharmonic Orchestra (1972–7). In the late 1970s he began to appear in the West, and was principal guest conductor for the Dallas Symphony Orchestra (1979–81) and the BBC Northern Symphony Orchestra in Manchester (1981–4). In 1984 he was appointed music director of the Detroit Symphony Orchestra, a position he held until 1990.

In addition to Jacques Israelievitch, the new concertmaster, and new principal violist Steven Dann, there were six new faces in the orchestra: violinist Marie Bérard (who had been concertmaster of the TSYO), violist Dan Blackman, cellist Kirk Worthington, bassist Charles Elliot, trumpeter James Spragg, and clarinettist Joseph Orlowski. Principal violist Osher Green resigned to take up a position with the Rochester Philharmonic Orchestra.

1988–1989 Everything looked promising for this new season. Subscriptions (totalling 45,247) were up more than 1,000 from the previous season. The long-standing dispute with Roy Thomson Hall on the amalgamation of box offices had been successfully resolved. Long-range planning was a top priority, covering all the issues important to the future of the orchestra. Many of the items up for discussion were linked with the ongoing 'Fund for the Future' campaign. The purpose of this venture was to build the Endowment Fund up to a level that could realistically meet the requirements of a present-day symphony orchestra. Other issues of vital importance included recording and broad-casting strategies and attracting a younger audience. Another project was the establish-ment of a summer home for the TS. In September, the Ontario Ministry of Culture announced they were prepared to fund 50 per cent of the cost for a feasibility study to investigate a suitable location.

The Toronto Symphony was asked by the Metropolitan Toronto Community Foundation to administer the Tom Thomas Scholarship Fund. This fund, set up by TS Board member Tom Thomas, was designed to provide financial assistance for serious young music students in Toronto. The scholarship fund has continued to allow many young talented musicians to develop their skills and become important participants in the Canadian music scene.

Günther Herbig conducted the opening concert of the 1988–9 season. The pro-gram opened with the overture to Carl Maria von Weber's opera *Oberon*. Violinist Midori joined the orchestra for the Violin Concerto in D minor by Sibelius, and the concert ended with a performance of Brahms's Symphony No. 1 in C minor – a good indication of Herbig's future plans for programming. His interpretation and intense rehearsal technique reminded the musicians of Karel Ančerl, with his demanding emphasis on detail and correct balance. On 26–7 July, during the 1989 summer season, Herbig and Midori were back on stage with the young and talented cellist Matt Haimovitz for a performance of the Brahms Double Concerto in A minor for violin and cello, op. 102.

Andrew Davis returned to the orchestra for the first time under his new designa-tion, Conductor Laureate, conducting a performance of Mendelssohn's *Elijah* – an oratorio often performed during the late nineteenth and early twentieth centuries but rather neglected these days. Davis brought together a group of artists with whom he had been closely associated during his time in Toronto: mezzo-soprano Florence Quivar, tenor Jerry Hadley, soprano Alessandra Marc, and treble Darren Dunstan. The Toronto Children's Chorus, the Toronto Mendelssohn Youth Choir, and the Toronto Mendelssohn Choir fulfilled the extensive choral requirements of the oratorio. The other major choral presentation of the season was the performance of J.S. Bach's magnificent *St Matthew Passion*, conducted by the pre-eminent German choral conduc-tor Helmuth Rilling. With the Toronto Mendelssohn Choir were soprano Sylvia McNair (making her TSO debut), mezzo-soprano Ursula Kunz, tenor Howard Crook, tenor Scot Weir, bass Philippe Huttenlocher, and baritone Daniel Lichti. These choral concerts were just a taste of the International Choral Festival to be held in Toronto during June.

Conductor Zubin Mehta at 'A Fusion of Harmonies,' March 1989

On 16 March the Toronto Symphony and the Israel Philharmonic Orchestra joined forces for a spectacular performance entitled 'A Fusion of Harmonies.' The two orchestras were conducted individually and collectively by Zubin Mehta, conductor of the Israel Philharmonic, and the two soloists represented the youth of both countries. The concert opened with the Israel Philharmonic playing *O Canada* followed by Weber's overture to *Oberon*. Corey Cerovsek, a young Canadian violinist, then joined the IPO for Mozart's Rondo in C major, K 373, and Saint-Saëns's *Introduction et rondo capriccioso*. Then the IPO left the stage, and the Toronto Symphony took their place, opening with the Israel national anthem, *Hatikvah*, followed by Beethoven's *Egmont Overture*. Sharon Kam, a young Israeli clarinettist, joined the TS for Weber's Clarinet

Concerto in E flat major. After the intermission, both orchestras were on stage for a most memorable performance of Berlioz's *Symphonie fantastique*. The concertmasters and principals of the two orchestras changed places after the third movement, so that they could all have the honour of leading this combined orchestra of 230 musicians. To accommodate this large orchestra, the stage area of RTH was enlarged by approximately twelve feet, covering the first six rows of the main-floor seating. This joint cultural event raised $340,000 for each orchestra. After the concert, about 200 musicians trooped over to Shopsy's Delicatessen for a post-concert dinner, and the guy at the end of the line did pay – after all, it was Zubin Mehta who had invited them for a midnight 'nosh.'

The 1989 International Choral Festival that took place in June had been the brainchild of entrepreneur extraordinaire Nicholas Goldschmidt, who has had the amazing vision, expertise, and insight to know when, where, and how to produce successful festivals. The Toronto Symphony participated in five Festival concerts. For the gala opening on 1 June Gennady Rozhdestvensky conducted a program featuring five scenes from Mussorgsky's opera *Boris Godunov* followed by Sergei Prokofiev's *Alexander Nevsky* with the Poliansky Choir of Moscow, the Obretenov Choir of Bulgaria, and boys from St Michael's Cathedral Choir School. The two soloists were bass Nikita Storojev and mezzo-soprano Mariana Paunova. On 4 June the TS was joined by the Ontario Choral Federation Choir and the Toronto Children's Chorus. For this concert Robert Shaw conducted four choral works by Brahms, including the *Alto Rhapsody* with contralto Maureen Forrester, but the major choral work in the program was Arrigo Boito's *Mefistofele* with bass Thomas Paul. On 11 June Robert Shaw conducted a performance of Beethoven's *Missa Solemnis*, with the Toronto Symphony, the Mennonite Festival Chorus, soprano Benita Valente, mezzo-soprano Janis Taylor, tenor Richard Margison, and baritone Tom Krause. The concert on 14 June, conducted by Elmer Iseler, featured Andrew Lloyd Webber's *Requiem* with the Toronto Mendelssohn Choir, soprano Jane Thorngren, tenor Vinson Cole, and treble Darren Dunstan. The Festival closed on 30 June with Giuseppe Verdi's *Requiem* presented by the TS and the Tanglewood Festival Chorus, conducted by Charles Dutoit, with soprano Alessandra Marc, mezzo-soprano Jard van Nes, tenor George Gray, and bass-baritone Simon Estes.

This season had been a busy but rewarding one. On the administration side, future plans looked promising. Meanwhile, the Toronto Symphony Youth Orchestra made history with an Arctic tour that included concerts in Whitehorse at the F.H. Collins High School and in Inuvik at the Sir Alexander Mackenzie School, along with a chamber music concert at Igloo Church. Three run-out concerts were planned to

The Toronto Symphony goes to Australia

Aklavik, Fort McPherson, and Tuktoyaktuk (although the Tuktoyaktuk event unfortunately had to be cancelled at the last minute as most of the town went hunting when a flock of geese flew into town). In Inuvik, the orchestra attended a party arranged by their billeting families. The food included roast caribou meat, and the musicians of the orchestra were entertained by the Grollier Hall Drummers.

1989–1990   Günther Herbig's second season saw a major change in the stability and fortunes of the orchestra. However, the event that dominated the season was the three-week Pacific Rim Tour that took the orchestra down the west coast of the Pacific Ocean from Vancouver to San Francisco before heading out over the Pacific to Australia, Singapore, Taiwan, and Japan.

The repertoire for the tour included a work by the talented Canadian composer Alexina Louie – *Music for Heaven and Earth*. The soloist on the tour was the renowned Canadian pianist Jon Kimura Parker, who played the Beethoven Piano Concerto No. 3 in C minor for eight concerts, giving the same immaculate performance at each. The repertoire also included Brahms's Symphony No. 2 in D major, Mahler's Symphony No. 7 in E minor, Tchaikovsky's Symphony No. 5 in E minor, and the overture to Carl

Pianist Louis Lortie and composer Alexina Louie with the Toronto Symphony on the Pacific Rim tour

Maria von Weber's opera *Oberon*. Herbig had wisely chosen compositions that reflected a broad spectrum of the symphonic repertoire, including works of which he was a recognized interpreter. The orchestra was well received everywhere it went and critics were full of praise. The Japanese audiences had one small complaint: they are avid collectors of recordings, and were disappointed that no CDs of the orchestra conducted by Maestro Herbig were available.

The Minnesota Orchestra was engaged to fill one subscription week while the orchestra was on tour. Edo de Waart conducted a program consisting of *Tromba Lontana* by John Adams followed by Beethoven's Piano Concerto No. 2 in B flat major with Peter Serkin as soloist, and *Eine Alpensinfonie* by Richard Strauss. In the same week, the Philadelphia Orchestra was engaged for a special concert. Riccardo Muti conducted Ferruccio Busoni's *Movements from the Turandot Suite*, Richard Strauss's *Don Juan*, and Tchaikovsky's Symphony No. 6, op. 74 ('Pathétique').

In November, the management of the Pantages Theatre approached the TS regarding the possibility of a joint venture to produce a five-concert classical pops series on Sundays. The concept was an exciting one – the TS would be the first 'non-Phantom' event to be held in this grand theatre. (*The Phantom of the Opera* was then in the first year of what became a ten-year run.) The TS management studied the economic feasibility of the series and the orchestra rehearsed a pops program in the theatre on

5 November. All agreed it was a terrific venue, but after much discussion and deliberation, it was felt that the series was not economically feasible. Perhaps there was a lack of vision and the possibilities for the future were not realized at the time.

Artistically the season had been successful. Jessye Norman was guest artist for the opening concert in a performance of Mahler's Symphony No. 3 in D minor, accompanied by the women's voices of the Toronto Mendelssohn Choir and the Toronto Boys' Choir, conducted by Günther Herbig. The subscription concerts on 22, 23, and 25 November were a choral tribute to Elmer Iseler, who was celebrating his twenty-fifth year as conductor of the Toronto Mendelssohn Choir. The program opened with the Symphony No. 7 in C by Jean Sibelius, followed by the world premiere of Derek Holman's *Tapestry* (*Five Medieval Lyrics for Chorus and Orchestra*) conducted by Iseler. The second half of the program was devoted to a performance of the *Mša Glagolskaja* (*Glagolitic Mass*) by Leoš Janáček conducted by Andrew Davis. The soloists were soprano Faye Robinson, mezzo-soprano Jean Stilwell, tenor John Mitchinson, and baritone John Cheek, with organist Michael Bloss. These concerts were a tribute to an eminent Canadian choral conductor.

Marilyn Horne, the distinguished American mezzo-soprano, sang the *Rückert Lieder* by Mahler with the TS on 26 January. In February, the Latvian conductor Mariss Jansons made his TS debut with a program consisting of the overture to Rossini's opera *La gazza ladra*, the Liszt Piano Concerto No. 1 in E flat major with soloist Jean-Yves Thibaudet, and a polished performance of Rachmaninoff's Symphony No. 2. This season included one of the most entertaining and enjoyable fund-raising gala events in the orchestra's history: Liza Minnelli gave an exuberant performance of songs associated with her and with her mother, Judy Garland. Minelli's enthusiasm and stage presence left the audience satisfied that the evening had indeed been well spent.

The end of this season, however, revealed a serious financial situation. The deficit had risen from $589,270 to $1,583,395. In his report at the Annual General meeting treasurer T. Iain Ronald said that the primary causes for the deterioration in financial stability were deficits from the Pacific Rim tour and a reduction in government grants. The high operating deficit was a concern to the Board, and further opportunities for expense reduction were actively pursued. The Board had been informed that all was under control, but the facts did not support this statement. Another costly tour was planned for the 1990–1 season – this time to Europe. In a memo to the Board of Directors, Managing Director J. Wray Armstrong expressed his concerns regarding the financial situation and recommended that the long-range planning approved during the season be scaled down and that all expenses be closely examined.

The 1990–1 season, in which Günther Herbig assumed the title of Music Director, was a busy one with a full complement of concerts in Roy Thomson Hall and a mini-tour to Ottawa, Montreal, and Carnegie Hall in New York, along with the much-discussed two-week tour in Europe. A number of guest artists and conductors made their TS debuts, including violinist Kyoko Takezawa, cellist Heinrich Schiff, soprano Christine Brewer, recorder player Michala Petri, pianist Cécile Ousset, and conductors Mark Elder and Velery Gergiev.

The mini-tour was well received. The program for Montreal and New York opened with Anton Webern's *Six Pieces for Orchestra*, op. 6. Cho-Liang Lin joined the orchestra for the Prokofiev Violin Concerto No. 1, and the concerts ended with Schubert's Symphony No. 9 in C major ('Great'). The two concerts in Ottawa – part of the National Arts Centre Orchestra subscription series – consisted of Claude Debussy's *La mer*, *Death and Transfiguration* by Richard Strauss, and Prokofiev's Violin Concerto No. 1, again played by Cho-Liang Lin.

There were a number of notable concerts in Toronto as well. On 5–6 October the orchestra gave the world premiere of Canadian composer Gary Kulesha's *The Midnight Road* with Simon Streatfield conducting. This work had been commissioned by the TS. Franz-Paul Decker conducted the TS premiere of Schoenberg's *Pelleas und Melisande*. A performance of Schoenberg's *Violin Concerto*, played by Christian Tetzlaff in his TS debut, was also a TS concert premiere. Returning guest artists included Yo-Yo Ma, Nigel Kennedy, Emanuel Ax, and André Watts.

In April of 1990, Herbig sent a memo to Wray Armstrong stating his personal concerns about the future of the orchestra and the delay in acting on issues that had been raised. Conductors have some degree of influence in orchestral administration. Herbig was noted for his knowledge in this area and was well aware of the challenges faced by board and management. Five main concerns had not been addressed: improvement to the Roy Thomson Hall acoustics, a recording contract, an increase in the orchestra's presence on television and radio, short tours, and a summer home. Herbig stated that unless some definite action was taken in these areas, he would postpone contract renewal negotiations until a later date. On 26 October the executive committee of the Board decided that because of the downturn of the economy it was not possible to proceed as rapidly as Herbig desired. After full and thorough discussion the Board reluctantly agreed that Maestro Herbig's contract would not be renewed after the 1991–2 season.

On 15 November, the Executive Committee of the Board had unanimously agreed to cancel the European tour but a short time later new information came to light that made them reconsider. For both artistic and financial reasons, the decision was reversed and the Board, with the executive committee's blessing, decided to proceed with the tour. The itinerary included two concerts in Britain (one at the Barbican in London and the other in the Royal Concert Hall in Glasgow), followed by concerts in Paris, Munich, Frankfurt, Hanover, Cologne, and Stuttgart. The repertoire consisted of *The North Wind's Gift* by Raymond Luedeke, Béla Bartók's *Viola Concerto* with Yuri Bashmet as soloist, Brahms's Symphony No. 1 in C minor, Anton Bruckner's Symphony No. 6 in A major, Beethoven's *Egmont Overture*, and Mendelssohn's Violin Concerto in E minor with Midori as soloist. The tour was well received. Critics praised the TS's performance but also commented on the orchestra's financial woes and internal problems.

Meanwhile back in Toronto the financial situation was not improving – on the contrary, things were getting worse. An accumulated deficit of over ten million dollars was considered unacceptable and various suggestions for future plans were tabled at Board meetings. Long-range planning was replaced with short-term survival. On 25 April Wray Armstrong, who had been Managing Director for the last four years, announced that he had accepted a post at ICM Artists (London) effective 1 August 1991. Armstrong later commented that the Board appeared to be split in its thinking. They had been supportive of the long-range plans that Armstrong had proposed, but when it came time to put these plans into operation, the Board was not prepared to give its approval.[1] Many Board members felt that Armstrong was making changes too fast. Armstrong also said that Günther Herbig was more and more frustrated by the Board's lack of vision and commitment, and indicated that Toronto was getting the orchestra it deserved.

Now the Board was searching for a new managing director in addition to a replacement for Maestro Herbig. To relieve the situation they asked Herbig if he would be willing to extend his tenure until the end of the 1992–3 season. Herbig agreed, but asked to retain the title of Music Director. His cooperation helped to provide much needed continuity and artistic strength. However, the annual financial report showed a season deficit of almost two million dollars.

1991–1992   This was the seventieth anniversary season of the Toronto Symphony, and the opening night was truly special. The Lieutenant Governor of Ontario, Lincoln M. Alexander, was in attendance. The concert, conducted by Günther Herbig, opened with two anthems – Godfrey Ridout's arrangement of *O Canada* and MacMillan's arrangement of *God Save the Queen* – followed by the world premiere of *Tradirunt me in manus*

Concertmaster Jacques Israelievitch and Second Concertmaster Jascha Milkis

impiorium II, a work by the TS composer-in-residence Walter Boudreau. The composition, a TS commission for the gala concert, was designed to incorporate extra players by doubling the wind parts, and on this occasion, the TS was joined by alumni of the Toronto Symphony Youth Orchestra. Canadian contralto Maureen Forrester followed with Brahms's *Alto Rhapsody*, and then Canadian pianist André Laplante and the Toronto Mendelssohn Choir joined forces with the Toronto Symphony for a brilliant performance of Beethoven's *Fantasia for Piano, Chorus and Orchestra*. The evening concluded with Dvořák's Symphony No. 9 in E minor ('From the New World').

The first concert of the subscription series was also an exciting season opener. Günther Herbig conducted a Richard Strauss–Wagner program with the celebrated soprano Jessye Norman. Richard Strauss's *Don Juan* was followed by Wagner's setting of five poems by Mathilde Wesendonck, known as the *Wesendonck Lieder*, sung by Jessye Norman. The balance of the program was devoted to excerpts from three of Wagner's operas: the Prelude to *Die Meistersinger von Nürnberg*, the Prelude to *Tannhäuser*, and the Prelude and Liebestod from *Tristan und Isolde*, again with Jessye Norman.

Two choral concerts were devoted to the music of Mozart, in commemoration of the 200th anniversary of his death. The first concert included the *Requiem*, K 626, with

Günther Herbig and a young fan

soprano Christine Brewer, contralto Catherine Wyn-Rogers, tenor Jon Garrison, and bass Thomas Paul, and the Toronto Mendelssohn Choir. The second was the annual performance of *Messiah*, on this occasion using the Mozart arrangement of Handel's masterpiece. The conductor was Vittorio Negri, considered to be one of Europe's foremost champions of the Baroque, and the soloists were soprano Faith Esham, mezzo-soprano Marietta Simpson, tenor John Mark Ainsley, and baritone Gary Relyea.

The financial situation was not improving. In August 1991 the Board announced that the cumulative deficit would be more than three and a half million dollars, primarily due to low subscription sales, cancelled summer concerts, and fund-raising expectations that were off by almost $400,000. Strategic plans made for the future were delayed until February 1992, and it seemed that any major plans had been placed on the back burner. At the beginning of the season Peter Ross, the Director of Development, had been appointed acting Managing Director until a new Managing Director could be found. In November William H. Broadhurst, the chairman of the Board, announced that Max Tapper had been appointed to the position. Tapper had been the executive director of the Winnipeg Symphony Orchestra. Prior to that appointment, which he had held for six years, he was director of development for the Royal Winnipeg Ballet. In an interview with Michael Crabb of the CBC, Tapper made several interesting statements that raised a few eyebrows within the TS. When asked by Crabb how he intended to deal with the accumulated debt of $3.7 million and how he intended to save the orchestra, his reply was that the TS did not need saving, and that he was of the opinion that the debt could be handled. At the end of the interview Crabb said, 'Max, you really are an idealist! Is that what got you into this business?' Tapper replied, 'I got into this business because I was a lousy actor. I was invited to begin some work in the management side of things and I guess I found my role.' The point in all of this, however, is that anyone who was engaged to take over the TS at this time would have been in for a formidable challenge.

Tapper's first goal was to stop the bleeding. The musicians' contract gave a 6 per cent raise in the second year and had a back-loading clause that would, with the increase from forty-eight to fifty weeks, add an effective 12 per cent in the third year. This was about to kick in. Tapper had a back-loaded three-year contract going into the depth of a recession. In four months he had to cut more than two million dollars out of the next season's budget. This meant a 15 per cent cut across the board. The musicians, naturally, were angry and upset and the threat of bankruptcy hung over the whole organization. No level of government offered a bailout. The offer made to the musicians meant that the minimum pay would drop from $57,000 to $48,300 for a forty-two-week season. On Thursday, 25 June, the musicians rejected the offer. On Friday, 26 June, the accountants added up the assets in preparation for filing for bankruptcy the following Monday morning. All staff and musicians were asked to remove personal belongings from the premises. During the weekend William Broadhurst, the chairman of the Board, received a call from the musicians asking for a delay in the filing. They wanted to discuss a plan of income sharing that Tapper had previously put forward. On 2 July, the negotiating teams met and reached an agreement under which management's offer was accepted along with a plan whereby any income over the break-even point would be shared between musicians and the organization. The musicians felt they had been made to bear the brunt of bad management, and quite possibly they were right. With a $15.5 million break-even budget set for the next year, the filing for bankruptcy was withdrawn. The accumulated deficit at the end of the season was $3.3 million.

1992–1993   With the economic difficulties being dealt with and a pledge made to reduce the cumulative deficit within three years, it was time to address the musicians' contract. The management had asked the musicians to recommend a mediator to settle a number of outstanding non-monetary issues, and during the summer months a representative of Mediations Dispute Services had been working to bring both parties together. A further session took place on 21 September. There were significant problems to be solved but a resolution seemed possible. Rehearsals had begun and both management and the musicians were operating in good faith. An agreement in principal had also been reached with Roy Thomson Hall whereby the rent was reduced by 15 per cent and other outstanding issues were resolved. In early November an agreement with the hall was signed. The Canada Council and Metropolitan Toronto grants were frozen for one year, and the Ontario Arts Council grant was reduced. Administrative staff was downsized to forty-one from a high of sixty-one in August 1990. Many guest artists agreed to a major reduction in their fees for the season, which resulted in a $350,000 savings, but a downturn in the Canadian dollar produced some slippage in this area. The end-of-the-season financial statement showed a surplus of $256,000, reducing the cumulative deficit of $3,345,904 to $3,089,688 – an encouraging step in bringing the TS finances to a more acceptable level.

The opening program of the 1992–3 season consisted of two major orchestral works: the Serenade No. 2 in A major by Johannes Brahms and *Eine Alpensinfonie* by Richard Strauss. Perhaps Herbig was making a statement that behind the mire of financial controversy there was an excellent orchestra that deserved magnanimous

Emanuel Ax

support. The season line-up of guest conductors and artists certainly endorsed the high distinction of the TS on the North American concert scene. Among the artists who appeared with the orchestra or in the Great Performers series were violinists Anne-Sophie Mutter, Isaac Stern, and Itzhak Perlman, and pianists Vladimir Ashkenazy, Emanuel Ax, and Alfred Brendel. Mariss Jansons conducted a superb performance of Mahler's Symphony No. 2 ('Resurrection') with soprano Alessandra Marc, mezzo-soprano Jard van Nes, and the Toronto Mendelssohn Choir. Hugh Wolff conducted two subscription concerts. Jukka-Pekka Saraste made his TS debut on 4 November in a program that included two pieces by fellow countryman Jean Sibelius – *Pohjola's Daughter* and *The Swan of Tuonela*. The soloist for Beethoven's Piano Concerto No. 5 in E flat major ('Emperor') was another fellow countryman – pianist Olli Mustonen. Helmuth Rilling conducted performances of Haydn's oratorio *The Seasons*.

The season ended with an abundance of choral activity. The last subscription concert was a performance of Mahler's Symphony No. 8 in E flat ('Symphony of a Thousand') conducted by Günther Herbig, with sopranos Faye Robinson, Edith Wiens, and Tracy Dahl, mezzo-sopranos Marietta Simpson and Jean Stilwell, tenor Richard Taylor, baritone Richard Stilwell, and bass-baritone Gary Relyea, supported by the Toronto Mendelssohn Choir, the Vancouver Bach Choir, and the Toronto Children's Chorus.

On 6 June the 1993 International Choral Festival opened in Roy Thomson Hall under the artistic direction of Nicholas Goldschmidt. This was the second such festival organized by Goldschmidt, and the TS was engaged to participate in four concerts. For the opening concert, Benjamin Britten's *War Requiem* was presented with Bramwell Tovey conducting. The choirs were the Mennonite Chorus and the Toronto Children's Chorus, with soloists soprano Lorna Heywood, tenor Ben Heppner, and bass William Stone. On 16 June, two works were programmed: Antonín Dvořák's *Te Deum* and Jean Sibelius's choral symphony *Kullervo*, both conducted by the eminent Russian conductor Gennady Rozhdestvensky. The two choirs participating were the

Tchaikovsky Conservatory Choir and the Kullervo Festival Chorus, with soprano Soile Isokoski and baritone Walton Grönroos. The work chosen for the third concert, also conducted by Rozhdestvensky, was Mendelssohn's oratorio *St Paul*, a composition that has been overshadowed by his more popular *Elijah*. The Toronto Mendelssohn Choir was indeed the appropriate choir for this performance. The soloists were soprano Wendy Neilson, mezzo-soprano Gabrielle Prata, tenor Richard Margison, and baritone Cornelius Opthof. The closing concert of the festival presented Beethoven's Symphony No. 9 in D minor. Soprano Henriette Schellenberg, mezzo-soprano Janis Taylor, tenor Michael Schade, and bass-baritone Gary Relyea, along with the Prague Philharmonic Choir, the Toronto Mendelssohn Choir, and the Toronto Symphony were all conducted by Jukka-Pekka Saraste. Artistically the festival was an overwhelming success. Choirs from many corners of the world enjoyed a wonderful experience, and the soloists were for the most part Canadian. Unfortunately, the festival was not a financial success. The TS finished their season with a small reduction in the overall deficit.

1993–1994   Maestro Günther Herbig had agreed to remain as Music Director for an extra season while the search committee continued to look for a suitable replacement. During the latter portion of the 1992–3 season, a successor was found. On 29 September Robert Gillespie, the chairman of the Board, announced that Jukka-Pekka Saraste had been appointed Music Director and would take over at the beginning of the 1994–5 season.

Günther Herbig had an extensive repertoire and he did not hesitate to take advantage of it during his tenure with the TS. Like Ančerl, Herbig was always prepared to give instructive and informative rehearsals and he worked to cultivate in the orchestra a rich 'European' tone. Like Ančerl, he was also a disciplinarian. He worked hard to balance the sound of the orchestra – not an easy task considering the deceptive acoustics of Roy Thomson Hall – and achieved a certain success that was evident when the orchestra performed in concert halls that were more conducive to orchestral playing. In addition to his broad knowledge of music, Herbig had an extensive understanding of orchestral administration, a valuable asset for preparing future programs. In the matter of personnel, however, there were occasions when more discretion would have been in order; it was in this area that some musicians had difficulty in accepting Herbig.

Herbig's interpretation of the works of Brahms, Beethoven, Tchaikovsky, Shostakovich, and Hindemith is still remembered by musicians and audience alike. He

Soprano Henriette Schellenberg

opened his last TS season with a concert performance of Beethoven's opera *Fidelio*. The highly acclaimed cast included tenor Ben Heppner, soprano Eva-Maria Bundschuh, bass John Macurdy, soprano Edith Wiens, tenors Benoît Boutet and André Clouthier, baritone Allan Monk, bass-baritones Gary Relyea and Brian McIntosh, narrator Werner Klemperer, and the Toronto Mendelssohn Choir. Herbig's final concert as Music Director of the Toronto Symphony featured two works by Brahms: the Violin Concerto in D major with Itzhak Perlman as soloist and the Symphony No. 1 in C minor. As always, he gave a deeply felt and impeccably musical interpretation. On 20 October when Herbig programmed the *Kammermusik*, op. 49, for piano, brass, and harp by Hindemith, the pianist was his charming wife, Jutta Czapski.

In December the Toronto Symphony gave a special concert in honour of the hundredth anniversary of Sir Ernest MacMillan's birth. The concert opened with Andrew Davis playing MacMillan's organ solo *Cortège académique*, then Davis conducted the TS for *Overture*, a work composed by MacMillan in 1924. The next piece in the program was *Altitude* by Claude Champagne, a close friend of MacMillan's. The concert ended with Holst's *The Planets*, a work that MacMillan had admired and had recorded in 1943 with the TSO for RCA Victor. This centennial celebration was commemorated by an exhibit in Ottawa at the National Library of Canada, and for December, a portion of the exhibit was transferred to the lobby of Roy Thomson Hall.

The concerts on 20, 21, 22, and 25 April included works by Johann Hertal, François-Adrien Boieldieu, Richard Strauss, and Mozart. The soloists chosen were all principals of the TS: violist Steven Dann, violinist Mark Skazinetsky, cellist Daniel Domb, clarinettist Joaquin Valdepeñas, bassoonist Michael Sweeney, timpanist David Kent, and harpist Judy Loman. It seemed this was Herbig's way of acknowledging his appreciation of the musicianship of the orchestra. In an interview, Herbig was asked about the status of the artist in Europe compared to North America. His answer was that in Europe the artist is more treasured, while in North America the artist is adored.

Herbig had, and still retains, a high regard for the Toronto Symphony, and when he returns for guest engagements the musicians are reminded of his unique artistry.

Unfortunately the financial situation had not improved. At the end of the 1993–4 season the overall deficit was still over three million dollars, due mainly to a reduction in subscription sales. Aggressive competition for the entertainment dollar in the Greater Toronto Area also contributed to the situation – a challenge that the TS had to address resolutely and expeditiously.

Jukka-Pekka Saraste

Music is well said to be the speech of angels; in fact, nothing among the utterances allowed to man is felt to be so divine. It brings us near to the infinite.

THOMAS CARLYLE

Jorma Panula, now retired as professor of conducting at the Sibelius Academy in Helsinki, is still in demand the world over as a juror and teacher. All teaching faculties and orchestras want something of the man and the method that launched Esa-Pekka Salonen, Osmo Vanska, Sakari Oramo, and Jukka-Pekka Saraste, to name but four successful students. Three of these young conductors have held positions with British orchestras. Vanska was chief conductor of the BBC Scottish Symphony Orchestra, and Oramo is music director of the City of Birmingham Symphony Orchestra. Saraste was principal conductor of the Scottish Chamber Orchestra before he was appointed Music Director of the Toronto Symphony Orchestra. All of these conductors have great admiration for Panula's unerring instinct for talent, and an appreciation of Finnish culture and music that goes back to Sibelius and before.

For the previous thirty years the succession of music directors for the TSO had followed a pattern of a young, developing conductor taking over from a older, experienced one: Seiji Ozawa took over from Walter Susskind, Andrew Davis from Karel Ančerl, and now Saraste was taking over from Günther Herbig. In each case, the younger conductor inherited an orchestra that played with a precision and style developed by an older and more mature maestro.

Max Tapper had begun searching for a music director to replace Herbig in the midst of the financial turmoil of 1991–2. The TSO needed a young, energetic, enterprising conductor with an interest in contemporary music. The aim was to develop more publicity, attract younger audiences, and create musical excitement. Saraste made his TSO debut in November 1992 to conduct a program of Beethoven, Sibelius, and Scriabin. The entire orchestra immediately sensed something special. The musicians liked Saraste, and Saraste liked the TSO. On 29 September 1993, it was announced that Jukka-Pekka Saraste would become the next Music Director of the TSO. With Saraste's arrival the orchestra reverted to the original form of its name – Toronto Symphony Orchestra.

Toronto Symphony Orchestra, Jukka-Pekka Saraste, Music Director

1994–1995

Jukka-Pekka Saraste's appreciation for his country's most famous composer, Sibelius, was immediately apparent. The first concert of the subscription series was devoted to three Sibelius Symphonies: No. 5 in E flat, No. 6 in D minor, and No. 7 in C major. For the final concert in the Masterworks Series, Sibelius was again represented with the suite from *Tempest*, the Violin Concerto with soloist Ida Haendel, and the Symphony No. 1. Saraste also had an interest in assembling new suites of well-known compositions: the concerts on 12, 13, and 15 October included his suite of selections from Prokofiev's *Romeo and Juliet*, arranged to convey the action and emotions of the story.

In November Andrew Davis conducted a program entitled 'A Celebration of Strauss.' Ben Heppner was the soloist for five arias, which later became the basis for an excellent CBC recording of Richard Strauss's music played by the TSO with Davis conducting.

Recordings are vital to the professional status of a major orchestra, but the TSO had been without a contract since the two recordings made with EMI in 1987. During the mid-1980s Naxos was beginning to broaden its recording base, and had approached the TSO, but after a consultation with the musicians the offer was turned down. This was unfortunate, especially now that Naxos is receiving worldwide acclaim for high quality budget-priced recordings. Both the Finnish Radio Symphony Orchestra and the Scottish Chamber Orchestra had secured recording contracts under Saraste's conductorship. On 5 April 1995 the TSO accepted a proposal from Warner Music to record seven discs over the next three years – one with Warner's Erato label and six with the Finlandia label, secured through Saraste's efforts.

The 1994–5 season also saw a sudden administrative change. In early April, Max Tapper informed Board chairman Robert Martin of his decision to resign as Managing Director of the TSO effective 30 April 1995, in order to pursue another career direction. Speculation, however, suggested that his reason for leaving may have been personal. Tapper had been faced with many problems, the worst being in 1993 when the orchestra narrowly avoided voluntary bankruptcy. The drastic measures he introduced at that time had saved the orchestra. The Board felt that the TSO should not be without executive leadership for an extended period. Someone who knew both the demands of the art form and the business of symphony orchestras was needed immediately. To that end, the Executive Committee unanimously recommended the temporary appointment of Stanley Shortt, a long-time member of the Board who had extensive experience within the business community, as Managing Director until a permanent replacement could be found.

1995–1996

In Canada during the 1990s various levels of government were reducing their support of performing arts organizations to such a degree that it seemed they were neglecting of the cultural heritage of the nation – or at least setting a new basis for funding whereby arts organizations were forced go to the corporate and private sectors for substantial financial support. Total cuts in government support for the 1995–6 season amounted to 13.9 per cent with a further 20.8 per cent anticipated for the 1996–7 season. In the United States, a support framework of corporate and private donors is commonplace and, to a certain extent, successful, owing to generous tax breaks given

Larry Weeks, Principal Trumpet, 1983–97

to sponsors of the arts. Advantages available to American orchestras also include postal subsidies, and exemptions from sales tax and from capital gains tax for gifts of appreciated property. Orchestras in cities such as New York, Boston, Cleveland, and Chicago have built up substantial endowments because of such advantageous arrangements.

Contract negotiations with the musicians were also scheduled during this season – the first contract negotiations since the 15 per cent cut in 1995. It would not be easy to reach a settlement when cash-flow difficulties were an ongoing challenge and reduced support from all levels of government was reflected in an overall deficit of $3.6 million by the end of the year. However the new four-year contract completed in March 1995 allowed for break-even budgets for all subsequent years. The musicians had agreed to an increase to forty-three weeks in the 1997–8 season and to forty-four in the 1998–9 season. They would receive a 1 per cent increase in 1996–7 and 2½ per cent in 1997–8. Stanley Shortt reported that this agreement had been achieved through hard work and cooperation from all parties.

While financial problems were being dealt with, the orchestra continued to present interesting and exciting concerts. On Saturday, 9 March, the TSO performed at Carnegie Hall, New York, with guest artist Frank Peter Zimmermann, who played Beethoven's Violin Concerto in D major. Two Sibelius symphonies – No. 6 in D minor and No. 7 in C major – completed a well-received program. The President's Evening on 21 May was a fund-raising gala concert in support of the TSO. Two internationally acclaimed artists – Itzhak Perlman and Pinchas Zukerman – played the J.S. Bach

Concerto for Two Violins in D minor and Mozart's Sinfonia Concertante in E flat major, and Jukka-Pekka Saraste conducted the Funtek and Gortchakov arrangement of Mussorgsky's *Pictures at an Exhibition* to complete the concert. This festive evening added a net profit of more than $200,000 to the TSO's depleted treasury.

1996–1997

After a season in which money problems had clouded the artistic scene, the celebration of the seventy-fifth anniversary of the TSO promised a refreshing change. The main theme for the season was an invitation to all previous music directors and assistant conductors to return for a visit and once again conduct the orchestra. On 29 November Seiji Ozawa came for a memorable program of Tōru Takemitsu's *Requiem for Strings*, Mozart's Piano Concerto in A major, K 414, with Leon Fleisher, and Dvořák's Symphony No. 9 in E minor ('From the New World'). This concert was the focal point for the launching of the Fund for the Future campaign – a project planned to raise $10 million to strengthen the Endowment Fund so that it could play a more significant role in the financial life of the orchestra. Andrew Davis, the TSO Conductor Laureate, returned for two consecutive weeks. His first week included Brahms's Piano Concerto No. 2 in B flat major, with Emanuel Ax as soloist, and Richard Strauss's *Ein Heldenleben* (A Hero's Life). In his second week he presented a choral work that had played an important part in his conducting career: Leos Janáček's *Glagolitic Mass* with soprano Eva Urbanová, mezzo-soprano Maria Popescu, tenor Gary Lakes, bass-baritone Gary Relyea, organist John Tuttle, and the Toronto Mendelssohn Choir. Between the main concerts Davis also conducted a Young People's Concert (a series he often led during his years as Music Director). The last work on the program was *Carnival of the Animals* by Camille Saint-Saëns, with pianists Andrew Davis wearing a lion costume and Patricia Krueger wearing a lion tamer's costume complete with black leather boots! Did those children enjoy the afternoon? Their laughter and screams of delight almost drowned out the music, and they will undoubtedly remember that day every time they hear this music.

Victor Feldbrill began his long association with the TSO in high school when he became his school's representative for the student concerts under Sir Ernest MacMillan. MacMillan also gave him an opportunity to conduct the TSO in 1943. Feldbrill was a violinist in the orchestra from 1949 to 1956. In the mid-1970s he created and developed the orchestra's Light Classics series. For this seventy-fifth season he conducted the opening concert of that series. Feldbrill also founded the TSYO and served as conductor from 1974 to 1978.

Andrew Davis in costume for a performance of *Carnival of the Animals*

Kazuyoshi Akiyama, who was an assistant conductor of the TSO during the Ozawa years, came back on 5, 6, and 8 March to conduct a program that included Rachmaninoff's Piano Concerto No. 2 with Arthur Ozolins as soloist, and Tchaikovsky's Symphony No. 4 in F minor. In the Great Composers series, Günther Herbig, who was well known for his interpretations of works by Brahms, returned to conduct two Brahms symphonies: No. 1 in C minor and No. 3 in F major.

For the opening concerts of this seventy-fifth season Yo-Yo Ma was the guest artist performing the Elgar Cello Concerto in E minor on 17 September and the Dvořák Cello Concerto in B minor on 18 September. In that same week, the TSO returned to Massey Hall for a special seventy-fifth anniversary concert, complete with nostalgic repertoire and a video produced by Norman Campbell portraying many of the orchestra's historical milestones. Shuter Street was closed between Victoria Street and Yonge Street to allow for further festivities after the concert. One work included in the concert was *A Summer Idyll* by Leo Smith, the principal cellist of the TSO from 1932 to 1940.

The President's Evening concert saw Anne-Sophie Mutter return to perform Mozart's Violin Concerto No. 4 in D major, K 218, and the *Carmen fantasie* by Pablo de Sarasate. During this season, the TSO participated in a week-long Canadian music celebration involving a collaboration of several new music organizations in Toronto and entitled 'Made in Canada.' The TSO also participated in the Northern Encounters Festival, a celebration of music and arts of the circumpolar nations. The TSO's contribution was three weeks of concerts, including a performance of Sibelius's *Kullervo* with the distinguished Polytech Choir of Finland.

The season closed with a free lunchtime concert in Metro Square on 20 June 1997. Mary Lou Fallis, dressed in the colours of the Canadian flag, joined Jukka-Pekka Saraste and the TSO to sing *O Canada* at the top of the program. Later, she entertained the audience with two of her favourite songs: *Paddle Your Own Canoe* and *Oh! What a Difference Since the Hydro Came.*

On 3 July, Stanley Shorrt welcomed and introduced Gary Kulesha to the TSO Board as Composer Adviser. This position had been established to support and review the many contemporary scores that were submitted to the orchestra.

1997–1998   Over the past few seasons, ticket prices had become a subject of much discussion. The TSO, like other performing arts organizations, realized that patrons were more budget conscious. In the 1950s, 1960s, and 1970s patrons who purchased subscription tickets for series of ten to twelve concerts considered it no great loss if they found they were unable to attend two or three performances. However with the less stable financial situation of the mid-1980s patrons had become more concerned about their entertainment dollar. If they purchased a series, they wanted to be sure that all the tickets would be used. Consequently, single tickets sales began to rise while subscriptions were on a downswing. This was especially true for large series; smaller series also were losing ground but not as quickly.

In his memoirs, Sir Georg Solti made the following observation about subscription series:

> Every system has its disadvantages, and to my mind a common disadvantage in the United States is the subscription series, which is needed because there are no state subsidies. If well over ninety per cent of the seats for an entire concert season are sold many months in advance by subscription, as was the case in Chicago during my time there, the organization enjoys a wide margin of financial safety, but subscriptions do not always create the best atmosphere for music-making. An ideal audience is made up of people who see that a certain programme is going to be given, are interested in hearing those pieces, and buy their tickets accordingly. Many subscribers attend concerts simply because they have already paid for their tickets. Regardless of the works being performed or who is performing them, they go every Tuesday, Thursday or Saturday, even if they aren't in the mood. Many are easily distracted and cough or clear their throats during soft passages or long-held notes. I found this so annoying once that I turned to the audience and said: 'If you knew how long we worked on this pianissimo phrase, you would control your coughing.'[1]

Solti may not be alone in his opinion. On one occasion, when an excessive amount of coughing during a slow movement of a symphony was followed by a crescendo of coughing during the short break, Andrew Davis turned to the audience and said, 'Let's all clear our throats so we can enjoy the music.' For the balance of the evening there was noticeable restraint.

The season opened with Mahler's Symphony No. 8 in E flat ('Symphony of a Thousand'). The large cast engaged for the three performances included sopranos Edith Wiens, Christine Brewer, and Valdine Anderson, mezzo-sopranos Sara Fulgoni and Christine Cairns, tenor Michael Sylvester, baritone Richard Zeller, and bass-baritone Gary Relyea, along with the Toronto Mendelssohn Choir, the Kitchener-Waterloo Philharmonic Choir, and the Toronto Children's Chorus. Including the orchestra, Saraste was conducting a gathering of about 400 performers.

The orchestra left town for concerts in several other venues. The first was a visit to the new Living Arts Centre in Mississauga. Hammerson Hall (its official title) was an extremely pleasant facility with good acoustic qualities. The TSO was conducted by Pinchas Zukerman, who also played the Mozart Violin Concerto No. 3 in G major, K 216, and Schubert's Rondo in A major for violin and string orchestra. The second out-of-town concert was at Carnegie Hall in New York. The orchestra was joined by the percussion ensemble Nexus for Tōru Takemitsu's *From me flows what you call time*, a work commissioned by Carnegie Hall for its 1990–1 centennial celebration. John Wyre, one of the five members of Nexus, had been a percussionist in the TSO for a number of years. The other work on the program was *Lemminkäinen Suite* by Jean Sibelius, with the English horn solos magnificently played by the TSO's Cary Ebli.

Under Andrew Davis, the TSO had been fortunate to be invited to Carnegie Hall on an annual basis. Unfortunately, during the recent financial struggles the orchestra management unwisely cancelled a booking, with the result that Carnegie Hall did not extend an invitation for the next few years. Concerts in this famous hall are of vital importance to the ongoing reputation of any orchestra – on a par with performances at the Salzburg Festival, the Edinburgh International Festival, or the BBC Proms in Royal Albert Hall. At these venues, the proficiency of an orchestra is demonstrated to the world, and excellent performances are remembered.

The Toronto Symphony Youth Orchestra was invited to participate in the highly regarded Guelph Spring Festival. Under conductor David Zafer, they gave a high-spirited and well-received performance of the overture to Mozart's opera *The Marriage of Figaro*, Mendelssohn's Violin Concerto in E minor with soloist Shane Kim (a former TSYO concertmaster), and Symphony No. 4 in F minor by Tchaikovsky.

The TSO also gave two concerts in the second 'Made in Canada' festival. The first concert presented a number of new compositions by Canadian composers. The second included the suite from Stravinsky's *L'oiseau de feu* (The Firebird). Perhaps festival organizers were thinking of Ralph Vaughan Williams, who wrote, 'Many young composers make the mistake of assuming that they can be universal before they had been local.' The Stravinsky suite is perhaps an example of what it takes to become universal.

On 25 June, George Tiviluk, the chairman of the Board, announced that Catherine Cahill had been appointed Executive Director as of the end of August. The 'Fund for the Future' campaign was also proceeding satisfactorily, with $6 million of a $10 million goal raised to date.

1998–1999   Catherine Cahill came from the New York Philharmonic Orchestra, where she held the position of general manager. She was energetic and enthusiastic, and was undoubtedly keen to undertake her new position. One of her first decisions was to cancel a performance of Schoenberg's *Gurrelieder*. Planning for the production was already at an advanced stage, due to the large choral forces needed for the work, but Cahill decided that in view of the expense involved, it would be more profitable to open the season with a three-week Beethoven festival. Cahill's decision did have some merit, considering the TSO's large accumulated deficit, but since the last season had closed with a Beethoven festival, it might have been better to present a Tchaikovsy or Schubert festival.

A tour to Florida, the first tour the orchestra had undertaken since its European tour of 1992, was the most exciting event of the season. The orchestra left Toronto on 25 January and gave its first concert in West Palm Beach. The soloist for the tour was the young Canadian pianist Stewart Goodyear, who played the Rachmaninoff *Rhapsody on a Theme of Paganini*. Other tour repertoire included Jean Sibelius's Symphony No. 1, Gary Kulesha's *The Gates of Time* (written in 1991 on a commission from CBC Radio), and Beethoven's Symphony No. 3 in E flat major ('Eroica').

Conductor Laureate Andrew Davis returned to lead two moving performances of Benjamin Britten's *War Requiem* with soprano Elena Prokina, tenor Ben Heppner, baritone Håkan Hagegård, the Toronto Mendelssohn Choir, and the Toronto Children's Chorus.

At the end of February 1999, the orchestra was surprised to learn that Catherine Cahill had given notice to the Board that she was resigning. She said that she was extremely sad to leave the orchestra, but because of family circumstances she had no

Tenor Ben Heppner

alternative but to take this step. This was an unfortunate situation, since the search committee set up by the Board had spent much time in finding a suitable person for this important job. The close of the season also meant that the musicians' current contract had expired, and there was every indication that the new round of negotiations would be extremely difficult.

The 1999–2000 season was one of the most controversial in the history of the Toronto Symphony Orchestra, and by the end, the organization was faced with many new challenges and conditions. With the departure of Catherine Cahill,

1999–2000

the Board decided to engage the services of Nick Webster as adviser to management. Webster had many years of experience on the administrative staff of the New York Philharmonic Orchestra dealing with musician-management negotiations.

At a Board meeting on 13 May 1999 Gary Labovitz, chairman of the Orchestra Committee, presented a statement reflecting the expectations of the musicians as they headed into negotiations. He reminded the Board of the sacrifices the musicians had already made. When bankruptcy was threatened in the mid-1990s, they took a 15 per cent cut in salary (equal to eight weeks of work) to ensure the future of the orchestra. The musicians had also agreed to reduce the orchestra's complement by three members in order to keep costs down, to perform eight donated services per year (the equivalent of one full week), and to virtually eliminate overtime payments by adding fifteen minutes to the length of concerts. Labovitz went on to state that the musicians felt it was unfortunate that the Board had not capitalized on these sacrifices.

On 18 August George Tiviluk, chairman of the Board, announced the cancellation of an eighteen-day European tour planned for February and March 2000. Two or three sources of significant funding that seemed certain a few months ago were now reluctant to confirm their support, and without appropriate funding the Board was forced to make this decision. Meanwhile, since contract negotiations were proceeding with no prospect of a firm deal, the musicians announced that they would go on strike as of Saturday, 25 September. The opening concert of the season on 23 September, with Kathleen Battle as soloist, and two run-out concerts (to Barrie on 18 September and Uxbridge on 19 September) were given before the strike deadline.

As of Saturday, 25 September, at 5:00 p.m. the TSO musicians were on strike for the second time in the orchestra's seventy-five-year history. The first concerts were cancelled immediately and cancellations continued as each week passed. In the midst of the strike, however, two concerts with pop singer James Taylor were already sold out. The musicians decided to suspend their strike just long enough to play the concerts, but at the last moment, the plan fell apart and the musicians were left in an uncomfortable situation with the union. The union had suggested to the TSO management that they play the two concerts as a benefit for the striking TSO musicians. Meanwhile, James Taylor had left Boston airport with the understanding that the concerts were on. Upon his arrival in Toronto he was informed that they had been cancelled, so he stayed in the airport and returned to Boston on the next flight. The many patrons who had bought tickets for these two shows were not impressed and expressed their displeasure in numerous letters, e-mails, and faxes.

As the strike continued through October and November, the musicians arranged their own concerts at various venues in the city. One concert took place in the warehouse of the Toronto Daily Bread Food Bank, and others were given in the Ford Centre for the Performing Arts, the Columbus Centre, and the Rex Hotel. In an interview on CBC Jukka-Pekka Saraste offered support for the musicians, but predicted disaster for Ontario's foundering arts institutions unless a consensus in the community was reached on how the arts were to be funded. 'If a society of culture wants to maintain a first-rate arts organization such as this orchestra,' he said, 'it has to be prepared to pay for it.' On Wednesday, 3 November, talks resumed for the first time since the strike began, but broke off hours later when the negotiating committee representing the striking musicians rejected what management called its final offer. At this point, the Board took an unusual and controversial step: they sent copies of the proposal by courier to each musician of the orchestra, advocating that the offer be put to a vote of the whole orchestra – a questionable tactic when tensions were running high on both sides. In early November, Jukka-Pekka Saraste called on Toronto mayor Mel Lastman to step in and help to negotiate a settlement. On 1 December, a closed meeting took place between management and City Hall. The mayor's office indicated they would help only if both sides showed an interest in working toward a solution, and now both parties appeared to be on board. On 7 December, the musicians and management met in an attempt to resolve the wage dispute and were able to reach to an agreement on a new four-year contract, which both sides consequently ratified. This meant that the scheduled TSO concerts could resume, beginning with the annual performances of Handel's *Messiah* conducted by Andrew Davis.

The agreement meant an increase in the minimum salary for the musicians from $53,169 to $69,000 in year four (an increase of 29.8 per cent over four years). Despite the savings on musicians' salaries, guest-artist fees, hall rental, and technicians' fees, the TSO lost about $500,000 during the seventy-four-day strike. If the strike had continued much longer, the shortened European tour that the Executive Committee had finally approved would also have been lost. The shortened tour included concerts in Germany, Austria, and Hungary; concerts in England and Spain that had been part of the original tour were cancelled.

The strike left much to contemplate, including whether or not Toronto really values its symphony orchestra. The quick answer is 'not much' – compared with the public support shown by the citizens of Detroit, Cleveland, and Boston. In his column in the *Toronto Star* on 18 December music critic William Littler commented that perhaps the real question was whether we truly do want such an orchestra. The musicians were surprised to learn of the apathy of the public towards their cause. Such a thing could not happen in Cleveland – a city that cares enough about its orchestra to have cushioned it with a multi-million dollar endowment and to have spent $36 million to expand, renovate, and restore Severance Hall, making it once again a state-of-the-art concert hall.

Early in 2000, preparations were made for the European tour. The soloists were all resident in Europe, which relieved the TSO of additional travelling expenses. One of the soloists was Sabine Meyer, a clarinettist who had for a short while been principal clarinet for the Berlin Philharmonic Orchestra under Herbert von Karajan. She had found it difficult to be the only female musician in the orchestra and had left to eventually become one of the leading wind soloists of her generation. Meyer joined the TSO for concerts in Berlin and Vienna, and at the Berlin Philharmonie she played Weber's Clarinet Concerto No. 1 in F minor. German violinist Christian Tetzlaff performed at four concerts: he played the Dvořák Violin Concerto in Stuttgart and Cologne, and the Bartók Violin Concerto No. 2 in Frankfurt and Vienna. The balance of the tour repertoire consisted of *Dance Suite* by Béla Bartók, Beethoven's Symphony No. 7 in A major, Gary Kulesha's *The True Colour of the Sky* (a TSO commission), Peter

Jukka-Pekka Saraste

Lieberson's *Fire*, and Rachmaninoff's *Symphonic Dances*. The third soloist was cellist Clemens Hagen, who played the Shostakovich Cello Concerto No. 1 in Vienna and Budapest.

The first concert in Europe was at the Liederhalle in Stuttgart. This was followed by performances at the Philharmonie in Berlin, the Philharmonie in Cologne, and the Patria Hall in Budapest. The tour culminated with the prestigious Triale at the Musikverein. One international orchestra is invited each season to give this series of three different programs. The visit to Vienna had been in question just before the orchestra left Toronto. The inclusion of Joerg Haider's far-right Freedom Party in Austria's coalition government had raised international concerns and the orchestra questioned whether or not they should perform in Austria. Finally the orchestra decided to go to Vienna, since the majority of Austria's population was not sympathetic towards Haider, and was very much concerned about the situation. Other performing organizations had the same dilemma, including the City of Birmingham Symphony Orchestra and the Scottish Opera, but they all decided not to boycott Austria.

In all tours there are unexpected problems, and on this tour the problems involved illness. Timpanist David Kent had to be admitted to a Berlin Hospital with a serious bout of pneumonia and composer Gary Kulesha suffered serious migraine headaches which forced him to return to Toronto. The most bizarre incident did not occur until the TSO arrived back at Toronto Airport. In the excitement of a reunion with her husband and daughter, violist Mary Carol Nugent left her valuable instrument on the floor of the parking garage at Terminal 2. Both she and her husband thought that the other had picked it up. On returning to the airport the viola was gone, but surprisingly it was returned intact two months later. The person returning the instrument said he had found it in the trunk of his car.

The tour proved a success, and demonstrated that the TSO produced a brilliant sound, given the right facility in which to perform. Reviews received from all cities where the orchestra played were highly appreciative and favourable.

At the beginning of April 2000, Jukka-Pekka Saraste announced to the Board that he would be resigning at the end of the 2000–1 season. His reasons were simply that he wished to return to Finland to continue to conduct the Finnish Radio Symphony Orchestra, and also to become more involved in the European music scene. This situation left the TSO without a music director to consult for the preparation of the 2001–2 season. The Board and management discussed the situation and decided to approach Conductor Laureate Sir Andrew Davis for advice as to who might be available. Davis quickly remedied the problem by offering to assist, and Saraste also offered to guest conduct the TSO for four weeks.

The opening of the 2000–1 season was a complete change from the usual format for TSO 'first nights.' The orchestra made its season debut with an acoustical reading session in the Apotex Theatre within the Toronto Centre for the Arts. The purpose of this exercise was to evaluate the possibilities of this 1,800-seat auditorium for future TSO use. In order to fulfil its mandate for more outreach the TSO was planning more concerts in the Greater Toronto Area, and the Apotex Theatre was one of the facilities chosen. The acoutistical reading sessions included excerpts from works by Samuel Barber, Leonard Bernstein, Johannes Brahms, Dmitri Shostakovich, Igor Stravinsky, Pyotr Il'yich Tchaikovsky, and John Williams, with the conducting shared between Errol Gay and Gary Kulesha. The results of the session were favourable and a group of programs were chosen to be performed there at the end of the season.

2000–2001

The second performance of the season was another 'first.' The TSO, conducted by Michael Lankester, was invited to play Prokofiev's memorable film score written for Sergei Eisenstein's classic 1938 silent film *Alexander Nevsky* for a screening in Massey Hall during the Toronto International Film Festival, as part of a special program for the festival's twenty-fifth anniversary. The third 'opening night' for the season was originally planned to include Kennedy but he had cancelled due to recording commitments. Christian Tetzlaff, who had performed with the orchestra on its recent European tour, fulfilled the engagement with an outstanding performance of Brahms's Violin Concerto in D major. For the Monday matinee repeat of the program, the talented young Catherine Manoukian gave a vivacious performance of Dvořák's Violin Concerto in A minor.

The 2000–1 season included two Canadian premieres. The first of these was the Symphony No. 3 by Edward Elgar. The symphony had been commissioned by the BBC in 1932, but was unfortunately left incomplete at Elgar's death in 1934. Elgar had asked for the incomplete score to be burnt, but this did not happen. Instead, his daughter

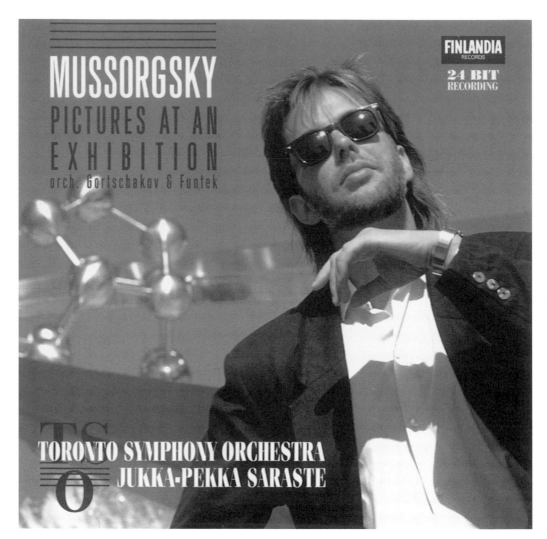

The TSO's first release on Finlandia/Warner

Caroline presented the assorted sketches to Sir Adrian Boult as a representative of the BBC. In 1993, after consultations with the Elgar family, Anthony Payne began working on a reconstruction of the symphony. The world premiere of the reconstructed work was given by the BBC Symphony Orchestra conducted by Andrew Davis on 15 February 1998 in the Royal Festival Hall, London. The North American premiere was given the following November by the Philadelphia Orchestra, again conducted by Davis. The Canadian performance, originally scheduled for December 1999, had been postponed because of the musicians' strike, but finally, on 6 December 2000, the Toronto Symphony Orchestra gave the Canadian premiere of Anthony Payne's reconstruction of Sir Edward Elgar's Symphony No. 3. The performance was an immense success. Andrew

Davis described the reconstruction as one of the greatest achievements of musical detection, and praised Payne's imaginative creativity in his use of Elgar's sketches. The musicians agreed that the score was woven together so well that it was difficult to recognize the portions that were not Elgar's original.

Schoenberg's song cycle *Gurrelieder* – settings of Danish poems by Jens Peter Jacobsen composed between 1900 and 1911 – requires an orchestra of 140 musicians – the largest individual orchestra assembled on Roy Thomson Hall's stage to date. The Toronto Mendelssohn Choir was augmented by the Victoria Scholars for a total of 200 voices and the stage was extended to allow room for the podium and the soloists. The soloists for this exciting performance were soprano Andrea Gruber, mezzo-soprano Lilli Paasikivi, tenors Ben Heppner and Benjamin Butterfield, bass-baritone Gary Relyea, and narrator Ernst Haefliger. This presentation of the *Gurrelieder* given on 14 and 16 June was the farewell performance for Jukka-Pekka Saraste as Music Director of the TSO.

In February 2001 the Toronto Symphony Orchestra was awarded its third Juno, this time for a recording of the *Four Lemminkäinen Legends* by Jean Sibelius. For both Saraste and the orchestra this was an honour to be cherished. During his tenure Jukka-Pekka Saraste had with justified pride conducted the entire Sibelius orchestral repertoire, with special emphasis on the less familiar works such as these legends. Audiences had been enriched by the opportunity to become closer acquainted with the music of Sibelius.

In the early spring the board and management of Roy Thomson Hall announced a major renovation to commence in March 2002. Plans included alterations to the interior of the hall to address the acoustic problems, adjustments to the ground-level seating to create two aisles to allow easier access, removal of the carpet from the ground floor, and installation of new adjustable sound baffles. The cost for these major alterations was estimated at $20 million.

The 2000–1 season closed with nine summer concerts in four different Toronto locations: four on Centre Island, two at Harbourfront, two at the Toronto Centre for the Arts, and a mid-day concert in Roy Thomson Hall. These concerts were conducted by Christopher Seaman, Carl Davis, and Errol Gay, and brought an inspiring end to a full season.

It is fitting that this chapter should close with an important reference to the future. From the early days, education has been an important element in the life of the TSO. Performance events have included Young People's Concerts on Saturday afternoons and an extensive series of school concerts, when thousands of students come to Roy

Thomson Hall for concerts. Under the Adopt-a-Player program, musicians lead a class of students in the creation of a new piece of music. The Toronto Symphony Youth Orchestra, formed in 1974 under Victor Feldbrill, has been perhaps the most prominent of the TSO's education projects. Many of these young musicians have gone on to join orchestras in North America and abroad, and some have 'graduated' to the senior orchestra. Recently the TSYO celebrated its twenty-fifth anniversary, and to commemorate this occasion the orchestra was invited to represent Canada at the International Festival of Youth Orchestras in Banff. Unfortunately there was little media coverage, especially in Toronto, of this important event in the lives of the many highly talented young musicians.

The 'torch' of education has passed from Emily Tedd and Sir Ernest MacMillan to dedicated personnel such as Barbara Manktelow, Loie Fallis, and Roberta Smith. The future of classical music rests in the hands of young, talented, enthusiastic, and dedicated purveyors. It is our task to provide and encourage them in their challenge in order to produce great music for years to come.

Toward the Unknown: 2001–2002

... toward the unknown region,

where neither ground is for the feet, nor any path to follow?

No map, there, nor guide,

nor voice sounding ...

— Walt Whitman

The future for symphony orchestras in Canada is, at best, unpredictable. It seems that governments at all levels have failed to realize the importance of cultural organizations and the benefits they bestow on the nation. The Toronto Symphony Orchestra is a great orchestra but it cannot maintain its high standards if it must constantly worry about where the next dollar is coming from. In the last week of September 2001 the Toronto Symphony Orchestra found itself in challenging circumstances.

Jukka-Pekka Saraste's tenure had been one of administrative turmoil. When Saraste took up the position of Music Director, Max Tapper was General Manager of the orchestra, but a year later Tapper suddenly resigned and for the next six years Saraste was without the support of a permanent Managing Director. Board member Stanley Shortt had been asked to take care of basic management duties for what was intended as a one-year arrangement while the Board searched for a suitable replacement. Three years later, Catherine Cahill was appointed, but she resigned after six months, to be followed by two management consultants. The first, Nick Webster, was an adviser who came from the New York Philharmonic. Eighteen months later Webster's place was taken by Jack Murta, who was brought in as chairman of the management team.

The long wait for a new Executive Director for the TSO came to an end in October 2000, when Robert Weiss announced the appointment of Ed Smith. Smith had begun his twenty-two years as chief executive of the City of Birmingham Symphony Orchestra at a time when that orchestra was facing difficulties due to the sudden departure of conductor Louis Frémaux. Smith took a bold step of putting the orchestra into the hands of a young conductor whom he had known from his days with the Royal Liverpool Philharmonic Orchestra. Simon Rattle was appointed principal conductor of the City of Birmingham Symphony Orchestra in 1979. Since then, the orchestra has become a highly regarded ensemble and Sir Simon Rattle is now one of the foremost international conductors. Ed Smith's management style was unobtrusive but strikingly imaginative and effective.

In early August 2001 Ed Smith forwarded an extensive and detailed memorandum to the chairman of the Board and the chairman of the finance committee. The memo posed a number of forthright questions addressing not only present problems but also challenges to be faced over the next five to ten years. Did the TSO have sufficient confidence to sustain itself artistically and fiscally and to work its way out of the deficit? What was the predicted viability of attracting an energetic and inspiring Music Director? During the 2000–1 season there had been a shortfall of $1,650,000. A number of reasonable assumptions made in 2000 had proved to be either unachievable in the short term or over-optimistic for the long term. This could also be said for the prior season. Smith listed several issues in the area of musician-management relationships. The agreement negotiated with the musicians contained ambiguities and negativism. Furthermore, management's ability to effect change through negotiation was compromised because the financial settlement with the musicians extended to 2003. Smith also pointed to evidence of a deep-seated culture of mistrust between musicians and management that manifested itself in either open hostility or suppressed frustration. With mistrust and deception comes a sense of fear and intimidation that, Smith said, was probably a result of a ten-year lack of realistic leadership within the body of musicians, both musically and politically.

Both Board and management were aware of this situation, but over thirteen years crucial matters had been swept under the carpet in hopes that they would be forgotten or would disappear. Instead, the situation had broadened and deepened. The sense of goodwill and trust that had existed among musicians, management, and the Board some fifteen to thirty years ago had been slowly and effectively destroyed by internal bickering and scepticism. It should also be noted that the situation facing the orchestra was not unique to the TSO, but was prevalent in other symphony orchestras, especially on the western side of the Atlantic Ocean.

At a Board meeting on 24 September 2001 Ed Smith announced his resignation. In early July he had indicated that he was not sure that the TSO would survive, and now he had come to the conclusion that the infrastructure of the TSO was not robust enough to support another crisis. Smith emphasized that this was not simply a financial issue. It is true that you can't have a great orchestra without substantial financial resources, but those resources alone will not guarantee excellence. Problems that began over a decade ago had insidiously eaten into the corporate body and embedded themselves firmly in the culture of the orchestra itself. During his short tenure, Smith had indeed pinpointed the problems within the organization. The Board agreed with his diagnosis and appreciated his honesty, but they disagreed with his statement that there was no cure. Board members felt that the diverse body of individuals who maintain and value the Toronto Symphony Orchestra had the ability to navigate a course that would restore, preserve, and consolidate their orchestra.

On the following day, 25 September, Board chairman Robert Weiss called a meeting of musicians and administration at Roy Thomson Hall. In the fiscal year ending 30 June 2001 the orchestra had incurred an operating deficit of over $2 million, which increased the overall deficit to $7 million. On 28 September the TSO would theoretically run out of money. In the light of this challenging situation the Board had decided on a restructuring plan that would come into effect within the next few days. A chief restructuring officer was to have full authority over TSO operations. The momentous task now facing the orchestra was to secure $1.5 million in new operating funds by 30 November and to increase the operating line of credit by more than $1 million.

The TSO press release issued on 28 September provoked an immediate reaction from orchestral associations across North America. When a major symphony orchestra is seriously threatened, other orchestras look to their own situations and study their financial positions closely. As Norman Lebrecht wrote in the *London Daily Telegraph*, 'Orchestras in North America are entering a nightmare zone. A crisis in Toronto has triggered shockwaves across the continent with even the mightiest fingering their inside collar.'[2] Orchestras in Britain and Europe received the disconcerting news via the Internet. As the affair became known internationally the press coverage, with varying degrees of sensationalism and truthfulness, increased to such a level that in mid-October a media black-out was imposed.

On 29 September Robert Weiss announced that Lambert Huizingh had been appointed chief restructuring officer. Huizingh, a former partner of Price Waterhouse Cooper, immediately formed a restructuring committee consisting of six board members, three musicians, and three individuals from the Toronto business community, along with Board Chairman Bob Rae as an adviser. At this point the TSO had run out of operating funds and needed $1.5 million to continue through until 30 November. This pressure was relieved somewhat when Douglas Derry, chairman of the Toronto

Symphony Foundation, announced that the foundation had agreed to advance $1.5 million to meet the orchestra's immediate needs.

By December the situation had become slightly clearer. The annual general meeting planned for mid-November was rescheduled for mid-December, owing to delays on the part of government departments in authorizing the payment of approximately $5 million from the foundation. The annual meeting date was again postponed, this time to early January 2002, at which time it was hoped that a new Executive Director would be appointed.

Meanwhile the orchestra had maintained its program schedule with concerts conducted by a distinguished group of guest conductors including Günther Herbig, Andrew Davis, Jiří Bělohlávek, Emmanuel Kirvine, Richard Hickox, and Yakov Kreizberg. Toronto Mayor Mel Lastman declared 13 December as 'Toronto Symphony Orchestra and Yo-Yo Ma Day.' The concert that evening was given as a benefit for the TSO. Ma played two well-known concertos: the Cello Concerto in C major, Hob. VIIb/5, by Franz Joseph Haydn, and the Cello Concerto in B minor, op. 104, by Antonín Dvořák. This concert also included a performance of Wagner's overture to *The Flying Dutchman* for which musicians from the TSYO joined the senior orchestra. With funding in place, the balance of the 2001–2 season now seemed secure, and plans for the 2002–3 season, the Toronto Symphony Orchestra's eightieth, were under way. In an open letter from the Toronto Symphony Orchestra dated 11 December 2001, Bob Rae stated that the Toronto Symphony Orchestra remained committed to providing the citizens of Toronto and Canada with a world-class musical experience.

In order to receive the special emergency funding the TSO had to produce a balanced budget. Both musicians and senior staff were asked to accept pay cuts in order to safeguard the continued survival of the orchestra, and the viability of maintaining a ninety-eight-member orchestra was also questioned. (It should be noted that many of the world's leading ensembles range between eighty-five and ninety musicians.) Finally, the Board accepted the need to update its own structure and operations. At the next annual general meeting the Board of sixty-plus members would be replaced by a significantly smaller body.

Where does the future lie for symphony orchestras? The plan proposed for the TSO looks good and gives the impression that many of the problems may be solved, but will the solution be long-lasting? In an article in the *Toronto Star* William Littler wrote, 'Why this roller coaster between solvency and panic? Because our orchestras lack financial security. They are so inconsistently funded that they lurch from crisis to resolution and back to crisis again with frightening ease.'[3] The need for and importance

When someone says to me, 'Can you imagine anything worse?' the answer is yes, I can. And I can also tell you how it happens: it happens because of neglect. It happens because people say it's somebody else's job to give; it's somebody else's job to go; it's somebody else's job to care. That is the beginning of civil neglect. That's the beginning of civic decline.

The choice is ours. We can begin a process of civil renewal – the kind of city we say we want to live in, one in which we can be proud. Where we will have great institutions. But not just great institutions: great experiences, great moments.

I don't think there is anyone who has not been moved – moved by great art, moved by great ballet, moved by great music. That's how we express ourselves. It's a language that we've now been able to define.

I want to close with a quotation from Duke Ellington, who said, 'We aren't worried about posterity; we just want it to sound good.'

The Honourable Bob Rae

Notes

THREE: 1931–1945: Sir Ernest MacMillan, Part 1

1 Ernest MacMillan, letter to Toronto Symphony Orchestra members, 24 October 1931.
2 Robertson Davies, 'Fifty-seven years of the TSO: Memories of a concert-goer,' *Toronto Symphony Magazine*, 23 April–15 June 1986.
3 Ernest MacMillan, 'Hitler and Wagnerism,' *Queen's Quarterly* (summer 1941), 97–105.
4 Ernest MacMillan, letter to J.E. Hahn, 11 September 1939, quoted in Ezra Schabas, *Sir Ernest MacMillan: The Importance of Being Canadian* (Toronto: University of Toronto Press, 1994), p. 163.

FOUR: 1945–1956: Sir Ernest MacMillan, Part 2

1 In 1945 the National Film Board made two films of the Toronto Symphony Orchestra conducted by Ernest MacMillan. *Toronto Symphony No. 1* presents Arthur Benjamin's *Jamaican Rhumba*, MacMillan's arrangement of the French Canadian folk song À *Saint-Malo* from his *Two Sketches for String Orchestra*, and the overture to the 1937 opera *Colas Breugnon* by Dmitri Kabalevsky. *Toronto Symphony No. 2* presents the third movement of Tchaikovsky's Symphony No. 6 in B minor ('Pathétique'). Both films were directed by Julian Roffman.
2 Ernest MacMillan, letter to Elie Spivak, n.d., quoted in Ezra Schabas, *Sir Ernest MacMillan: The Importance of Being Canadian* (Toronto: University of Toronto Press, 1994), 195.

FIVE: 1956–1965: Walter Susskind

1 Revenue for the season was $223,878. Expenditures of $384,133 resulted in an excess of expenses over revenue of $160,255. This initial deficit was reduced by donations and grants of $158,322 to $1933, which when added to the accumulated deficit totalled $6,552.23. However, this deficit was erased by an anonymous donation of $7,100, giving a surplus of $547.77.

EIGHT: 1975–1982: Andrew Davis at Massey Hall

1 Andrew Davis, interview with Richard Warren, 1978.
2 Murray Ginsberg, *They Loved to Play: Memories of the Golden Age in Canadian Music* (Toronto: Eastendbooks, 1998), p. 179.
3 Review in *La Nouvelleste*, quoted in *The Toronto Symphony News*, 14 (1980–1), no. 7, p. 2.
4 Johnny Cowell, note in program for Gala Concert, 4 June 1982.

NINE: 1982–1987: Andrew Davis at Roy Thomson Hall

1 'Programme Notes,' Toronto Symphony program for 24–5 October 1984.

2 Jack Brymer, *In the Orchestra* (London: Hutchinson, 1987), 172.

3 Andrew Davis, interview with Richard Warren, 1978.

TEN: 1988–1994: Günther Herbig

1 Wray Armstrong, interview with Richard Warren in London, England, 1998.

ELEVEN: 1994–2000: Jukka-Pekka Saraste

1 Georg Solti, *Solti on Solti: A Memoir*, with assistance from Harvey Sachs (London: Chatto and Windus, 1997), p. 169.

TWELVE: 2001–2002: Toward the Unknown

1 Walt Whitman, from opening two stanzas of the poem 'Darest Thou Now, O Soul,' from *Leaves of Grass*. The entire poem was set for SATB chorus and orchestra under the title *Towards the Unknown Region* by Ralph Vaughan Williams in 1904–6, during the time he was also working on *A Sea Symphony* (Symphony No. 1).

2 Norman Lebrecht, 'A crescendo of cash crisis,' *London Daily Telegraph*, 7 November 2001.

3 William Littler, 'There's a price to pay for excellence,' *Toronto Star*, 12 November 2001.

APPENDIX A

Musicians of the Toronto Symphony Orchestra

Note: Several musicians listed below were engaged as occasional players, especially before 1960.

Name	Instrument	Years	Notes
Aaron, H.	violin	1923/4	
Adaman, Anatoly	violoncello	1957/8–1959/60	
Adams, Patricia	violin	1951/2–1957/8	
Adaskin, John	violoncello	1925/6–1926/7; 1928/9–1937/8	
Adaskin, Murray	violin	1923/4–1935/6	
Adaskin, Harry	violin	1923/4	
Addison, L.F.	double bass	1923/4–1926/7; 1929/30–1945/6	
Adeney, Marcus	violoncello	1925/6; 1928/9–1948/9	
Ainley, Ernest	percussion	1923/4–1926/7; 1928/9–1938/9; 1945/6–1956/7; 1959/60–1962/3	
Aitken, Robert	flute	1965/6–1969/70	Co-Principal
Alexander, Ivan, aka Paul Thompson	violin	1981/2–present	
Anderson, George	trumpet	1945/6–1956/7; 1967/8–1982/3	Principal 1945/6–1956/7
Anderson, W.T.	violin	1931/2	
Andrews, F.W.	tuba	1932/3–1939/40	
Angelo, M.	trumpet	1933/4	
Angus, Robert	trombone	1960/1	
Annetts, Madge	violin	1936/7–1944/5	
Antonacci, Anthony	flute/piccolo	1953/4–1955/6; 1958/9–1988/9	
Armin, Adele	violin	1997/8–present	
Armin, Richard	violoncello	1965/6–1968/9	
Ash, Peter	trombone	1958/9–1959/60	
Atkinson, Keith	oboe	1985/6–present	Associate Principal
Aylward, Albert E.	violin	1923/4; 1925/6; 1927/8–1929/30; 1932/3; 1942/3–1950/1; 1961/2–1962/3	
Babiak, Walter	viola	1957/8–1959/60	

APPENDIX A

Musicians of the Toronto Symphony Orchestra – *continued*

Name	Instrument	Years	Notes
Bankas, Atis	violin	1982/3–present	
Barclay, Hugh	percussion	1959/60	
Barker, Geoffrey	double bass	1943/4–1950/1	
Barkin, Leo	pianoforte	1946/7–1962/3	
Barrow, B.H.	French horn	1927/8–1931/2	Principal
Barrow, R.H.	French horn	1925/6; 1927/8–1932/3; 1934/5–1957/8	Principal 1932/3
Barshtz, B.	viola	1923/4–1926/7	
Bartmann, Erich	violoncello	1932/3–1940/1	
Bauman, Perry W.	oboe	1940/1–1955/6; 1964/5–1970/1	Principal 1940/1–1955/6; Co-Principal 1964/5–1970/1
Baxtresser, Jeanne	flute	1978/9–1983/4	Principal 1978/9–1983/4
Beard, H.	violin	1923; 1923/4	
Bedford, H.	viola	1929/30–1945/6	Principal until 1930/1?
Bell, Goldie	violin	1946/7–1952/3; 1957/8; 1962/3–1963/4	
Benac, Andrew	violin	1951/2–1957/8; 1987/8–1990/1	
Bennett, Margaret	violoncello	1938/9	
Berard, Marie	violin	1988/9–1989/90	
Bergart, Harry	violin	1938/9–1959/60; 1962/3–1977/8	
Berul, G.J.	violin	1923/4–1926/7	
Biloshysky, Halina	violin	1959/60	see also Bobrow
Biloshysky, Leon	double bass	1952/3–1971/2	
Bilton, Lionel H.	violoncello	1923/4	Principal
Biniowsky, Morris	violin	1951/2–1970/1	
Blachford, Frank	violin	1932/3–1945/6	
Blackburn, A.	violin	1923/4–1931/2	
Blackman, Daniel	viola	1988/9–present	
Blackstone, Milton	viola	1923; 1923/4–1925/6	Principal 1923/4–1924/5
Blackwell, G.T.	trombone	1923; 1923/4–1926/7	Principal 1923/4–1925/6
Blenkin, Frank	French horn	1928/9–1945/6	
Bloomer, Barbara	French horn	1966/7–1984/5	
Bobrow, Halina	violin	1960/1–1966/7	see also Biloshysky
Boltyansky, Eduard	viola	1975/6–1984/5	
Booth, C.E.	bassoon	1925/6–1926/7	
Bosman, J.	violin	1923/4–1924/5	
Boucher, E.	trumpet	1923; 1923/4–1927/8; 1929/30–1935/6	Principal 1923; 1923/4–1927/8; 1929/30–1930/1
Bourque, David	bass clarinet	1983/4–present	

APPENDIX A
Musicians of the Toronto Symphony Orchestra – *continued*

Name	Instrument	Years	Notes
Bower, Bruce	contrabassoon	1975/6–1978/9	
Boyko, Lisa	viola	1989/90–1990/1	listed as Nelson for 1989/90
Bradfield, H.H.	flute/piccolo	1924/5; 1931/2–1940/1	Principal 1937/8–1940/1
Braunstein, Steven	contrabassoon	1979/80–1988/9	
Brennand, T.E.	violin/viola	1928/9–1936/7	
Bridges, E.	French horn	1923/4–1926/7	
Broadfoot, Hugh	violin	1925/6–1926/7	
Browne, R.O.	bassoon	1923/4	
Bruce, George A.	violoncello	1923/4–1931/2; 1933/4–1956/7	Personnel Manager 1938/9–1955/6
Bruce, Alfred	viola	1928/9–1945/6	
Budd, Philip	oboe	1942/3–1945/6	
Budd, Ruth	double bass	1964/5–1988/9	
Bugaeva, Galina	violin	1974/5–1989/90	
Burghauser, Hugo	bassoon	1938/9–1940/1	Principal
Burgin, Arthur	French horn	1961/2–1969/70	
Burry, Thomas J.	timpani	1923; 1923/4–1939/40; 1945/6–1963/4	Principal 1962/3–1963/4
Bursh, J.	viola	1923	
Burul, J.	violin	1923/4	
Busby, H.	double bass/tuba	1925/6–1931/2	
Cadesky, Macey	viola	1957/8–1970/1	
Cahill, John	French horn	1971/2–1972/3	
Capper, Vair	percussion	1954/5–1966/7	
Carter, Harold	viola	1944/5–1951/2; 1963/4–1974/5	
Carter, W.	violoncello	1923/4; 1924/5	
Carver, Frank	double bass	1922/3–1923/4; 1927/8–1929/30; 1933/4–1937/8	
Cassidy, Varia	violin/viola	1933/4–1941/2; 1947/8–1953/4	see also Niemiec
Caston, Paul	timpani/percussion	1972/3–1974/5	
Caswell, W.A.	percussion	1929/30	
Causton, Clarence	violin	1932/3	
Causton, C.	violin	1942/3–1945/6	
Causton, C.P.	violin	1923/4	
Causton, R.O., Jr	clarinet	1923/4–1931/2	
Chambers, L.	French horn	1932/3–1933/4	
Chang, Yoon Im	violin	1978/9–1980/1	
Charles, W.A.	violin	1957/8	
Chenhall, Martin	violoncello	1925/6–1926/7	

APPENDIX A
Musicians of the Toronto Symphony Orchestra – *continued*

Name	Instrument	Years	Notes
Chomyk, Stephanie	viola	1953/4–1980/1	
Chuchman, Josephine	violin	1952/3–1956/7	see also Toth
Chun, Sydney	violin	1999/2000–present	
Clark, B.	violin	1922/3–1924/5	
Clark, T.	violin	1922/3	
Clarke, Benedick	violin	1923/4–1925/6	
Clarke, G.C.	violoncello	1922/3	
Clarke, Henry	viola	1925/6–1926/7	
Clarke, Mitchell	bassoon	1973/4–present	
Cochrane, Robert	double bass	1923/4–1925/6; 1929/30–1945/6	Principal 1923/4–1925/6; 1938/9–1941/2
Coghill, Eugene	French horn	1957/8–1958/9	
Cohen, Richard	French horn	1972/3–present	
Cooper, Archie	percussion/ timpani	1940/1–1953/4	
Corrin, Gary	librarian	1991/2–present	Principal
Cowell, John	trumpet	1952/3–1990/1	
Cox, Roy	oboe	1956/7–1976/7	
Craig, Maude C.	harp	1935/6; 1937/8; 1940/1–1948/9	see also Watterworth
Crang, Frank L.	French horn	1922/3–1927/8	1923 listed as Krang, L.
Creech, Robert	French horn	1952/3–1954/5	
Crewe, Murray	bass trombone	1989/90–1993/4	
Cross, William	trombone	1985/6–present	
Crown, J.C.	French horn	1923/4	
Crowther, H.	bassoon	1927/8–1945/6	Principal 1927/8–1929/30; 1936/7–1937/8
Culbert, Arlene	violin	1960/1	
Culley, Charles E.	timpani	1923/4–1927/8	
Culley, H.T.	flute	1924/5; 1933/4	
Culley, William R.	trombone	1934/5; 1940/1–1954/5	Principal 1934/5
Curtis, Charles H.	violoncello	1922/3–1926/7; 1928/9–1929/30; 1932/3	
Daminoff, Peter	violin	1963/4–1994/5	
Dann, Steven	viola	1987/8–2000/1	Principal
Darida, Ladislau	viola	1981/2–2000/1	
Davidson, Castor	violin	1923/4–1935/6; 1937/8	
Davidson, Erica	violin	1967/8–1972/3	see also Zentner
Davidson, Rosalind	violoncello	1961/2–1964/5	see also Sartori
Davis, Sam	double bass	1963/4–1982/3	Principal 1965/6
Dawson, Timothy	double bass	1979/80–present	
Day, Gordon	flute	1941/2–1948/9	Principal
De Bystrice, Count	violin	1933/4–1935/6	

APPENDIX A
Musicians of the Toronto Symphony Orchestra – *continued*

Name	Instrument	Years	Notes
Dembeck, John	violin	1941/2–1947/8; 1957/8–1960/1	
Dementev, Tanya	violin	1977/8–Dec. 1997	
Dempster, Agnes	violin	1959/60; 1963/4–1965/6	see also Roberts
Dennis, F.E.	bassoon	1922/3–1926/7; 1931/2–1933/4	Principal 1923; 1925/6–1926/7
DeSotto, Peter	violin	1986/7–1992/3	
Desser, Isidor	violin	1931/2–1972/3	Assistant Concertmaster 1959/60–1972/3
Diamond, Hillel	violin	1948/9–1950/1	
Dineen, D.	violin	1923/4	
Dixon, R.J.	trombone	1923/4; 1927/8	
Dlouhy, Jonathan	oboe	1977/8–1978/9	Associate Principal
Dobias, Charles	violin	1961/2–1969/70	
Domb, Daniel	violoncello	1974/5–2001/2	Principal
Donnellan, Muriel F.	harp	1923/4; 1924/5–1927/8; 1932/3–1941/2	
Dorsey, Richard	oboe	1979/80–present	Associate Principal 1979/80–1981/2; Principal 1982/3–2000/1
Dowell, E.	violin	1932/3–1935/6	
Dubinsky, Isadore	violin	1922/3–1971/2	
Dudley, William	clarinet	1923/4–1924/5; 1933/4–1935/6	Principal 1923; 1923/4–1924/5
Dunk, F.C.	double bass	1924/5	
Ebli, Cary	English horn/ oboe	1991/2–2000/1	
Elliott, Anthony	violoncello	1970/1–1972/3	
Elliott, Charles	double bass	1988/9–present	
Elton, H.J.	flute/piccolo	1922/3–1930/1	Orchestra Manager 1924/5–1926/7
Emerson, Carla	harp	1957/8	
Engelman, John	percussion	1968/9–1971/2	Principal
Evens, Clifford	violin	1961/2–1968/9	Principal Second 1965/6–1968/9
Evens, Mary	violoncello	1961/2–1969/70	
Everson, R.	trumpet	1924/5–1925/6; 1928/9; 1936/7–1943/4	Principal 1928/9
Eyles, Christine	violin	1931/2–1941/2; 1960/1	
Fancher, Joelle	double bass	1989/90	
Farquhar, Susan	viola	1970/1–1972/3	see also Lipchak
Feldbrill, Victor	violin	1949/50–1956/7	Resident Conductor 1973/4–1974/5

APPENDIX A
Musicians of the Toronto Symphony Orchestra – *continued*

Name	Instrument	Years	Notes
Fenbogue, A.E.	flute	1922/3–1924/5	1924/5 – 9 or 10 concerts
Fenwick, John	librarian	1981/2–1989/90	Principal 1982/3–1989/90
Fetherston, Douglas E.	violin	1931/2–1961/2	
Fetherston, John	clarinet	1956/7–1987/8	Principal 1956/7–1957/8
Figelski, Cecil	violin/viola	1932/3; 1934/5–1935/6; 1937/8–1943/4	Principal 1938/9–1943/4
Findlay, William	violoncello	1963/4; 1969/70–present	
Finney, P.S.	double bass	1936/7–1937/8; 1942/3–1946/7	
Fiore, Nicholas	flute	1952/3–1977/8	Principal, 1952/3–1964/5; 1970/1–1977/8; Co-Principal 1965/6–1969/70
Fischer-Byfield, Betty-Ann	violin	1963/4–1978/9	1978/9 listed as Fischer
Fleisher, Martin	oboe	1939/40	Principal
Fogle, Meyer	violin/viola	1923/4–1926/7; 1929/30–1962/3	
Fontana, N.J.	flute/piccolo	1922/3–1930/1; 1934/5–1952/3	
Forsyth, Amanda	violoncello	1990/1	
Franks, C.	violin	1924/5–1930/1; 1931/2	
Freedman, Harry	oboe/English horn	1946/7–1969/70	
Friedlander, Fowler	bassoon	1941/2	Principal
Fryer, Simon	violoncello	1989/90–present	
Fujino, Carol Lynn	violin	1992/3–present	
Furer, Rafael	violoncello	1973/4–1989/90	
Fusco, Francesco	violin	1928/9–1941/2; 1946/7–1952/3; 1957/8–1959/60; 1962/77	
Galper, Avrahm	clarinet	1947/8–1955/6; 1958/9–1978/9	Principal 1952/3–1955/6, 1958/9–1972/3; Co-Principal 1973/4–1978/9
Gardiner, James	trumpet	1999/2000–present	
Garten, Moe	violin	1922/3; 1923/4–1925/6; 1940/1–1945/6	Concertmaster 1923/4–1925/6
Garten, N.	violin	1922/3; 1923/4–1924/5	Principal Second violin
Gartner, Esther	violoncello	1972/3–2000/1	
Gay, Errol	librarian	1982/3–present	Associate Principal 1982/3–1988/9; 1991/2–present; Acting Principal 1989/90–1990/1
Gelinas, Marie	violoncello	1980/1–2000/1	

APPENDIX A
Musicians of the Toronto Symphony Orchestra – *continued*

Name	Instrument	Years	Notes
Gelsin, L.	violin	1930/1–1937/8	
Geringas, Yaakov	violin	1975/6–1989/90	
Gesensway, Louis	violin	1922/3; 1923/4–1925/6	
Gesensway, A.S.	violin	1922/3; 1923/4	
Gibson, Georgina	celesta/ violoncello	1951/2–1952/3	see also Roberts
Ginsberg, Murray	bass trombone	1961/2–1978/9	
Ginter, Anthony	violin	1957/8–1963/4	
Ginzler, Seymour	trombone	1935/6–1939/40	Principal
Girard, Keith	flute	1958/9–1983/4	
Glionna, M.A.	viola	1923/4–1931/2	
Glover, Lorna	violin	1967/8–1970/1	
Godwin, Kenneth	French horn	1946/7–1970/1	
Goldberg, Grigory	violoncello	1986/7–1988/9	
Gomberg, H.	oboe	1938/9	Principal
Gongos, Christopher	French horn	1998/9–present	
Goodman, Erica	harp	1964/5–1965/6	
Goodman, Hyman	violin	1932/3–1941/2; 1946/7–1947/8	Concertmaster 1948/9–1966/7
Goodman, Nathan	oboe/ English horn	1944/5–1945/6	
Gorevic, Ronald	violin	1972/3–1973/4	
Goroshin, Naum	violoncello	1925/6–1926/7	
Gowen, John	double bass	1972/3–present	
Gray, J.W.	trombone	1927/8–1935/6	Principal 1927/8–1931/2
Green, B.	violin	1922/3–1923/4	
Green, Nathan	viola	1942/3–1972/3	
Green, Osher	viola	1985/6–Sept. 1988	Principal 1985/6–1986/7
Greenwood, Charles	double bass/ tuba	1925/6–1949/50	Principal 1932/3–1937/8
Greenwood, W.	oboe	1932/3–1935/6; 1937/8	
Griss, Murray	violin	1922/3; 1923/4–1925/6; 1929/30–1932/3	1923 listed as Griss, N.
Groob, Jacob	violin	1946/7–1948/9; 1953/4–1958/9; 1964/5–1981/2	
Grunsky, Wolfgang	violoncello	1953/4–1970/1	
Guise, Clifford	English horn/ oboe	1923/4–1926/7; 1928/9; 1931/2–1933/4	
Hale, Leonard	French horn	1950/1–1951/2	
Hall, Jeffrey	bass trombone	1994/5–present	
Halperin, B.	violin	1936/7–1950/1	
Hansen, Andrea	violin	1977/8–2000/1	
Hardwick, Fred	violin	1923/4–1926/7	

APPENDIX A
Musicians of the Toronto Symphony Orchestra – *continued*

Name	Instrument	Years	Notes
Haris, E.	violin/viola	1928/9–1929/30	Principal
Harmantas, Frank	trombone	1971/2–2000/1	Associate Principal 1990/1–2000/1
Harper, James	librarian	1966/7–1974/5	
Harrisay, Vino	violin	1931/2	
Hart, Arthur	clarinet	1946/7	
Harwick, Fred	violin	1923/4–1926/7	
Hashizume, Miho	violin	1992/3–1996/7	
Haslam, H.	percussion	1923/4–1924/5	
Hawe, H.E.	trombone	1923/4–1926/7; 1936/7–1950/1	Principal 1926/7; 1940/1–1946/7
Hayes, Edward	violoncello	1970/1–1988/9	
Hearn, Miles	French horn	1970/1–1971/2	
Heins, Donald	violin/viola	1927/8–1947/8	Concertmaster 1927/8–1930/1; Principal 1931/2–1937/8
Henderson, Floyd	tuba	1949/50–1950/1	
Henniger, Harcus	French horn	1985/6–present	
Hersenhoren, S.	violin	1925/6–1943/4	
Hetherington, David	violoncello	1970/1–present	Assistant Principal 1996/7–1997/8, 1999/2000; Acting Principal 1998/9, 2000/1–present
Himbury, Lola	violin	1948/9–1951/2	
Hoffman, Sidney	violin/viola	1923/4–1935/6	
Holowach, Terry	violin	1970/1–1971/2; 1974/5–present	
Hornyansky, Joyce	violoncello	1931/2–1935/6	
Horvath, George	violoncello	1950/1–1987/8	
Hossack, Donna	harp	1953/4–1958/9	Principal 1957/8–1958/9
Hudson, Eugene	viola	1957/8–1973/4	see also Rosenfield, P. in violins
Huggins, Ernest	contrabassoon	1934/5–1958/9	
Hunt, Bridget	violin	1995/6–present	
Hunter, James	violoncello	1948/9–1955/6	
Hurwitz, Ronald	viola	1975/6–present	
Hutcheon, D.S.B.	English horn/oboe	1924/5; 1926/7–1928/9; 1933/4; 1935/6–1937/8; 1939/40–1943/4	Principal 1926/7–1928/9
Hutchings, Edward	oboe	1954/5–1955/6	
Imajishi, Fujiko	violin	1973/4–1976/7	
Inkman, Pamela	viola	1980/1	
Innes, James Jr.	violin	1947/8–1949/50	

APPENDIX A
Musicians of the Toronto Symphony Orchestra – *continued*

Name	Instrument	Years	Notes
Innes, James	violin	1944/5–1956/7	
Isenbaum, M.	trumpet	1942/3–1947/8	Principal 1942/3–1943/4
Israelievitch, Jacques	violin	1988/9–present	Concertmaster
Jackson, Fraser	contrabassoon	1990/1–present	
Jansonn, Glen	French horn	1961/2	
Jansonn, Julia	violin	1961/2	
Jennings, H.	violoncello	1922/3; 1923/4–1926/7; 1930/1–1931/2; 1936/7–1937/8	
Jennings, H.	bassoon	1926/7–1929/30	
Jewell, Jeffery	bass clarinet	1937/8–1954/5	
Joanou-Canzoneri, Amalia	violin	1994/5–present	
Johnson, Donald	trumpet	1946/7; 1948/9–1951/2	
Johnson, Ernest	violin	1923/4–1957/8	
Jones, A.J.	trumpet	1929/30–1931/2; 1936/7–1944/5	Principal 1931/2; also listed as Jones, Bert
Jones, T.B.	tuba	1922/3; 1923/4–1925/6	
Jose, R.L.	French horn	1922/3–1927/8	Principal 1923/4–1924/5, 1926/7
Jun, Sonia	violin	1993/4–1999/2000	Principal 1995/6–1998/9
Kantarjian, Gerard	violin	1967/8–1969/70	Concertmaster
Karp, D.	French horn	1923/4	
Kash, Eugene	violin	1934/5–1941/2	1934/5–1935/6 listed as Kash, J.
Keetbrass, D.	flute	1949/50–1951/2	Principal
Kent, David	timpani	1981/2–present	Principal; Personnel Manager 1986/7–present
Kernerman, Morry	violin	1973/4–1988/9	Assistant Concertmaster
Kersting, Boris	double bass	1961/2–1962/3	
Keyho, W.A.G.	double bass	1924/5	
Kilburn, Michael	violoncello	1956/7–1963/4	
Kilburn, Nicholas	bassoon	1959/60–1990/1	Principal 1959/60–1967/8; Co-Principal 1968/9–1984/5; Associate Principal 1985/6–1990/1
Kim, Mi Hyon	violin	1988/9–present	
King, Audrey	violoncello	1971/2–present	
Kirshner, Debbie	violin	1989/90	
Klepacki, Veronica	double bass	1953/4–1958/9	
Knaggs, E.S.	violin	1923/4	
Knaggs, F.E.	double bass	1924/5–1926/7	
Knowles, Leslie	violin	1977/8–present	see also Ryker

APPENDIX A
Musicians of the Toronto Symphony Orchestra – *continued*

Name	Instrument	Years	Notes
Koldofsky, Adolph	violin	1922/3; 1923/4–1924/5; 1927/8; 1932/3–1937/8	
Kolkowski, Julian	violin	1957/8–1968/9; 1972/3–1999/2000	Principal Emeritus 1995/6–1999/2000
Kolt, Stanley	violin	1958/9–1959/60; 1968/9–1987/8	
Kowalski, Eugene	violin	1969/70	
Krang, L.	French horn	1923/4	
Kregal, Jesse	timpani	1964/5–1965/6	
Kreit, F.	double bass	1922/3	
Kreit, D.F.	bassoon	1922/3–1923/4	
Krueger, Patricia	keyboard/ percussion	1978/9–present	Principal 1990/1–present
Kuehn, Donald	percussion	1973/4–present	Principal 1973/4–1992/3
Kuinka, William	double bass	1951/2	
Kuyvenhoven, Cora	violoncello	1988/9–1990/1	
Kwasniak, Olga	violoncello	1957/8–1959/60	
Labovitz, Gary	viola	1973/4–present	
Langeley, W.	violin	1923/4	
Langley, John	violin	1923/4–1928/9	
Langley, John	bass trombone	1979/80–1988/9	
Lasserre, Henri	violoncello	1923/4–1925/6	
Laurie, Ronald	violoncello	1956/7–1995/6	Assistant Principal 1975/6–1995/6; Assistant Personnel Manager 1983/4–1986/7
Lechow, Ross	viola	1949/50–1957/8	
Lee, R.E.	trombone	1924/5–1926/7; 1929/30–1931/2	Principal 1932/3–1933/4
Lenzer, Hyman	violin	1925/6	
Letvak, Philip	violin	1935/6–1956/7	
Levine, Sam	double bass	1949/50–1978/9	
Levy, Sidney	viola	1932/3–1969/70	
Lieberman, Carol	violin	1971/2	
Lipchak, Susan	viola	1973/4–present	Assistant Principal 1975/6–1983/4, 1985/6–2000/1; Acting Co-Principal 1984/5; Acting Principal 2000/1–present; see also Farquhar
Locksley, Roy	trumpet	1924/5–1928/9; 1931/2; 1933/4–1935/6	

APPENDIX A

Musicians of the Toronto Symphony Orchestra – *continued*

Name	Instrument	Years	Notes
Neal, Ronald	trumpet	1946/7–1974/5	Stage Librarian 1968/9–1975/6; Librarian 1975/6–1981/2
Neilsen, J.	violin/viola	1932/3–1935/6; 1939/40–1941/2; 1945/6–1952/3	1932/3 listed as Neilson, J.
Nelson, Lisa	viola	1989/90	see also Boyko
Nelsova, Zara	violoncello	1940/1–1942/3	Principal
Newham, George	percussion	1929/30–1931/2	
Nichols, R.G.	bass clarinet	1932/3–1935/6	
Nicholson, H.	timpani	1922/3–1923/4	
Niemiec, Varia	viola	1954/5–1956/7	see also Cassidy
Nikonov, Sergei	violin	1999/2000–present	
Norton, Earl	percussion	1930/1; 1932/3; 1940/1	
Nugent, Mary Carol	viola	1987/8–present	
Obercian, Leslie	double bass	1956/7–1970/1	
Obercian, Teresa	violin	1964/5–1993/4	
Orbach, Daniel	viola	1974/5–1975/6; 1983/4	Principal 1983/4
Orlowski, Joseph	clarinet	1988/9–present	
Pack, Roland	violoncello	1948/9–1956/7	Principal 1953/4–1956/7
Paik, Hyung-Sun	violin	1980/1–present	
Palmason, Pearl	violin	1941/2–1946/7; 1948/9–1959/60; 1972/3–1980/1	Principal Second 1960/1–1961/2
Palmer, H.F.	violoncello	1923/4	
Palmer, Harry	violoncello	1936/7	
Palmer, W.H.	violoncello	1923/4	
Palyga, Katherine	violin	1992/3–1994/5	
Park, Young-Dae	violin	1979/80–present	Acting Assistant Principal 1988/9
Parkinson, Harry C.	viola	1923/4	also H.G.
Peel, J.	trombone	1923/4–1924/5; 1927/8–1929/30	
Pelletier, Maurice	viola	1973/4–1985/6	Acting Assistant Principal 1984/5
Pelletieri, V.F.	violin	1922/3–1931/2	1923 listed as Pelletiere, J.
Perit, Roland	French horn	1955/6–1956/7; 1959/60–1960/1	
Perras, John	flute/piccolo	1956/7–1957/8	
Pertsovsky, Semyon	violin	1979/80–present	
Peters, George F.	violin	1923/4–1927/8	
Pilcher, C.V.	bass clarinet	1923; 1923/4–1931/2	
Pohjola, Larry	double bass	1964/5	
Polley, Victoria	violin	1967/8–1970/1	see also Richards

APPENDIX A
Musicians of the Toronto Symphony Orchestra – *continued*

Name	Instrument	Years	Notes
Pollock, H.	violin	1922/3–1923/4	
Poole, Gordon	oboe	1946/7–1953/4	
Poure, M.	viola	1930/1–1932/3	
Powdermaker, Frank	violin	1989/90–1990/1	
Pratz, Albert	violin	1933/4–1940/1, 1969/70–1978/9	Acting Concertmaster 1970/1; Concertmaster 1971/2–1978/9
Prystawski, Walter	violin	1953/4–1957/8	
Puchtiar, Philip	violin	1951/2–1965/6	
Pulis, Gordon	trombone	1958/9–1964/5; 1968/9	Principal, portion of 1968/9
Purvis, Douglas	tuba	1985/6	
Pye, Herbert C.	clarinet	1925/6–1945/6	Principal 1925/6–1935/6
Pyper, George E.	violin	1957/8; 1959/60–1962/3	
Quarrington, Joel	double bass	1991/2–present	Principal
Radcliffe, Frank	violin	1952/3–1961/2	
Ranson, A.E.	double bass	1923/4–1925/6	
Ranti, Julie	flute	1985/6–present	Associate Principal 1990/1–present
Rapson, Anne	violin	1973/4	
Rapson, Peter	violoncello	1990/1–1991/2	
Ravening, Jan	violin	1957/8	
Ray, Marcel	violoncello	1938/9–1946/7; 1962/3–1968/9	
Redfield, Christopher	viola	1989/90–present	
Reeves, Anthony	French horn	1959/60–1960/1	
Reid, Duncan	percussion	1941/2–1944/5	
Reilly, Raymond	percussion	1967/8–1991/2	Acting Principal 1972/3
Reynolds, Frank	trombone	1967/8–1979/80	
Richards, Victoria	violin	1971/2–1973/4; 1975/6–present	see also Polley
Richardson, Florence	violin/viola	1931/2–1943/4	
Richer, L.	viola	1923/4–1929/30	
Riddleswick, A.	trombone/ double bass	1923/4–1926/7; 1928/9; 1930/1–1944/5	
Rini, Michael	violoncello	1960/1–1962/3	
Rittich, Eugene	French horn	1952/3–1988/9	Principal 1952/3–1972/3; Co-Principal 1973/4–1984/5; Associate Principal 1985/6–1988/9
Rizner, Fredrick	French horn	1965/6–present	Associate Principal 1970/1–1972/3; Co-Principal 1973/4–1984/5; Principal 1985/6–present

APPENDIX A

Musicians of the Toronto Symphony Orchestra – *continued*

Name	Instrument	Years	Notes
Robb-Barrow, Mary	French horn	1939/40–1950/1	Principal 1939/40–1944/5
Roberts, Agnes	violin	1958/9; 1966/7; 1968/9; 1970/1–1974/5; 1989/90	see also Dempster
Roberts, Georgina	violoncello/ celesta	1953/4–1955/6; 1960/1; 1963/4–1985/6	see also Gibson
Roberts, Oswald	violoncello	1923/4–1935/6; 1937/8– 1950/1	Principal 1923/4–1931/2
Roberts, Richard	violin	1971/2–1972/3	Associate Concertmaster
Robertson, John	trumpet	1931/2–1932/3	Principal
Robin, Bertrand	violin	1997/8–1998/9	
Roderman, T.	trombone	1957/8	Principal
Rogers, Nora	harp	1949/50–1952/3	
Rogers, Paul	double bass	1989/90–present	
Rogers, Robert	clarinet	1936/7–1957/8	Principal 1936/7–1951/2
Rose, Charles	double bass	1923/4–1926/7; 1933/4– 1934/5; 1937/8–1941/2; 1947/8–1951/2	Principal 1923/4–1926/7
Rose, Wendy	violin	1981/2–present	Assistant Principal 1984/5– present
Rosenfield, P.	violin	1922/3–1925/6	
Ross, Ruth	double bass	1947/8–1951/2	see also Budd
Roth, M.	violin	1923; 1923/4	
Rowe, Carol	viola	1971/2–1972/3	
Ruddick, Daniel	percussion	1973/4–present	
Rudolph, John	percussion	1997/8–present	Principal
Ryker, Leslie	violin	1975/6–1976/7	see also Knowles
Sands, Joyce	violoncello	1940/1–1944/5	
Sargous, Harry	oboe	1971/2–1981/2	Principal 1971/2–1981/2
Sartori, Rosalind	violoncello	1965/6–1969/70	see also Davidson
Sauer, Ralph	trombone	1968/9–1973/4	Principal
Saunders, H.S.	violoncello	1923; 1923/4–1937/8	
Savoie, Marc-André	violin	1990/1–present	Assistant Concertmaster
Schenkman, Peter	violoncello	1967/8–1973/4	Principal
Scherman, Issay	violin	1931/2–1932/3; 1934/5– 1943/4	
Scherman, Paul	violin	1944/5–1951/2	
Schmidt, D.	double bass	1922/3; 1923/4	
Schwalm, Charles	double bass	1924/5–1928/9; 1932/3– 1935/6; 1939/40–1940/1	
Schweers, James	tuba	1952/3–1954/5	
Scuse, J.F.	violin	1923/4–1925/6	

APPENDIX A
Musicians of the Toronto Symphony Orchestra – *continued*

Name	Instrument	Years	Notes
Sera, Josef	violin	1946/7–1959/60, 1961/2–1982/3	Principal Second 1957/8–1959/60; Assistant Principal 1975/6–1982/3; Assistant Personnel Manager 1977/8–1982/3
Shea, D'Arcy	violin	1971/2–1976/7	
Sherman, Isidore	violin	1925/6; 1926/7	
Sherman, Louis	violin	1925/6–1941/2; 1945/6–1947/8	
Shrubsole, E.W.	violin	1922/3–1926/7	
Shulman, Nora	flute	1974/5–present	Associate Principal 1974/5–1983/4; Acting Principal, 1984/5–1985/6; Principal 1986/7–present
Simonelli, John	French horn	1962/3–1964/5; Mar. 1976–1996/7	
Sinden, Mark	trumpet	1945/6	
Skazinetsky, Mark	violin	1980/1–present	Associate Concertmaster 1988/9–present
Skura, Harry	viola	1975/6–present	
Slater, Harold	percussion	1929/30; 1933/4–1958/9	
Smeall, E.	trumpet	1922/3–1923/4; 1929/30; 1932/3	1923 listed as Smeal, E.
Smith, E.T.	flute	1923/4; 1925/6–1932/3; 1938/9–1956/7	Principal 1925/6–1930/31
Smith, Frank Converse	viola	1923/4–1927/8; 1932/3–1935/6	Principal 1925/6–1927/8
Smith, Leo	violoncello	1932/3–1939/40	Principal
Sobel, M.	violin	1923/4–1924/5	
Solomon, Stanley	viola	1946/7–1987/8	Principal 1949/50–1982/3; Principal Emeritus 1983/4–1987/8
Solway, Maurice	violin	1923/4–1925/6; 1933/4–1948/9	
Sommerville, Buena	violin	1942/3–1944/5	
Sommerville, James	French horn	1997/8	
Sparkes, Doug	bass trombone	1993/4	
Sparling, Lillian	violin	1932/3–1946/7	
Spearing, Clifford C.	French horn	1925/6; 1932/3–1938/9; 1940/1–1970/1	Principal 1936/7–1938/9; 1945/6–1949/50
Spergel, Robert	violoncello	1947/8–1948/9; 1965/6–1971/2	
Spivak, Elie	violin	1931/2–1947/8	Concertmaster

APPENDIX A
Musicians of the Toronto Symphony Orchestra – *continued*

Name	Instrument	Years	Notes
Spivak, Philip	violoncello	1931/2–1961/2	Principal 1950/1–1952/3
Spragg, James	trumpet	1987/8–present	
Stansfield, B.	violin	1923/4	
Staryk, Steven	violin	1950/1–1951/2; 1982/3–1986/7	Concertmaster 1982/3–1986/7
Steinberg, Albert	violin	1936/7–1945/6	
Steinberg, M.	trumpet	1924/5–1925/6	
Steinberg, Sigmund	violin	1934/5–1977/8	
Sterin, J.	violoncello	1922/3–1923/4	Principal 1923, 1923/4
Stevenson, Harry	trombone/ bass trombone	1951/2–1966/7	
Stevenson, Wilma	celesta	1934/5	
Stimpson, George	French horn	1971/2	
Sturm, K.	violin	1923/4; 1924/5	
Sturm, Vaughn	violoncello	1923/4; 1924/5–1962/3	
Sugarman, Berul	violin	1925/6–1937/8, 1942/3–1982/3	
Sullivan, Peter	tenor trombone	1984/5	
Sumberg, Harold	violin	1928/9–1956/7, 1961/2–1974/5	Principal Second
Sweeney, Gordon	trombone	1974/5–present	Principal
Sweeney, Michael	bassoon	1989/90–present	Principal
Tait, Edward	double bass	1971/2–present	Assistant Principal 1975/6–present
Tait, Malcolm	violoncello	1957/8–1966/7	Principal
Tarnowsky, Vera	violin	1961/2–1968/9; 1976/7–1985/6	
Taylor, H.J.	violin	1922/3–1926/7	
Teeple, Kent	viola	1977/8–present	Assistant Personnel Manager 1987/8–1992/3
Temoin, Bernard	clarinet/ bass clarinet	1955/6–1982/3	
Tetel, Mihai	violoncello	1990/1–present	
Tetreault, Mark	tuba	1986/7–present	Principal
Thomas, Rachel	trombone	1990/1	
Thompson, Jack	tuba	1951/2	
Thompson, Jennifer	violin	1999/2000–present	
Titmarsh, Gurney	tuba/ double bass	1940/1–1948/9	
Tobias, Fred	violin	1925/6–1927/8	
Tobias, Norman	bassoon	1965/6–1972/3	
Todd, Jean	violin	1964/5–1967/8	see also Wulkan, Jean
Toews, Angelique	violin	1996/7–present	

APPENDIX A

Musicians of the Toronto Symphony Orchestra – *continued*

Name	Instrument	Years	Notes
Tong, W.	trumpet	1923/4	
Toth, Josephine	violin	1957/8	see also Chuchman
Tweedie, H.S.	violin	1923/4; 1924/5–1927/8	
Umbrico, Joseph	trumpet	1957/8–1998/9	Principal 1957/8–1982/3; Principal Emeritus 1983/4–1998/9; Assistant Personnel Manager 1972/3–1976/7
Valdepeñas, Joaquin	clarinet	1980/1–present	Co-Principal 1980/1; Principal 1981/2–present
Van Sickle, H.L.	violin	1922/3; 1923/4–1924/5	
Van Sickle, R.	double bass	1952/3	
Van Vugt, John	violin	1922/3–1967/8	Assistant 18 concerts 1923/4, 1924/5–1935/6, 1938/9–1945/6; Librarian 1946/7–1967/8
Vearncombe, H.	viola	1922/3–1923/4	Assistant Librarian 1923/4
Veary, A.	piccolo	1925/6	
Voisey, W.	French horn	1922/3–1926/7	
Vopni, F.B.	French horn	1923/4–1925/6; 1933/4–1950/1	Principal 1933/4–1935/6
Vrba, Cenek	violin	1971/2–1975/6	
Waddington, Geoffrey	violin	1925/6–1927/8	
Wahlberg, Elver	bassoon/ contrabassoon	1942/3–1967/8	Principal 1942/3–1958/9
Waizman, Louis	viola	1923/4–1931/2	Librarian 1923/4–1945/6; Honorary Librarian 1946/7–1948/9
Wakefield, William	percussion	1963/4	
Wallenberg, James	violin	1978/9–present	
Warburton, Robert	viola	1932/3–1948/9; 1957/8–1977/8	Principal 1944/5–1948/9
Warnaar, Brad	French horn	1972/3–1974/5	
Warrington, Martha	viola	1979/80	
Watkin, Fenwick	trombone	1955/6–1956/7	
Watson, Joan	French horn	1988/9; 1991/2–2001/2	Associate Principal 1991/2–2001/2
Watterworth, Maude	harp	1930/1–1934/5	see also Craig
Watts, Eugene	trombone	1965/6–1967/8	Principal
Watts, Camille	flute/piccolo	1989/90–present	
Weait, Christopher	bassoon	1968/9–1984/5	Co-Principal
Webber, Winston	violin	1972/3–1978/9	

APPENDIX A
Musicians of the Toronto Symphony Orchestra – *continued*

Name	Instrument	Years	Notes
Weeks, Larry	trumpet	1975/6–1996/7	Associate Principal 1975/6–1981/2; Principal Elect 1982/3; Principal 1983/4–1996/7
Wegiel, Annette	violin	1960/1	
Wells, Sydney D.	double bass	1931/2–1960/1	Principal 1942/3–1960/1
Wells, Virginia Chen	violin	1991/2–present	
Werner, Michael	percussion	1993/4–1994/5	Principal 1993/4–1994/5
Wherry, Donald	percussion	1960/1–1972/3	
Whitaker, Walter	flute	1931/2–1936/7	Principal
Whitnall, Frank	violoncello	1943/4–1947/8	
Whitney, E.C.	percussion	1922/3–1923/4	
Whitton, Don	violoncello	1949/50–1959/60	
Whyte, Jan	violin	1958/9–2000/1	
Wiebe, Thomas	violoncello	1993/4–2000/1	
Wigdorchik, Leo	violin	1974/5–1990/1	
Williams, A.J.	trumpet	1932/3–1939/40	Principal 1933/4–1939/40
Wilson, Scott	French horn	1973/4–present	
Witham, A.E.	violin	1922/3–1928/9; 1930/1–1932/3	
Witte, Monica	violin	1970/1	
Wood, Alan	tuba	1956/7	
Wood, Alfred	trombone	1945/6–1956/7	Principal 1947/8–1956/7
Wood, Reginald H.	double bass	1946/7–1948/9; 1957/8–1974/5	Principal 1964/5
Wood, Stanley	oboe/ English horn	1956/7–1990/1	Principal 1956/7–1963/4; Co-Principal 1964/5; Principal 1988/9–1990/1
Woods, J.J.	double bass	1922/3–1923/4	
Woods, Maxine	bassoon	1934/5–1935/6	
Wood, Oliver E.	oboe/ English horn	1922/3–1925/6; 1931/2	Principal 1925/6; 1931/2
Woomert, Barton	trumpet	1982/3–present	Associate Principal 1983/4–1997/8, 1999/2000–present; Acting Principal 1998/9
Worthington, Kirk	violoncello	1988/9–present	
Wotherspoon, H.C.	Orchestra Manager	1923/4	1927/8–1945/6 and after 1956/7
Wulkan, David	violin	1952/3–1986/7	
Wulkan, Jean	violin	1968/9–present	see also Todd
Wunder, Kathryn	violin	1973/4–1974/5	

APPENDIX A
Musicians of the Toronto Symphony Orchestra – *continued*

Name	Instrument	Years	Notes
Wyre, John	timpani	1966/7–1971/2; 1975/6–1980/1	
Wyshniowsky, B.	double bass	1952/3–1955/6; 1959/60–1962/3	
Yanivker, Arkady	violin	1978/9–present	
Yates, Marjorie	flute	1971/2–1973/4	Associate Principal 1971/2–1973/4
Ysselstyn, C.G.	violoncello	1927/8; 1945/6–1947/8	
Zafer, David	violin	1956/7–1958/9	
Zentner, Erica	violin	1958/9–1967/8	see also Davidson
Zuchter, Victor	viola	1946/7–1950/1; 1963/4–1973/4	
Zuckert, Leon	violin/viola	1952/3–1956/7; 1961/2–1962/3	

While every effort has been made to ensure the completeness and accuracy of this list, some errors or omissions may exist. The publisher would be grateful to be notified of such errors so that they may be corrected in future printings.

Music Directors, Conductors, and Composers

Toronto Symphony Orchestra

Luigi von Kunits	Music Director and Conductor	1923–31
Ernest MacMillan	Music Director and Conductor	1931–56
Donald Heins	Assistant Conductor	1931–42
Ettore Mazzoleni	Assistant Conductor	1942–8
Paul Sherman	Assistant Conductor	1947–55
Walter Susskind	Music Director and Conductor	1956–65
Boris Brott	Assistant Conductor	1963–4
Seiji Ozawa	Music Director and Conductor	1965–9
Nicklaus Wyss	Assistant Conductor	1966–7
Kazuyoshi Akiyama	Assistant Conductor	1968–9
Karel Ančerl	Music Director and Conductor	1969–73
Victor Feldbrill	Resident Conductor	1973–8
Andrew Davis	Music Director and Conductor	1975–88
	Conductor Laureate	1988–
Ermanno Florio	Apprentice Conductor	1976–9
John Kim Bell	Apprentice Conductor	1980–1
Eric Hall	Apprentice Conductor	1984–6
Günther Herbig	Artistic Advisor	1988–9
	Music Director Designate	1989–90
	Music Director and Conductor	1990–4
Jukka-Pekka Saraste	Music Director and Conductor	1994–2001

Toronto Symphony Youth Orchestra

Victor Feldbrill	Conductor	1974–8
Leonard Atherton	Conductor	1978–9
Ermanno Florio	Conductor	1979–86
Nurhar Arman	Conductor	1986–7
David Zafer	Conductor	1988–1999
Joaquin Valdepeñas	Conductor	1988–1999
Susan Haig	Conductor	2001–

Composers

Harry Freedman	Composer-in-residence	1970–1
Walter Boudreau	Composer-in-residence	1990–2
Gary Kulesha	Composer adviser	1995–present
Barbara Croall	Composer affiliate	1998–2000
Paul Steehuisen	Composer affiliate	1998–2000
Eric Morin	Composer affiliate	2000–2
Jeffrey Ryan	Composer affiliate	2000–2

Presidents/Chairmen of the Board of Directors

Albert E. Gooderham	1923–31
Vincent Massey	1931–4
James E. Hahn	1934–6
Arthur E. Bishop	1936–9
William G. Watson	1939–53
Trevor F. Moore	1953–7
Thomas S. Johnson	1957–61
Trevor F. Moore	1961–3
R. William Finalyson	1963–4
Edward A. Pickering	1964–7
Robert F. Chisholm	1967–9
Frank F. McEachren	1969–73
James W. Westaway	1973–5
Terence A. Wardrop	1975–8
Alan R. Marchment	1978–82
William G. Boggs	1982–5
H. Tom Beck	1985–7
Geoffrey G. Mckenzie	1987–9
David E. Howard	1989–91
William Broadhurst	1991–3
Robert Gillespie	1993–5
Robert Martin	1995–8
George Tiviluk	1998–2000
Robert Weiss	2000–2
The Hon. Bob Rae	2002–

APPENDIX D

Canadian Works Commissioned by the
Toronto Symphony Orchestra (since 1960)

Composer	Premiere	Title
Oskar Morawetz	2 February 1960	Symphony No. 2
Harry Somers	19 March 1963	*Stereophony* for Orchestra
Otto Joachim	10 October 1967	*Contrastes for Orchestra*
Luigi Nono	31 October 1967	*Per Bastiana Tai-Yang Chin*
Jacques Hétu	14 May 1967	*L'apocalypse*, op. 14
Norman Symonds	18 March 1969	*Impulse*
R. Murray Schafer	16 February 1971	*No Longer than Ten Minutes*
Harry Freedman	26 October 1971	*Graphic I ('Out of silence...')*
John Beckwith, text by James Reaney	7 April 1973	*All the Bees and All the Keys*
Norma Beecroft	1973	*Improvvisazioni concertanti no. 3*
Walter Buczynski	1973	*Three against Many*
Lothar Klein	24 February 1976	*Musica Antiqua*
Morris Surdin	23 October 1976	*Eine kleine 'Hammer Klapper' Musik*
Harry Somers	2 June 1981	*Elegy, Transformation, Jubilation*
Harry Freedman	29 September 1982	Concerto for Orchestra
John Weinzweig	13 October 1982	*Divertimento #9 for Orchestra*
Steven Gellman	16 February 1983	*Awakening*
*Anne Lauber, text by Paule Tardif-Delorme	5 November 1983	*Beyond the Sound Barrier* (joint commission of the TSO and the Quebec Symphony Orchestra)
Godfrey Ridout	18 January 1984	*No Mean City: Scenes from Childhood*
Raymond Luedeke	8 February 1984	*Shadow Music*
Michael Colgrass	27 September 1984	*Chaconne for Viola and Orchestra*
*Raymond Luedeke	6 March 1985	*The Moon in the Labyrinth*
Glenn Buhr	11 September 1985	*Beren and Lúthien*
Steven Gellman	8 January 1986	*Universe Symphony*
Alexina Louie	14 May 1986	*The Eternal Earth*
Raymond Luedeke	10 December 1986	*The Transparency of Time*
Glenn Buhr	30 March 1988	*Lure of the Fallen Seraphim*
R. Murray Schafer	6 April 1988	Concerto for Harp and Orchestra
*Raymond Luedeke	22 February 1989	*Tales of the Netsilik* (commissioned by the TSO, with joint support of the orchestras from Montreal, Edmonton, London, Calgary, and Quebec, and with the financial assistance of the Canada Council)

APPENDIX D
Canadian Works Commissioned by the Toronto Symphony Orchestra since 1960 – *continued*

Composer	Premiere	Title
*Istvan Anhalt	13 September 1989	*Sonance Resonance: Welche Töne?*
Derek Holman	22 November 1989	*Tapestry*
*R. Murray Schafer	21 March 1990	Concerto for Guitar and Orchestra (co-commissioned by the TSO, the Montreal Symphony Orchestra, and the Calgary Philharmonic Orchestra)
Alexina Louie	25 April 1990	*Music for Heaven and Earth*
*Michael Conway Baker	2 June 1990	*Timedancers*
Stephen Chatman	20 September 1990	*Piano Concerto*
Gary Kulesha	5 October 1990	*The Midnight Road* (Third Essay for Orchestra)
**Tomas Dusatko	31 January 1991	*Eine kleine Traummusik*
**Walter Boudreau	28 February 1991	*Encore ces questions sans réponses (Again, those unanswered questions)*
R. Murray Schafer	17 April 1991	*The Darkly Splendid Earth: The Lonely Traveller*
Raymond Luedeke	24 April 1991	*The North Wind's Gift* (co-commissioned by the TSO, the Calgary Philharmonic Orchestra, and the Vancouver Symphony Orchestra)
Walter Boudreau	7 September 1991	Tradiderunt me in manus imporium II
Walter Boudreau	19 September 1991	*Berliner Momente, Zweiter Teil*
*Glenn Buhr	8 January 1992	*Double Concerto for Flute, Harp, and Orchestra* (co-commissioned by the TSO, the Hamilton Philharmonic Orchestra, and the National Arts Centre Orchestra)
Srul Irving Glick	15 January 1992	*The Reawakening*
*Michael Colgrass	6 May 1992	*Arias for Clarinet and Orchestra*
*Peter Lieberson	17 February 1993	Viola Concerto
Alex Pauk	26 March 1993	*Portals of Intent*
R. Murray Schafer	31 March 1993	*Concerto for Accordion and Orchestra*
Ian McDougall	6 December 1993	Concerto for Bass Trombone and Orchestra
Omar Daniel	5 October 1995	*Strategies against Architecture*
Barbara Croall	11 June 1997	*The Four Directions (inspired by Vivaldi)*
Raymond Luedeke	8 November 1997	Concerto for Double Bass and Orchestra
Gary Kulesha	11 February 1998	Symphony
Barbara Croall	12 November 1998	*When Push Came to Shove* (excerpt)
Henry Kucharyk	12 November 1998	*Prosthetic (Part 3)*
Paul Steenhuisen	12 November 1998	*Ciphering in Tongues*
Alexander Levkovich	15 April 1999	*There is no end for my sorrow*
Gary Kulesha	16 February 2000	*The True Colour of the Sky*
Stewart Goodyear	4 March 2000	*Allegro brillante for String Orchestra* (commissioned by the TSO Volunteer Committee in honour of their 75th anniversary and the TSYO's 25th Season)

APPENDIX D

Canadian Works Commissioned by the Toronto Symphony Orchestra since 1960 – *concluded*

Composer	Premiere	Title
Éric Morin	27 September 2000	*Bombs Away*
Barbara Croall	7, 8, 10 June 2000	*When Push Came to Shove* (completed)
Paul Steenhuisen	2 February 2000	*Airstream*
Peter Lieberson	24 May 2000	*The Six Realms*[1]
Derek Holman	1 June 2000	*The Invisible Reality*[2]
James Rolfe, text by Dennis Lee	7 October 2000	*Mechanical Danny and How He Saved the Children*
Jeffrey Ryan	18 April 2001	*Violet Crumble*
Éric Morin	16 May 2001	*Elegy*
Jeffrey Ryan	17 April 2002	*The Chalice of Becoming*
Paul Steenhuisen	29 May 2002	*Pensacola*
*Kelly-Marie Murphy	12 June 2002	*And Then at Night I Paint the Stars* (joint commission of the TSO and the CBC)

*joint commissions
**commissioned for 'Evening Overtures'
[1]Commission for Music Canada Musique, patron: The Fleck Family Foundation
[2]Commission for Music Canada Musique, patron: The Roy Thomson Hall Founders Fund

Since 1982, the Toronto Symphony Orchestra has commissioned new works annually for the 'Evening Overtures' chamber music series.

Discography

Conducted by Sir Ernest MacMillan

William Byrd	*Jacob Suite*	1942	RCA Victor 11-8726-A
Jean Coulthard	*A Winter's Tale*	1942	RCI No. 2
Franz Joseph Haydn	*Serenade*	1942	RCA Victor 11-8726-B
Edward Elgar	*Pomp and Circumstance Marches 1–4*	1942	RCA Victor M911
Gustav Holst	*The Planets*	1943	RCA Victor CM 928
John Weinzweig	*Interlude in an Artist's Life*	1946	RCI
Oskar Morawetz	*Carnival Overture*	1947	RCI No. 41
Eldon Rathburn	*Cartoon No. 2*	1947	RCI No. 41
John Weinzweig	*Our Canada*	1947	RCI No. 41
Robert McMullin	'Pass River' (from *Sketches from the Rocky Mountains*)	1950	RCI No. 19
Eldon Rathburn	*Images of Childhood*	1950	RCI No. 19
Harry Freedman	*Symphonic Suite*	1950	RCI No. 19
Serge Rachmaninoff	Piano Concerto No. 3	[1950?]	IPA 507
Darius Milhaud	*Suite française*	1950	RCI 18
Benjamin Britten	*Canadian Carnival*	1950	RCI 18
Arthur Benjamin	*Red River Jig*	1950	RCI 18
George Frideric Handel	*Messiah*	1952	Beaver LPS-001 (USA – RCA Victor)
Herbert Elwell	*Pastorale* for voice and piano	1953	Hallmark CS-2
Robert Fleming	*Shadow on the Prairie*	1953	RCI No. 129
Wolfang Amadeus Mozart	*Exultate jubilate*	1953	Hallmark CS-S
Giuseppe Verdi	'Pace Pace'	1953	Hallmark SS-1
Pyotr Il'yich Tchaikovsky	Symphony No. 5	1954	Beaver LP 1001

Conducted by Geoffrey Waddington

Murray Adaskin	*Ballet Symphony*	1952	RCI No. 71
Alexander Brott	*Concertino for violin and Orchestra*	1952	RCI No. 71
Harry Freedman	*Nocturne*	1952	Music Canada RM222

Conducted by Victor Feldbrill

Norma Beecroft	*Improvisation concertanti*	1961	Audat 477-4001
Harry Freedman	*Tangents*	1961	Audat 477-4001

Appendix E
Discography – *continued*

John Weinzweig	*Concerto for Piano and Orchestra*	1966	CBC SM-104
Norman Symonds	*The Nameless Hour*	1966	CBC SM-104
Godfrey Ridout	*Fall Fair*	1966	Audat 477-4001
Godfrey Ridout	*'Scenes from Childhood'*	1990	Centre Disc 3890
Godfrey Ridout	*No Mean City*	1990	Centre Disc 3890
Godfrey Ridout	*Music for a Young Prince*	1990	Centre Disc 3890
Godfrey Ridout	*Cantiones mysticae*	1990	Centre Disc 3890
Godfrey Ridout	*Ballade for Viola and Orchestra*	1990	Centre Disc 3890
Godfrey Ridout	*La Prima Ballerina*, Suite No. 1	1990	Centre Disc 3890

Conducted by Walter Susskind

Gabriel Pierné	*The Children's Crusade*	1960	Beaver LPS003
Oskar Morawetz	*Piano Concerto No. 1*	1965	Capitol SW 6123
Roger Matton	*Concerto for Two Pianos*	1965	Capitol SW 6123

Conducted by Jean Deslauriers

Oskar Morawetz	*Symphony No. 2*	1966	CBC SM-104
Turner	*Three Episodes*	1966	CBC SM-4

Conducted by Seiji Ozawa

Hector Berlioz	*Symphonie fantastique*	1967	CBS M2S-756
Harry Freedman	*Images*	1967	CBS M2S-756
Pierre Mercure	*Triptyque*	1967	CBS M2S-756
François Morel	*L'étoile noire*	1967	CBS M2S-756
Olivier Messiaen	*Turangalila Symphony*	1968	RCA LSC-7051
Tōru Takemitsu	*November Steps*	1968	RCA LSC-7051
Tōru Takemitsu	*Asterism*	1970	RCA LSC-3099
Tōru Takemitsu	*Requiem*	1970	RCA LSC-3099
Tōru Takemitsu	*Green (November Steps II)*	1970	RCA LSC-3099
Tōru Takemitsu	*The Dorian Horizon*	1970	RCA LSC 3099

Conducted by Karel Ancerl

Healey Willan	*Symphony No. 2*	1970	CBC SM-133
Bohuslav Martinů	*Symphony No. 5*	1971	CBC SM-218
Ludwig van Beethoven	*Symphony No. 6 ('Pastoral')*	1972	CBC SM-150
Clermont Pepin	*Guernica*	1972	Audat 477 4002

Conducted by Kazuyoshi Akiyama

Ottorini Respighi	*The Fountains of Rome*	1972	CBC SM-218
Igor Stravinsky	*The Firebird*	1980	CBC SM-5004

Appendix E
Discography – *continued*

Conducted by Hermann Scherchen

Gustav Mahler	Symphony No. 7 (recorded 1965)	1991	Music & Arts CD 695

Conducted by Andrew Davis

Alexander Borodin	Symphony No. 1	1977	CBS M2-34587
Alexander Borodin	Symphony No. 2	1977	CBS M2-34587
Alexander Borodin	Symphony No. 3	1977	CBS M2-34587
Alexander Borodin	*Prince Igor: Overture*	1977	CBS M2-34587
Alexander Borodin	*Polovtsian Dances*	1977	CBS M2-34587
	(Borodin set re-released on CD)	1989	CBS WMDK 44910
Johannes Brahms	Symphony No. 4	1977	CBC SM-327
Johannes Brahms	Symphony No. 2	1978	CBC SM-336
Leoš Janáček	*The Cunning Little Vixen*	1978	CBS M-35117
Leoš Janáček	*Taras Bulba*	1978	CBS M-35117
Johannes Brahms	Symphony No. 1	1979	CBC SM-353
Pyotr Il'yitch Tchai-kovsky	*The Nutcracker* (complete)	1979	CBS M2-35196
	(re-released)	1990	Sony VMK-38975
Georges Bizet	*Carmen: Suite No. 1*	1980	CBC SM-5003
Jules Massenet	*Scenes pittoresques*	1980	CBC SM-5003
Richard Strauss	*Der Rosenkavalier Suite*	1980	CBC SM-5003
Georges Bizet	*L'arlésienne Suites Nos 1 and 2*	1981	CBS IM-36713
Antonín Dvořák	Symphony No. 9 ('New World')	1981	CBC SM-5007
Ottorini Respighi	*La boutique fantastique*	1981	CBS IM-35842
Jean Sibelius	Symphony No. 2	1983	CBS IM-37801
Igor Stravinsky	*The Rite of Spring*	1983	CBC SM-5019
Ludwig van Beethoven	Piano Concertos Nos 1–5	1984	CBC SM-5027 (Digital)
Antonín Dvořák	*Slavonic Dances*, op. 46	1984	CBC SM-5012 (Digital)
Dmitri Shostakovich	Violin Concerto, op. 99	1984	CBC SM-5037 (Digital)
Richard Strauss	*Ein Heldenleben*	1984	CBC SM-5036 (Digital)
Richard Strauss	*Salome* (highlights)	1985	CBS IM-42019 (Digital)
Richard Strauss	*Four Last Songs*	1985	CBS IM-42019 (Digital)
Richard Strauss	*Malvern*	1985	CBS IM-42019 (Digital)
Ludwig van Beethoven	Piano Concerto No. 5	1986	CBC SMCD-5155
Ludwig van Beethoven	Fantasia for Piano, Chorus and Orchestra	1986	CBC SMCD-5155
Ludwig van Beethoven	*King Stephen* Overture	1986	CBC SMCD-5155
Ludwig van Beethoven	Piano Concerto No. 3	1986	CBC SMCD-5179
Ludwig van Beethoven	Piano Concerto No. 4	1986	CBC SMCD-5179
Ludwig van Beethoven	Piano Concerto No. 1	1986	CBC SMCD-5182
Ludwig van Beethoven	Piano Concerto No. 2	1986	CBC SMCD-5182
Gustav Holst	*The Planets*	1986	EMI DS-4DS-37362
			EMI CD-CDC-7 474172
George Frideric Handel	*Messiah*	1987	EMI DSB-49027
			EMI CDCB 49027

Appendix E
Discography – *continued*

George Frideric Handel	*Messiah*	1988	EMI4DS-49407
			EMI CDC 7494072
Orchestra Spectaculars		1988	CBC SM-5068
			CD SMCD-5068
Michael Colgrass	*Chaconne for Viola and Orchestra*	1990	CBC SM-5087
			CBC SMCD-5087
Ernest Bloch	*Suite Hebraïque*	1990	CBC SM-5087
			CBC SMCD-5087
Paul Hindemith	*Trauermusik*	1990	CBC SM-5087
			CBC SMCD-5087
Benjamin Britten	*Lachrymae*	1990	CBC SM-5087
			CBC SMCD-5087
Richard Strauss	*Die Liebe der Danae*, op. 83	1990	CBS WMDK-45804 CD
R. Murray Schafer	Harp Concerto	1992	CBC SMCD-5114
R. Murray Schafer	*The Darkly Splendid Earth: The Lonely Traveller*	1992	CBC SMCD-5114
R. Murray Schafer	Concerto for Flute and Orchestra	1992	CBC SMCD-5114
Richard Strauss	eight songs (Ben Hepner)	1995	CBC SMCD-5142

Conducted by Günther Herbig

Ludwig van Beethoven	Symphony No. 3 ('Eroica')	1992	Analekta AN 2 8201
Ludwig van Beethoven	Romance No. 1 for Violin & Orchestra	1992	Analekta AN 2 8201
Ludwig van Beethoven	Romance No. 2 for Violin & Orchestra	1992	Analekta AN 2 8201

Conducted by Mario Bernardi

Ernst van Dohnányi	*Variations on a Nursery Song*	1987	CBC SMCD-5052
Serge Rachmaninoff	Piano Concerto No. 1	1987	CBC SMCD-5052
Henry Litolff	Scherzo	1987	CBC SMCD-5052
Serge Rachmaninoff	Piano Concerto No. 2	1991	CBC SMCD-5108
Healey Willan	Piano Concerto	1991	CBC SHCD-5108
Serge Rachmaninoff	Concerto for Piano and Orchestra No. 4	1993	CBC SMCD-5129
Serge Rachmaninoff	*Rhapsody on a Theme of Paganini*	1993	CBC SMCD-5129
Serge Rachmaninoff	*Cinq études-tableaux* (arr. Respighi)	1993	CBC SMCD-5129
Serge Rachmaninoff	Piano Concerto No. 3	1993	CBC SMCD-5128
Richard Strauss	*Burleske for Piano and Orchestra*	1993	CBC SMCD-5128

Conducted by Jukka-Pekka Saraste

Modest Mussorgsky	*Pictures at an Exhibition*	1996	Finlandia 2-14911
Modest Mussorgsky	*Night on Bald Mountain*	1996	Finlandia 2-14911

Appendix E
Discography – *concluded*

Modest Mussorgsky	Prelude to *Khovanschina*	1996	Finlandia 2-14911
Modest Mussorgsky	Scherzo in B flat	1996	Finlandia 2-14911
Modest Mussorgsky	*March: The Capture of Kars*	1996	Finlandia 2-14911
Alexander Scriabin	*Prometheus*	1997	Finlandia 2-17277
Serge Rachmaninoff	Piano Concerto No. 4	1997	Finlandia 2-17277
Igor Stravinsky	Concerto for Piano and Winds	1997	Finlandia 2-17277
Sergei Prokofiev	*Romeo and Juliet Suite*	1997	Finlandia 2-19050
Béla Bartók	*The Wooden Prince Suite*	1998	Finlandia 2-21029
Béla Bartók	*Music for Strings, Percussion and Celeste*	1998	Finlandia 2-21029
Béla Bartók	*Dance Suite*	1998	Finlandia 2-21029
Henri Dutilleux	Symphony No. 2	1999	Finlandia 2-25324
Henri Dutilleux	*Métaboles*	1999	Finlandia 2-25324
Henri Dutilleux	*Timbres, espace, mouvement*	1999	Finlandia 2-25324
Jean Sibelius	*Night Ride and Sunrise*	2000	Finlandia 2-27890
Jean Sibelius	*Lemminkäinen Suite*	2000	Finlandia 2-27890
Peter Paul Koprowski	Concerto for Flute and Orchestra	2001	CBC SMCD-5206
Peter Paul Koprowski	Concerto for Accordian and Orchestra	2001	CBC SMCD-5206
Peter Paul Koprowski	Concerto for Viola and Orchestra	2001	CBC SMCD-5206

Select Bibliography

Benson, Eugene, and L.W. Conolly. *Oxford Companion to Canadian Theatre*. Toronto: Oxford University Press, 1989.

Catalogue of Canadian Music for Orchestra. Toronto: Canadian Music Centre, 1976.

Catalogue of Canadian Music for Orchestra: Supplement 1979. Toronto: Canadian Music Centre, 1979.

Ginsberg, Murray. *They Loved to Play: Memories of the Golden Age in Canadian Music*. Toronto: Eastendbooks, 1998.

Kallman, Helmut, Gilles Potvin, and Kenneth Winters, eds. *Encyclopedia of Music in Canada*, 2nd ed. Toronto: University of Toronto Press, 1992.

MacMillan, Keith, and John Beckwith, eds. *Contemporary Canadian Composers*. Toronto: Oxford University Press, 1975.

Randel, Don Michael, ed. *The Harvard Biographical Dictionary of Music*. Cambridge, MA: Belnap Press of Harvard University Press, 1996.

Sadie, Stanley, ed. *The New Grove Dictionary of Music and Musicians*, 2nd ed. 29 vols. London: Macmillan, 2001.

Schabas, Exra. *Sir Ernest MacMillan: The Importance of Being Canadian*. Toronto: University of Toronto Press, 1996.

Slonimsky, Nicola, rev. *Bakers Biographical Dictionary of Musicians*, 8th edition. New York: Schirmer, 1992.

Solti, Georg, with assistance from Harvey Sachs. *Solti on Solti: A Memoir*. London: Chatto and Winds, 1997.

Index